"CHINK!"

ETHNIC PREJUDICE IN AMERICA SERIES

General Editor—Michael Selzer

"*CHINK!*"—*Anti-Chinese Prejudice in America*, edited by Cheng-Tsu Wu

"*KIKE!*"—*Anti-Semitism in America*, edited by Michael Selzer

"*MICK!*"—*Anti-Irish Prejudice in America*, edited by Joan McKiernan and Robert St. Cyr

"*WOP!*"—*Anti-Italian Prejudice in America*, edited by Elihu Smith

A Documentary History of
Anti-Chinese Prejudice in America

Edited and with an Introduction
by Cheng-Tsu Wu

Foreword by Ben Fong-Torres

A Straight Arrow Book

"CHINK!"

WORLD PUBLISHING
TIMES MIRROR
NEW YORK

My deep appreciation extends to Sandra Leoung, John Hon, Terry Tjon, and Shanlon Wu. Their assistance was indispensable in the preparation of this volume.

The picture appearing on the cover of this book was selected solely by the publisher and not by the editor, Cheng-Tsu Wu.

Published by The World Publishing Company
Published simultaneously in Canada
by Nelson, Foster & Scott Ltd.

First printing—1972

Copyright © 1972 by Straight Arrow Books
All rights reserved
ISBN 0-529-04472-2
Library of Congress catalog card number: 78-183096
Printed in the United States of America

WORLD PUBLISHING
TIMES MIRROR

Contents

Foreword ix
Introduction 1
1. Institutionalization of Prejudice 11
2. Overt Agitation 104
3. Chinaman's Chance 145
4. Have They Made It?—A Conclusion 213
   Notes 271
   Bibliography 282

Foreword

"How come," I asked my mother just the other family gathering, "Chinese call black people *hok guey* [black devils] and white people *bok guey* [white devils]?"

She'd never been asked that before. It was obvious by the quickness of her response.

"I don't know," she said, in Chinese. "Always we've called them that. People were calling them that when I got here." She got here and settled right into Oakland's Chinatown, an area separated by the city's downtown boulevard from the "colored" sector. My mother worked in a garment factory when she wasn't needed at my father's restaurant. The factory was owned by a Caucasian, but staffed with all Chinese. Mom had hardly any contact with whites or blacks; all she knew was what she'd heard.

And when I was fourteen and a waiter at a Chinese takeout place in Emeryville, a black-pocket town between Oakland and Berkeley, the manager's mother always called Negroes *see-yow gwai* (or *see-yew guey*, in my dialect). Which means "soy sauce devils." But here, there *was* contact. Negroes were her customers, her delivery men, her neighbors. Perhaps more important, another minority. But there was more to it than simplistic power controls, the man on top keeping the lessers clawing each other weak. The fact is, whites were taught Chinese stereotypes, and somewhere along the line, here in America, land of the golden mountains, the Chinese were fed—and lapped up—fearful stereotypes about blacks and other slummers. Boxed in, roped off, and kept down, the Chinese began to teach each other.

So long before we began to slink into the marching lines of Vietnam Day protestors, long before we were formulating *our* fifteen nonnegotiable demands to the administration, and thinking of *us* as part of an oppressed "Third World," we were being drilled.

"What are you hanging around the white devils for? Just go home and study."

"You don't need to go to any party. Plenty of work at the restaurant. Plenty of time to have fun later—when you get big." Later, it becomes: "When you get married."

"Speak Chinese, for God's sake. Can't even talk with your own parents."

"Hok guey, bok guey, ky-doy" (bad boys). This axiom was among the first we heard, at age five or six. And *guey* meant ghosts, too. And ghosts, in our confused youth, might mean the witch in the cellar, or the devil in the pantry, among all the jarred roots and medicines.

So no, we would never be like those weird, clumsy white kids playing football and making model jets and dressing for church and fighting after school. You wouldn't see *us* writing all over 49-er jackets and rolling up T-shirt sleeves and hanging out and threatening, "Man, gimme nickel" . . . Me, I'd be going back to the restaurant, shell some prawns, strip spines off some pea pods, refill Bireley's and Pabst Blue Ribbons into the icebox, then sling on a pouch and head off to Chinese school, bow to the teacher, for three hours. And at eight, either go home and study or back to the restaurant, Chinatown Oakland, and eat and work some more. We'd study in a room set up just around from the droning refrigerator and next to the chicken-wired rice bin, four of us around the big table doing homework till we were called out for a chore. For fun, I'd put the paper sack a yard or so from me and aim the stripped peas at it. Basketball at the New Eastern Café. Ben vs. the Bag . . .

We were being told, in so few words—talking different tongues, after all—that we were *above* social mixing, or church, or sports, this American stuff. You call me "Ching Chong Chinaman" sometimes? Hell, evil bull-jive asshole DEVIL is the only name I have for you—the only name I've ever been *taught*. There is, in fact—not that I've been told, anyway—no Chinese translation for "Negro," or "African," or even "colored people." It's *hok guey,* and my folks, my teachers, my Chinese doctors and friends, they join me in calling you that, and we can't fight about it, and I can't stop now and explain it. Always we've called you that, and I gotta go peel some shrimp.

Today, young Chinese are angry. Conditions in Chinatown, meaning every facet of simple human existence, are intolerable. And the reports from the various community-agency studies and from the various magazine articles have turned the troubles into a jingular litany. *Newsweek* shouted it out this way in February 1970:

One third of the families earn less than the federal poverty level.

The unemployment rate is 12.8 percent, vs. 6.7 percent for San Francisco and 3.9 for the country as a whole.

The density rate is 885.1 people per acre, ten times the city's average.

The suicide rate is three times the national average.

The rate of substandard housing is 67 percent, vs. 19 percent for the rest of San Francisco.

I've seen families of six, eight people living in hotel rooms, shopping bags hanging off nails as closets, a plank of plywood over the bathtub as a dining table. Outside, people starve and kill and steal from each other while tour-bussed whites click clumsily away with their 'matics.

I put in time as volunteer editor of the bilingual paper in San Francisco's Chinatown in 1970, wanted to help relieve just one of the problems—factionalism—and ended up crying, from frustration, months later, having been beat up down the block by a Chinatown gang. The gang didn't want any mention of their existence or affairs—even, or especially, criminal. And I'd gone and opened up my big front page. Their "letter to the editor" was a good ass-stomp. And I was frustrated because I work and play with words, and sometimes, especially in Chinatown, words aren't enough.

The Chinese don't even speak the same language with each other. Dialects: depending on your native district in China; Chinese or English, depending on your age and generation, on whether you're fresh off the boat, or "F.O.B.s" as the American-borns derisively called Hong Kong immigrants, or *jook sing,* as the immigrants put down the crazy Americanized native-borns. And semantics, depending on your politics, on your love of or hate for Nationalist China, city hall, the property-owning elite . . . or the *revolution.* And among the reformists there are so many chasms, depending on whom each group, agency, or club represents (the government? the church? the old people? the poor? the street people?), how much power it holds and/or wants, and how much money it has and/or wants.

A Chinatown crisis, as the media put it. But the early Chinese workers sculpted their own community, excluding the hatefully, mercilessly violent Americans—"the foreigners," as the Chinese saw them. ("Self-determination." Isn't that the term for it now?)

Young Chinese are angry about Chinatown, about *bok gueys,* about lack of jobs and opportunities. Of course there's been, there is, prejudice. Read this book. Look at TV or listen to radio. Look around you. We ain't exactly stuck in grocery stores and six-booth cafés, all of us. But we sure ain't everywhere.

And yet I can't help thinking back again. "You're going to be a doctor—aren't you?" asked with such certainty, as if the question is, "You *do* get into the tub after running the bath water—don't you?" Lawyer or engineer would be all right, too. Or some other respectable-sounding, high-salaried job, good face for the family name and a measure of independence from the American mainstream. Study for yourself, work for yourself and family—parents, children, yourself. Which meant politics were out. Mass media were out. "What—you *need* to be famous?" "Nobody does that stuff. Don't be so fancy. You be a doctor. Look at Bill Young. His parents are so proud."

Victor Wong, a talented photographer at KQED, the PBS station in San Francisco, wrote once about how his parents were never satisfied with their children, always putting them down in front of other people. *All B's—so what? How come no A's, stupid, lazy boy?* . . . And when I chose media work, I had to go through all that. White space and dead air at home, of all places. "Your name and story's in the magazine? You get paid?" "I heard you on the radio. You sound like a white devil."

We must go ahead and demand those jobs in those weird endeavors. Be able to join the unions, to get civil service jobs, to be a cop, if we want to. Simple justice. But if we remember our parents—and we were raised to remember—remember? —we'll admit that they were about as encouraging as the white folks.

I am ashamed now that I felt so despondent that time, sitting in front of the library at SF State, wondering why I had to be Chinese. After all, all I wanted was to be a radio announcer, and here, in my sophomore year, I'm being told "You're not pronouncing your final *l*'s" and not differentiating between soft and hard *ch* and *th* sounds. And to me, of course, it was all because I was Chinese.

Within the next couple of years, I was a DJ on the campus station and an editor of the campus paper, and after that, all-night man on the top "good music" FM station in town, and I was despondent again, out-of-synch, when Asians began pitching themselves into the call for yellow-powered, off-white revolution. Something must be wrong with me, I thought, because I simply cannot recall an instance of white racism against me. Not even in Amarillo, Texas, where I spent my thirteenth year and fell in love with radio, rock 'n' roll, and newspapers. Except for the PE teacher at Horace Mann Junior High who'd yell "Chop Chop!" at me to get me running faster . . . and, thinking about it, it was rather delicate when I first arrived with my father (who was part-owning a new restaurant in town), and someone had to call the school district office to ask whether I should be sent to Horace Mann or George Washington Carver. But, of course, there was no question. My mother would have walked from Oakland, California, to Amarillo, Texas, to take me back home if they'd said Carver.

But whatever I have experienced, I cannot pretend to speak for my fellows. I can only report what I have lived, along with what I've learned in Chinatown.

And what people there have said, what is being said today, is documented and collected in this very important volume, which tells the history of the massacres—legal, social, verbal, and physical—on Chinese in America. But it also gives insight into the Chinese way in America, to our walled-in sub-cities and subsocieties. Ethnic prejudice, both sides now. My parents, my past taught me the Chinese way, but beyond that. . . . Well, there was always that tongue wall. And one can speak from his own experiences only so long.

"Chink!" gives me the substance of an important new understanding of my race and hard times. For now, I am appalled for what it is telling me. Later, with luck, I'll be thankful for what it is teaching me.

BEN FONG-TORRES
October 1971

Introduction

The Chinese started to come to the United States around the middle of the nineteenth century. Their subsequent experience in this country, as Harold Isaacs has observed, was largely to be "a story of brutal bigotry of Americans" against them.[1]

The Chinese arrived first on the West Coast during the period when the extermination of Indians and agitation against Spanish-Americans was being intensified—and when, presumably, there were still fewer restraints than usual against the development and expression of hostile views regarding "alien" ethnic groups. However, the Chinese were initially brought into the United States to meet the serious labor shortages which then affected economic growth, particularly in California. As a rule, they performed unskilled labor, the kind of strenuous and menial jobs which whites tended to shy away from. For a short while, the Chinese immigrants were generally welcomed; racial prejudice gave way temporarily to economic necessity. The Chinese were admired as "our most orderly and industrious citizens," "the best immigrants in California," "law-abiding," "inoffensive," and "tractable."[2]

However, the Chinese showed the tendency to establish themselves as equals with white Americans in various aspects of industry and business, and to compete with white laborers for jobs which the latter wished to keep to themselves. Samuel Becker, writing in 1877, vividly perceived the consequences of this development:

> *With the exclusion of the surface diggings, or ... as soon as prospecting got played out, . . . it became manifest that the Chinaman could and did suit himself to the changed circumstances; that he could and did wash over old abandonded tailings, and make not only a living, but a profit upon them. Driven from those by exorbitant taxes leveled solely at and ruthlessly exacted from him, he undertook the getting up of linen as laundryman; did it so well and so cheap that the business soon fell altogether in his hands. Many Chinese became employed as cooks, or slop-boys, as domestic servants of all sorts. So sober, so obedient, so punctual and reliable were they, that those who employed them would have no others. By these qualities and a superior deftness, they soon got hold of the business of the cigar makers. From remnants of misfit carpets and strips of sole leather, they made and sold slippers at 50¢ the pair which the noble Caucasian would not deign to make for less than $1.50. But the noble race bought the cheaper slipper, and California ceased to import slippers from France. The woolen mills were then in their infancy in*

> San Francisco, and the employees would get drunk;
> would keep "blue Monday" and many other blue days;
> insisted upon such high wages that the nascent industry
> stood no chance of success, while the workmen varied
> performances by going on occasional strikes by way of
> enlivening the business prospect. Chinamen were then
> employed, who were always on hand, invariably sober,
> contented if they received the wages promised, and they
> soon proved themselves adept in the art of manipulating the wool at every stage, from the fleece to the finest
> manufactured article. Employers are not slow to perceive their own wants, nor more unlikely than the rest
> of the world to suit themselves, and thus the Chinese
> always found remunerative employment, while their
> sullen antagonists (for the miners by this time hated the
> Chinaman) refused work unless at their trade (if they
> had one), prospected vaguely and of course unsuccessfully over the country, and were largely to be found
> playing "poker" or practicing at the bar of the saloons.
> "Say, lend us a half?" began to be a not unusual form of
> address. Clothes grew seedier, more dilapidated, while
> the occasional sight of John's (every Chinaman is called
> John in California) neatly clad figure on his way to or
> from his work added fuel to the smoldering indignation
> of the superior race. What a vile passion in human nature is that which makes the idle, slinking sot hate so
> bitterly his fellow (perhaps otherwise his inferior)
> merely for being industrious, thrifty, and sober![3]

The Chinese then were accused as "dangerous," "deceitful and vicious," "criminal," "coward," and "inferior from a mental and moral point of view."[4] A San Francisco newspaper constantly attacked the Chinese as, for example, "that nature and custom should so combine to manufacture so much individual ugliness."[5] In congressional testimonies, Chinese were cursed as "inferior to any race God ever made."[6] A California attorney-general had this remark on record in print: "I believe that the Chinese have no souls to save, and if they have, that they are not worth the saving."[7]

In addition to the enormous amount of verbal attacks on Chinese, a large number of discriminatory laws were specifically enacted against them. For example, a Foreign Miner's License Tax of four dollars per month was specifically imposed on Chinese in 1853, with the law officially translated into the Chinese language. Those Chinese who were not engaged in mining then had to pay a "Chinese Police Tax." After 1854 Chinese were not allowed to give evidence in the court against a white man on the West Coast. San Francisco's "Cubic Air" ordinance, requiring 500 cubic feet of space for every adult in his or her apartment, drove scores of Chinese into prison during the 1870s; then a "Queue Ordinance" was passed and required every male prisoner to have his hair cut to within one inch of his scalp. And under the California Constitution of 1879, no public officer, corporation, attorney, contractor, etc., was allowed to employ any Chinese.

The tragic situation of Chinese on the West Coast during the latter half of the nineteenth century was well described by Mark Twain in the 1870s:

> *They [the Chinese] are a harmless race when white men either let them alone or treat them no worse than dogs; in fact, they are almost entirely harmless anyhow, for they seldom think of resenting the vilest insults or the cruelest injuries. They are quiet, peaceable, tractable, free from drunkenness, and they are as industrious as the day is long. A disorderly Chinaman is rare and a lazy one does not exist. . . . He is a great convenience to everybody—even to the worst class of white men, for he bears most of their sins, suffering fines for their petty thefts, imprisonment for their robberies, and death for their murders. Any white man can swear a Chinaman's life away in the courts, but no Chinaman can testify against a white man. Ours is "the land of the free"— nobody denies that—nobody challenges it. (Maybe it is because we won't let other people testify.) As I write, news comes that in broad daylight in San Francisco, some boys have stoned an inoffensive Chinaman to death, and that although a large crowd witnessed the shameful deed, no one interfered. . . .* [8]

Unlike Negroes, the Chinese in America supposedly enjoyed treaty protection, the Burlingame Treaty of 1868 and the treaty of 1880 between the United States and China providing for "most favored nation" privileges for the Chinese in America. But the treaty rights of the Chinese were totally ignored. The discrimination against the Chinese, as Carey McWilliams pointed out, "squared perfectly with the policy of placing Indians on reservations, and segregating Negroes by force of law. Modes of aggression which had been tried out against Indians and Negroes were easily transferred to the Chinese, and a Californian on the Supreme Court had little difficulty in convincing his colleagues that it was as easy to breach a treaty with China as with the Indian tribes."[9]

The Chinese, however, tried to defend their rights along strictly legal and constitutional lines, but that effort ended with the national Exclusion Law in 1882. This law marked the beginning of the official national policy of racial discrimination against the Chinese in the United States. Not only were Chinese workers excluded from this country but also the Chinese in the United States were denied the right of citizenship.

After the Exclusion Law was enacted by Congress, the Chinese in America were further massacred, murdered, robbed, and banished in groups from their living quarters. "Their timidity, unaggressiveness, and lack of protest provoked further attacks, simply because such characteristics were interpreted by Westerners as signs of weakness."[10] There was no protection for the victims and no punishment for the crimes. "A Chinaman's chance" came to be a figure of speech for referring to a hopeless situation.

A series of racial discriminatory laws against the Chinese was enacted by Congress shortly after the Exclusion Law of 1882. Each law subjected the Chinese in America to further injustice and inhumanity. In a period of two decades, from 1882 to 1902, the U.S. Congress passed thirteen discriminatory laws against the Chinese—and this despite the fact that the total number of Chinese in America amounted to only a small fraction of 1 percent of the population of the United States.

Under the laws and regulations of the Immigration Bureau, Supreme Court Justice David Brewer pointed out in 1905, "the Chinese were deprived of due process of law for the protection of their liberty and property, of the right of trial by jury, of being confronted with the witnesses, and of having the assistance of Counsel...."[11] Not surprising, then, that an American writer in the late nineteenth century should have observed that John Chinaman "seldom smiles!"[12]

Besides the political and legal discrimination against the Chinese there were also persistent assaults on the Chinese character in motion pictures, newspapers, popular fiction, comic strips, school textbooks, folklore, etc. These were very successful in creating the stereotype of the Chinese as inscrutable, mysterious, rat-eating, "pidgin" English-speaking, Fu-Manchu types of the most evil and sinister people. The stereotype for Chinatown was a filthy and loathsome ghetto area which was full of vices and crimes, secret trapdoors and underground passageways, etc. In 1929, Bruno Lasker made a survey of American children's race attitudes. The typical answer regarding the Chinese was: "I don't like Chinese, because they have such a bad reputation."[13]

The agitation of racial prejudice against the Chinese was tuned down a bit in the 1940s, as China became the heroic ally of America after Pearl Harbor. In the meantime, Pearl Buck's *Good Earth* and Carl Glick's *Shake Hands with the Dragon*, in addition to many other writings, had corrected the image of Chinese and Chinatown, respectively, to some extent. But in Harold Isaacs' survey, conducted during the 1940s, one still found the following prejudiced image of the Chinese: "A Congressman said he had an idea of the Chinese as a 'savage people' from the comic strip, 'The Gumps,' and, a public opinion specialist thought that the Chinese might be 'untrustworthy in business' because he had heard repeatedly in his boyhood that one should 'Never trust a Chink!' "[14]

The repeal of the Exclusion Law in 1943 may have marked

the beginning of the deinstitutionalization of racial prejudice against the Chinese. But the annual quota of 105 immigrants established in the same law was for "persons of Chinese ancestry." In other words, while immigration quotas for other peoples were based on their "country of origin," for the Chinese it was based on race and took no account of whether a potential immigrant had lived in China or in one of the many large Chinese communities elsewhere in the world.

The erosion of institutionalized racial prejudice in America finally began to take place, however, in the postwar years, especially in the 1960s. A great number of highly dedicated white Americans of all walks of life, especially the younger generation, and the awakening mass of all the minorities, blacks, Jews, Puerto Ricans, Asians, etc., have concurrently launched the great civil liberties movement in America. A significant amount of civil liberties legislation was enacted. Confronted with the rising tide of social reform, American racism is facing its inevitable defeat and is already conspicuously waning. Chinese in America for the first time have the hope of being equal partners with other American citizens in this country. Nevertheless, it is still premature to say that the Chinese "have made it," as the *New York Times* claimed in 1970 in reporting "the almost total disappearance of discrimination against the 400,000 Chinese and 500,000 Japanese Americans since the end of World War II and their assimilation into the mainstream of American life."[15]

At the present time the economic and social problems of the Chinese communities in American cities are mounting, and possible solutions are practically beyond the reach of those communities. But no adequate action for assistance has been taken at any level of government.

Prejudice in job opportunities still is serious in both public and private quarters. In December 1970, for example, the City and County Human Rights Commission of San Francisco issued a report on the participation of minorities in the San Francisco civil service system which indicated that only 4.3 percent out of the total city employees are Orientals

(Chinese and Japanese), whereas out of the total population in the same geographical area there is an estimated 14 percent Oriental population.[16]

Some of the present television programs and commercials, movies, and novels still perpetuate, consciously or unconsciously, Chinese stereotypes.[17] In short, racial prejudice, though no longer as blatant as in the past, "is still ubiquitous," as James Chin pointed out, "although now couched in very sophisticated, subtle form."[18]

In view of the past history of Chinese suffering in this country, a revival of anti-Chinese activities might possibly occur in the event of violent confrontation between Communist China and the United States. "If the present Chinese government in China," C. Marden wrote, "becomes a major target for finding a devil, there may be repercussions on American Chinese as scapegoats."[19] Harold Isaacs, in an attempt to classify changing American attitudes toward the Chinese, chronologically suggested that the period from 1949 on is "the Age of Hostility."[20] A possible hostile attitude toward the Chinese may further be illustrated by the following event:

> In Woodland, California, a family lost their son recently in the battlefield in Korea. When the Defense Department notified them, parents, wife, and brother were deeply grieved. Filled with a desire for revenge, they gathered their friends and relatives and headed toward a Chinese restaurant in that town. They broke into the establishment and destroyed everything within. Dishes, glasses, furniture, etc., were all ruined. The damages were estimated to be very great.[21]

More frightening to the Chinese in America was FBI chief J. Edgar Hoover's testimony before the Congress that "There are 300,000 Chinese in the United States, some of whom might be susceptible to recruitment by Red China as spies."[22] By implication, in case of international conflict between Communist China and the United States, every Chinese in America could automatically be suspected as a "spy."

Aware of the frightening oppression in the past and the tragic experience of the American Japanese in World War II, many Chinese, especially in the older generation, are extremely cautious in expressing their views regarding anything concerning communists. Many leaders of the Chinese community in this country are rather reluctant about freely uttering their opinions. In other words, the Chinese today are still politically living in fear. Apparently the "total disappearance of racial prejudice against the Orientals" in this country is yet to be seen.

Since the 1960s, however, the great struggle for civil liberty in this country has set American society in crisis. The Kerner Commission, established by former president Lyndon B. Johnson in 1967 to inquire into the causes of civil disorders, has reported recently that "what white Americans have never understood—but what the Negroes can never forget—is that white society is deeply implicated in the ghetto, white institutions created it, white institutions maintain it, and white society condons it." Undoubtedly in reality the word "Negro" used in this report applies to all other minorities including the Chinese, Indians, Puerto Ricans, Chicanos, Jews, and Japanese, just to mention a few. "Today, most Americans," the Kerner report continued, "know little of the origins of the racial schism separating our white and Negro citizens." The same statement, of course, can be applied perfectly to the case of the Chinese.

In conclusion, what Senator Oliver Morton, who was the chairman of the Congressional Investigating Committee on Chinese Immigration in 1876, said about the cause of the anti-Chinese movement on the West Coast remains valid as the explanation of the Chinese experience in America since the nineteenth century. "If the Chinese in California were the white people," Senator Morton stated, "being in all other respects what they are, I do not believe the complaints and warfare made against them would have existed to any considerable extent."[23]

The Chinese in this country, being so small a group, have suffered so much for so long simply because they are nonwhite. It is incredible, but it is true. This book presents a bit of the history of the racial prejudice against the Chinese, which white Americans may have "never understood," but which the Chinese "can never forget." This bit of history may help us to know a little more of "the origins of the racial schism," which has prevented the Chinese from entering the mainstream of American life.

—CHENG-TSU WU

1. Institutionalization of Prejudice

The institutionalization of racial prejudice against the Chinese started in California during the 1850s, when they began to arrive in large numbers. The first law of prejudice applied to the Chinese was the Foreign Miner's License Tax Act, enacted in 1853, which required four dollars per month for each license. Since most of the Chinese who came to the United States in the early 1850s were to work in the gold mines, the Foreign Miner's License Tax was, of course, chiefly aimed at the Chinese, and, therefore, this tax law was specifically authorized in another act to be translated into the Chinese language (see pp. 20 and 25). The Chinese payment amounted to 85 percent of this total tax paid in 1869. When the Chinese gradually diversified into other occupations, other special taxes followed them. Chinese engaged in fishing, for example, were required to pay a tax of four dollars per month in 1860, and in 1862, a peculiar "Chinese Police Tax" was imposed on each member of the "Mongolian race" over eighteen years of age who was not engaged in mining or some other industries (see p. 26).

In order to discourage the immigration to California of Chinese persons, the state legislature passed an act requiring owners of ships bringing them there to pay fifty dollars for each passenger who was "incompetent . . . to become citizens"—meaning the Chinese (see p. 31). And in 1858 the legislature simply passed an act to "prevent further immigration of Chinese or Mongolians" to California (see p. 32).

Ostensibly as an antiprostitution measure, the state legislature passed another act in 1870 to prevent the immigration of a Mongolian, Chinese, or Japanese female unless she could present "satisfactory evidence" that she was a person of correct habits and good character (see p. 33).

Since the 1858 act preventing Chinese immigration to California was inadequately enforced, the legislature passed a new act in 1870 forbidding the immigration of Chinese under the pretense of preventing importation of Chinese criminals and coolie slave-labor. This law required a Chinese or Mongolian to present evidence satisfactory to the commissioner of immigration that he was a person of correct habits and good character (see p. 35).

The California state superintendent of public institutions protested against the attempt to force "Africans, Chinese, and Niggers" into white schools in 1859, and the California Statute of 1860 excluded Mongolians, Indians, and Negroes from the public school. Later, in 1870, the California school laws were reorganized into one act which provided separate schools for the white and for other races.

The most brutal instance of legal discrimination against the Chinese was established in 1854, not by the legislature, but by the state supreme court. A man convicted of murder on the testimony of a Chinese witness appealed to the supreme court. Chief Justice Hugh C. Murray held that Chinese belonged to the category of Negro, mulatto, and Indian, who were not allowed by law to give evidence in favor of, or against, a white man. The chief justice further explained that the Chinese, Negroes, and Indians are, respectively, "a race of people whom nature has marked as inferior, and who are incapable of progress or intellectual development . . . as their history has shown. . . ." "If we would admit them to testify," the chief justice warned, we "would admit them to all the equal rights of citizenship, and we might soon see them at the polls, in the jury box, upon the bench, and in our legislative halls" (see p. 36).

The result of the exclusion of Chinese testimony from the courts was most disastrous for the Chinese. It "opened the way for almost every sort of discrimination against the Chinese," as Dr. Sandmeyer pointed out. "Assault, robbery, and murder, to say nothing of lesser crimes, could be perpetrated against them with impunity, so long as no white person was available to witness in their behalf. Without a doubt, this decision must bear a large part of the responsibility for the outrages committed against the Chinese."[1]

Efforts to amend the law so as to provide the Chinese with equal protection under law were unsuccessful. In fact, the court ruling was enacted into a law in 1863, which declared: "No Indian or person having one half or more Indian blood, or Mongolian or Chinese, shall be permitted to give evidence in favor of, or against, any white man." It is amazing to see how the courts defended the racially prejudiced law as being not in conflict with the Fourteenth Amendment to the Constitution. In 1871, for example, in one of several cases, a white man was convicted of the crime of robbery in San Francisco committed upon Hing Kee, a Chinese who was permitted to testify against the defendant in the trial. The white man appealed and won a new trial (see p. 43).

In addition to these prejudiced laws, a great variety of anti-Chinese ordinances were also established in cities in California. The "Cubic Air" ordinance, for example, passed in San Francisco in 1870 and soon to become the law of the state, required a lodging house to provide at least 500 cubic feet of clear atmosphere for each adult person in his or her apartment (see p. 65). This law was enforced, of course, only in the Chinese quarters. Consequently, the prisons became filled with Chinese when the Chinese landlords and lodgers failed to pay the fines. The Board of Supervisors responded quickly and passed the infamous "Queue Ordinance," with the drastic requirement that every male prisoner sentenced to jail should have his hair cut to within one inch of his scalp (see p. 66).

In the same year that the "Queue Ordinance" was passed, many Chinese, driven out from employment in many industries and businesses, had turned to making a living in small, shabby hand-laundry shops. The white racists then passed another ordinance which required all laundries employing a horse-drawn vehicle to pay a license fee of two dollars a quarter, those employing two such vehicles four dollars a quarter, and those using none—which included practically all of the Chinese laundries—fifteen dollars a quarter. This discriminatory law was thus obviously against the Chinese.

In the 1870s on the West Coast it was common for some individuals, firms, or corporations to hire "special police" officers for the protection of persons or property. But the California legislature passed an act in 1878 to prevent special police officers being appointed from the Chinese quarter of a city or county (see p. 66).

In 1878, Chinese were even denied naturalization. Actually, naturalization had been restricted in the United States since 1790 to "free white persons" only. A federal district court judge in California, in a case involving a Chinese, had ruled the word "white" referred to a person of the Caucasian race only. This important decision affected the Chinese in the United States as a whole for decades to come.

The new Constitution of California, adopted in 1879, was fully discriminatory against the Chinese. Mongolians were forbidden employment on public works. Chinese were subject to removal by the legislature to regions beyond the limits of cities and towns, and the legislature was empowered to prohibit any corporation from employing Chinese or Mongolians (see p. 67). Soon after the Constitution was ratified, the legislature passed a law providing that "any officer, director, manager, member, stockholder, clerk, agent, servant, attorney, employee, assignee, or contractor of any corporation . . . who shall employ in any manner or capacity . . . any Chinese or Mongolian is guilty of a misdemeanor . . ." (see p. 69.)

The Chinese sought redress against California's "barbarous and obnoxious anti-Chinese legislations" through strictly legal and constitutional measures. The federal courts were thus constantly preoccupied with California's outrageous "Hottentot," or race, legislation during the period from the 1850s to 1876. As a result of these court actions, most discriminatory legislation adopted in California was declared unconstitutional, as being in violation of treaty provisions, the Fourteenth Amendment, or the federal civil rights statutes. But racial discrimination was still popular and deeply entrenched in American society and, therefore, the agitators of racial prejudice found no difficulty in advancing the local anti-Chinese legislation to national laws. In 1876, the California state legislature appointed a committee of investigation of the Chinese and published its findings in a memorial to Congress. Also "An Address to the People of the United States upon the Evils of Chinese Immigration" was distributed to governors, editors, and legislators throughout the United States. The evils enumerated in the address are very much the same as those in the memorial, but are described in greater detail. Both the address and the memorial together became the basis of a nationwide anti-Chinese campaign.[2]

"As was expected, the report [the Address] was violently anti-Chinese in character," Theodore Hittel pointed out, "and suited the popular prejudice so well that 20,000 copies were ordered printed. Matters had so far advanced that nobody, particularly nobody that held or even expected to hold office, dared say a word in favor of the Chinese; but on the contrary, everybody, the Republicans as well as the Democrats, seized every opportunity to make public profession on the anti-Chinese side."[3]

In the same year Congress established a special committee to investigate the Chinese problem. Their report, as Mary R. Coolidge analyzed, "reveals the intentional perversion of the testimony in order to produce the desired anti-Chinese campaign document."

Finally, the Congress of the United States passed the Exclusion Law in 1882, and the nationwide institutionalization of racial prejudice against the Chinese thus began (see p. 70).

"With the adoption of the 1882 Act," Carey McWilliams stated, "the United States was formally committed to a policy of racial discrimination at variance with its tradition and principles as well as its prior policies. The measure also sanctioned state discriminations, since it denied the Chinese the protection of citizenship, and seriously undermined the philosophy upon which the federal civil rights legislation rested. Indeed one year later, in 1883, the Supreme Court declared the general civil rights act unconstitutional."[4]

It is to be noted that in the Exclusion Law of 1882, it was emphatically stated (in Article 14), that "no state court or court of the United States shall admit Chinese to citizenship."

An amendment of the above law was passed in 1884 which created further hardships for the Chinese living in the United States and also placed harsh obstacles in the way of Chinese seeking to reenter the country after temporarily having left it. And it made the Chinese certificate (Section 6 of the Exclusion Law) much stricter and more specific (see p. 75).

The Scott Act, passed in Congress in 1888, simply prevented the Chinese who had temporarily left the United States from returning to this country. At least 20,000 Chinese who, at the time, had a legitimate right of reentry, were thus prevented from doing so. And about 600 persons who were already on their way back to the United States when the law was enacted were denied permission to return (see pp. 82 and 85).

At the expiration of the Exclusion Law, the Geary Act of 1892 was passed in Congress and not only provided for the suspension of Chinese immigration for a further period of ten years, but also denied bail to Chinese in habeas corpus proceedings. In addition, this law required certificates of residence from the Chinese within one year. Those Chinese who failed to hold the certificate could be deported (see pp. 86 and 89).

Chinese were also excluded from the Hawaiian Islands in a joint congressional resolution of July 7, 1898 (see p. 90). This resolution also excluded from the U.S. mainland the Chinese who already resided in Hawaii.

The Act of April 30, 1900, which was to provide a government for the Territory of Hawaii, declared all Hawaiians to be citizens of the United States, but required the Chinese in Hawaii to apply for certificates of residence (see p. 91). This act also specified that Chinese laborers who held certificates of residence in Hawaii were not allowed to enter any state, territory, or district of the United States.

At the end of the extended ten years' suspension of Chinese immigration to the United States in 1902, Congress immediately passed another act which extended indefinitely the exclusion of Chinese and the denial to the Chinese in the United States of the privilege of naturalization (see p. 91). Chinese in the Philippine Islands were required by the same act to apply for certificates of residence and also were not allowed to enter the U.S. mainland and other territories. The Philippine Commission was authorized and required to make all regulations for the enforcement in the Philippine Islands of this act (see p. 93).

From 1882 to 1902, the Chinese population of the United States remained minute, and indeed actually shrank—from 105,465 in 1880 to 89,863 in 1900. Nevertheless, in those two decades, the United States passed at least thirteen racial discrimination laws against the Chinese. These laws may be summarized chronologically as follows:

U.S. LAWS RELATING TO THE EXCLUSION AND
PERSECUTION OF CHINESE, 1882–1902.

1. The Exclusion Law, May 6, 1882
(Officially entitled: An Act to Execute Certain Treaty Stipulations Relating to Chinese.)
Chinese laborers are excluded from the United States, and the Chinese living in the United States are denied citizenship.

2. An Amendment to the Exclusion Law, July 5, 1884
(Officially entitled: An Act to Amend an Act Entitled "An Act to Execute Certain Treaty Stipulations Relating to Chinese," approved May sixth, eighteen hundred and eighty-two.)
Creating further hardships for the Chinese living in the United States, and more harassments for Chinese reentry.

3. The Scott Act, October 1, 1888
(Officially entitled: An Act, a Supplement to an Act Entitled "An Act to Execute Certain Treaty Stipulations Relating to Chinese," approved the sixth day of May, eighteen hundred and eighty-two.)
Prohibiting not only the immigration of Chinese laborers to the United States, but also the return of Chinese who had temporarily left the United States.

4. The Geary Law, May 5, 1892
(Officially entitled: An Act to Prohibit the Coming of Chinese Persons into the United States.)

Extending the Exclusion Law for another ten years, and requiring certificates of residence for Chinese in the United States.

5. Act of February 15, 1893
(Officially entitled: An Act Granting Additional Quarantine Powers and Imposing Additional Duties upon the Marine-Hospital Service.)
Empowering the president to prohibit persons or property moving to the United States from a foreign country by reason of the existence of cholera or other infectious or contagious disease. This act was specifically aimed at the Chinese in that time.

6. Act of November 3, 1893
(Officially entitled: An Act to Amend an Act Entitled "An Act to Prohibit the Coming of Chinese Persons into the United States," approved May fifth, eighteen hundred and ninety-two.)
Making the immigration of Chinese businessmen more difficult, and creating more hardships for those already here.

7. Joint Resolution of December 7, 1893
(Officially entitled: Joint Resolution Providing for the Payment of Salaries and Expense of Additional Deputy Collectors of Internal Revenue to Carry Out the Provision of the Chinese Exclusion Act of May 5, 1892, as amended by the Act of November 3, 1893.)

8. Act of August 18, 1894
(Officially entitled: An Act Making Appropriations for Sundry Civil Expenses of the Government for the Fiscal Year Ending June 13, 1895, and for Other Purposes.)
Empowering the immigration officers to debar an alien from entering the United States.

9. Joint Resolution of July 7, 1898
Excluding Chinese from Hawaii.

10. Act of April 30, 1900
(Officially entitled: An Act to Provide a Government for the Territory of Hawaii.)
Chinese in Hawaii should apply for certificate of residence.

11. Act of June 6, 1900
(Officially entitled: An Act Making Appropriations for Sundry Civil Expenses of the Government for the Fiscal Year Ending June 13, 1901, and for other purposes.)

Empowering the immigration commissioner in charge of the administration of the Chinese Exclusion Law and other related regulations.

12. Act of March 3, 1901
(Officially entitled: An Act Supplementary to an Act Entitled "An Act to Prohibit the Coming of Chinese Persons into the United States," approved May 5, 1892.)

13. Act of April 29, 1902
(Officially entitled: An Act to Prohibit the Coming into and to Regulate the Residence Within the United States, Its Territories and All Territory under Its Jurisdiction, and the District of Columbia, of Chinese and Persons of Chinese descent.)
Extended the Chinese Exclusion Law indefinitely. Chinese in Philippine Islands were restricted.

In addition to the national discrimination laws, numerous laws and institutional regulations discriminating against the Chinese were established in various localities of this country.

In the meantime, immigration offices of the United States subjected the Chinese who had come through the legitimate way to the most humiliating and inhuman treatment. They were subject to a thorough searching by customs officials in San Francisco, where most of them arrived. The incoming Chinese immigrant was usually asked detailed questions pertaining to his family and village life in China. Sometimes from 2,000 to 5,000 questions were asked at a hearing. "Regulations Governing the Admission of Chinese" and a sample of the questions and answers are included on pages 95 and 97, respectively.

When Chinese arrived in San Francisco, they were lodged in the loft of a wooden house to await this examination. It was practically an imprisonment, lasting sometimes for weeks and even months. They were not allowed to see their friends. Cases are reported where persons became sick and no doctor was allowed to see them, and, indeed, deaths occurred.[5]

In 1926, for example, "The daughter of an American citizen applied for admission. She was twenty-four years of age, unmarried. She was asked why she has not married, the assumption and suspicion being that she was entering here for immoral purposes. She has been in the immigration station for five months. The case has been taken to the United States Court. Meanwhile, she is never allowed to go to the home of her friends but may only take walks with the matron and must return to the immigration station at night."[6]

Congress continued to pass laws prejudicial to all Asians, with the Chinese, of course, specifically included. The Immigration Act of 1924, for example, excluded aliens "ineligible to citizenship," defined in Section 28 of that act as "when used in reference to any individual, includes an individual who is debarred from becoming a citizen of the United States" under the Exclusion Law (see p. 102).

In the same year, American citizens of Chinese ancestry were refused the right to bring their Chinese wives to this country. The Supreme Court (in the case of *Chang Chan et al.* v. *John D. Nagle*) decided in October 1924 that Section 13(c) of the 1924 Immigration Act excludes the Chinese wives of American citizens. It is also important to note the fact that by 1928 eleven states prohibited intermarriage with Chinese.

California Taxes the Foreign Gold Miner (1853)

An Act to Provide for the Protection of Foreigners, and to Define Their Liabilities and Privileges.
[Approved March 30, 1853]

The People of the State of California, represented in Senate and Assembly, do enact as follows:

SECTION 1. That from and after the passage of this Act, no person, not being a citizen of the United States (California Indians excepted) shall be allowed to take gold from the mines of this State, unless he shall have a license therefor, as hereafter provided.

SEC. 2. It shall be the duty of the Comptroller of State to procure a sufficient number of blank licenses, which shall be substantially in the following form and numbered consecutively, and a record thereof be filed in his office. He shall deliver said licenses to the Treasurer of State and take his receipt for the same upon the books of his office:

FORM OF LICENSE

No. *County (date)* 185 *has paid four dollars mining license, which entitles him to work in the mines one month.*	No._____ County, (date.) This certifies that . . . . has this day paid the Sheriff of . . . . . . County, four dollars, which entitles him to work in the mines of this State for one month from date. *Comptroller of State.* By . . . . *Sheriff.*

(To be renewed upon expiration of term.)

Every subsequent license after the first, shall be dated from the expiration of the former license issued by the Sheriff or his Deputy to any foreign miner who shall have been engaged in mining, from the expiration of such former license.

SEC. 3. The Sheriff of each County shall be the Collector of License Tax, under the provisions of this Act, who, before entering upon the duties herein provided for, shall enter into bond to the State, with two or more sureties, to be approved by the Board of Supervisors, if any such Board exists in his county; if there be no such Board, then by the County Judge, in the sum of fifteen thousand dollars, conditioned for the faithful performance of the duties required of him by this Act, which bond shall be filed in the office of the Clerk of said county.

SEC. 4. The Treasurer of State shall fill the blanks for the numbers and counties which have been left in the printed form, and shall be liable on his bond for all licenses delivered to him by the Comptroller, except for such as he may have issued to the Recorders of counties, under the provisions of the following section.

SEC. 5. The Treasurer of State shall issue, as soon as practicable, to the Recorder of each mining county, and thereafter previous to the fifteenth of December of each year, such number of licenses as may be deemed sufficient for the use of said county, taking a receipt therefor, which receipt shall be recorded by the Treasurer, in a book to be provided for that purpose, and shall stand as a charge against said Recorder; and said Recorder shall execute a bond to the State, conditioned for the faithful performance of all the duties required of him by this Act, in the sum of ten thousand dollars; said bond to be approved by the Governor and Comptroller.

SEC. 6. The amount to be paid for each license shall be at the rate of four dollars per month, and said license shall in no case be transferable.

SEC. 7. The Recorder shall deliver to the Sheriff of his County such number of licenses as said Sheriff may require, charging him therewith, and taking his receipt therefor. The Sheriff shall make monthly returns to the Recorder of his County, of the number of licenses issued, and to whom, and the amount of money received. The first returns shall be made to the Recorder on the first Monday of May next, and thereafter, a return shall be made on the first Monday of each succeeding month as herein specified.

SEC. 8. It is hereby made the duty of the Treasurer of each County to which licenses have been issued, to report to the Treasurer of State on the first Monday of August next, and on the first Monday of every third month thereafter, the amount of money received by him on account of foreign miners' licenses.

SEC. 9. Fifty percent of the net proceeds of all moneys collected under the provisions of this Act, shall be paid into the State Treasury, and shall constitute a part of the General Fund; the remaining fifty percent of the net proceeds shall be paid into the General Fund of the County; and it shall be the duty of the Sheriff to pay over to the County Treasurer, monthly, the amounts specified in this section.

SEC. 10. The collector may seize the property of any person liable to, and refusing to pay such tax, and sell at public auction, on one hour's notice, by proclamation, and transfer the title thereof to the person paying the highest price therefor, and after deducting the tax and necessary expenses incurred by reason of such refusal and sale of property, the collector shall return the surplus of the proceeds of the sale, if any, to the person or persons whose property was sold:

Provided, That should any person liable to pay such tax in any County of this State escape into any other County with intent to evade the payment of such tax, then and in that event it shall be lawful for the collector to pursue such person, and enforce the payment of such tax in the same manner as if no such escape had been made. Any foreigner representing himself to be a citizen of the United States, shall, in absence of his certificate to that effect, satisfy the collector of the correctness of his statement by affidavit, or otherwise, and that the collector be and is empowered to administer such oath or affirmation. All foreigners residing in the mining districts of this State shall be considered miners under the provisions of this Act, unless they are directly engaged in some other lawful business avocation.

SEC. 11. Immediately preceding the time provided by law for the final settlement of the County Treasurer with the Treasurer of State, it shall be the duty of each Recorder to whom licenses have been issued to report to the Comptroller of State the number of licenses on hand in his office, as also the number in the hands of the Sheriff, who is hereby required to report to said Recorder the number of licenses not disposed of, for which he has receipted to the said Recorder.

SEC. 12. The Treasurer and Comptroller of State shall, as soon as practicable, compare the returns of the Sheriff with the reports of the County Recorder, and if there shall be any discrepancy in the statements, it shall be the duty of the Comptroller to immediately inform the prosecuting Attorney of the county in which such delinquent resides, who shall commence suit against such delinquent and his sureties forthwith.

SEC. 13. Any Sheriff or his Deputy who shall neglect or refuse to pay over the money collected by him or them, under the provisions of this Act, or shall appropriate any part thereof to his or their use, other than the percentage they are entitled to retain by the provisions of this Act, shall be deemed guilty of embezzlement, and upon conviction thereof shall be punished by imprisonment in the State

Prison any time not less than one year, nor more than ten years.

SEC. 14. Any officer charged with the collection of the tax provided to be collected by this Act, who shall give any receipt other than the receipt prescribed in this Act, or receive money for such license without giving the necessary receipt, shall be deemed guilty of a misdemeanor, and upon conviction shall be fined in a sum not exceeding one thousand dollars, and be imprisoned in the county jail not exceeding six months.

SEC. 15. It shall be the duty of the different Sheriffs to return all unsold licenses to the County Recorder prior to the fifteenth day of December of each year, and receive new licenses, and the County Recorders shall immediately transmit to the Comptroller of State said licenses, who shall deliver them to the Treasurer of State. Such licenses so returned shall be placed to the credit of the different County Recorders on the books of the Treasurer, and the licenses destroyed in presence of the Comptroller of State, who shall also make a record of the same.

SEC. 16. Any person who shall make any alteration, or cause the same to be made, in any license, shall be deemed guilty of a misdemeanor, and upon conviction shall be fined in a sum not exceeding one thousand dollars, and imprisonment in the State Prison not exceeding six months.

SEC. 17. Any person or company hiring foreigners to work in the mines of this State shall be liable for the amount of the licenses for each person so employed.

SEC. 18. The Sheriff shall have power, and it is hereby made his duty to appoint a sufficient number of Deputy Collectors to assist him in the collection of the tax provided to be collected by this Act, said Deputy Collectors to be paid not less than fifteen (15) percent on all sums collected by them; and the Sheriff shall be responsible for the acts of said Deputy Collectors, and may require from them such bond and surety as he may deem proper for his own indemnification, and for such service he shall be entitled to receive three percent on all sums collected by them. Should the Board of Supervisors, or in the event of there being no such Board, then the County Judge, deem the percentage to be paid to Deputy Collectors by the provisions of this section to be insufficient, an order may be entered by the Board of Supervisors or the County Judge providing that an additional sum shall be paid such Deputy Collector, not to exceed in all twenty-five percent to be paid as herein provided. The County Recorder of each County shall receive three percent on all sums collected under the provisions of this Act.

SEC. 19. That the Sheriff be required to receive good clean gold dust when tendered at seventeen dollars per ounce in payment for licenses, and be required to pay the same into the Treasury at the same rate.

SEC. 20. That the Act entitled "An Act to Provide for the Protection of Foreigners, and to Define their Liabilities and Privileges," approved May fourth, one thousand eight hundred and fifty-two, and all laws or parts of laws conflicting with the provisions of this Act be and the same are hereby repealed.

From *California Statutes*, 1853

The Foreign Miner's Tax Translated into Chinese (1853)

An Act to Authorize the Secretary of State to Procure the Translation and Lithographing, into the Chinese Language, of the Act to Provide for the Protection of Foreigners, and to Define their Liabilities and Privileges.
[Approved April 12, 1853]

The People of the State of California, represented in Senate and Assembly, do enact as follows:

SECTION 1. That the Secretary of State be, and is hereby authorized to have translated into the Chinese language, and lithographed for the use of the State, the first, sixth, ninth, tenth, fourteenth, sixteenth, seventeenth, nineteenth, and twentieth sections of the law, entitled "An Act to Provide for the Protection of Foreigners and to Define their Liabilities and Privileges," as also form No. one, of Section one: *Pro-*

vided, That four thousand lithographed copies of said Act, with the translation, shall not cost more than six hundred dollars. And further, that as soon as said lithographed copies shall be delivered to the Secretary of State, it is hereby made his duty to send to the clerks of the several mining counties, by some conveyance deemed safe, a number of such copies in proportion to the number of Chinese in said county. It is hereby made the duty of said clerks to distribute to the sheriffs of their several counties, such number of said copies as may be necessary to supply each Deputy Collector with one copy of said Act.

SEC. 2. The sum of six hundred dollars be, and is hereby appropriated out of the General Fund, to defray the expense of said translation and lithographing, according to the provisions of the first section of this Act.

From *California Statutes,* 1853

California Protects Free White Labor Against Chinese Competition (1862)

An Act to Protect Free White Labor against Competition with Chinese Coolie Labor, and to Discourage the Immigration of the Chinese into the State of California.
[Approved April 26, 1862]

The People of the State of California, represented in Senate and Assembly, do enact as follows:

SECTION 1. There is hereby levied on each person, male and female, of the Mongolian race, of the age of eighteen years and upwards, residing in this State, except such as shall, under laws now existing, or which may hereafter be enacted, take out licenses to work in the mines, or to prosecute some kind of business, a monthly capitation tax of two dollars and fifty cents, which tax shall be known as the Chinese Police Tax; *provided,* That all Mongolians exclusively engaged in the production and manufacture of the following articles shall be exempt from the provisions of this Act, viz: sugar, rice, coffee, tea.

SEC. 2. It shall be the duty of the Controller of State to procure a sufficient number of blank "Police Tax Receipts," which shall be substantially in the following form; these tax receipts shall be numbered consecutively, and a record thereof be made and filed in his office:

CHINESE POLICE TAX.

No.. . . . .
. . . . COUNTY,. . . . . 18. . . .
This certifies that. . . . . has this day paid the Tax Collector of. . . . . County, two dollars and fifty cents, the same being his police tax for the month commencing. . . . ., and ending. . . . . , both inclusive.
. . . ., Controller of State.
. . . . , Collector.

SEC. 3. The Controller of State shall, with ink, fill the blank which has been left in the printed form, with the name of the proper county, and shall sign and issue to the Treasurer of each County, from time to time, when required by the Treasurer, a sufficient number of police tax receipts for the use of such County, and take a receipt therefor, and charge the Treasurer with the same. The County Treasurer shall, in a book to be by him kept for the purpose, keep an account of all Chinese police tax receipts received by him, and shall, from time to time, deliver them to the County Auditor, taking his receipt therefor. And the Auditor shall, on the first Monday in each month, write the name of the month in all police tax receipts issued by him for that month, and shall deliver to the Tax Collector of his County a sufficient number of said tax receipts for the use of his County for that month; *provided*, That in counties where there are Township or District Collectors, said tax receipts shall be delivered to such Collectors, who shall discharge the duties imposed in this

Act, in their respective townships or districts.

SEC. 4. The Collector shall collect the Chinese police tax, provided for in this Act, from all persons liable to pay the same, and may seize the personal property of any such person refusing to pay such tax, and sell the same at public auction, by giving notice by proclamation one hour previous to such sale; and shall deliver the property, together with a bill of sale thereof, to the person agreeing to pay, and paying, the highest therefor, which delivery and bill of sale shall transfer to such person a good and sufficient title to the property. And after deducting the tax and necessary expenses incurred by reason of such refusal, seizure, and sale of property, the Collector shall return the surplus of the proceeds of the sale, if any, to the person whose property was sold; *provided,* That should any person, liable to pay the tax imposed in this Act, in any County in this State, escape into any other County, with the intention to evade the payment of such tax, then, and in that event, it shall be lawful for the Collector to pursue such person, and enforce the payment of such tax in the same manner as if no such escape had been made. And the Collector, when he shall collect Chinese police taxes, as provided for in this section, shall deliver to each of the persons paying such taxes a police tax receipt, with the blanks properly filled; *provided,* further, That any Mongolian, or Mongolians, may pay the above named tax to the County Treasurer, who is hereby authorized to receipt for the same in the same manner as the Collector. And any Mongolian, so paying said tax to the Treasurer of the County, if paid monthly, shall be entitled to a reduction of twenty percent on said tax. And if paid in advance for the year next ensuing, such Mongolian, or Mongolians, shall be entitled to a reduction of thirty-three and one third percent on said tax. But in all cases where the County Treasurer receipts for said tax yearly in advance, he shall do it by issuing receipts for each month separately; and any Mongolian who shall exhibit a County Treasurer's receipt, as above provided, to the Collector, shall be exempted from the payment of said tax to the Collector for the month for which said receipt was given.

SEC. 5. Any person charged with the collection of Chinese police taxes, who shall give any receipt other than the one prescribed in this Act, or receive money for such taxes without giving the necessary receipt therefor, or who shall insert more than one name in any one receipt, shall be guilty of a felony, and, upon conviction thereof, shall be fined in a sum not exceeding one thousand dollars, and be imprisoned in the State Prison for a period not exceeding one year.

SEC. 6. Any Tax Collector who shall sell, or cause to be sold, any police tax receipt, with the date of the sale left blank, or which shall not be dated and signed, and blanks filled with ink, by the Controller, Auditor, and Tax Collector, and any person who shall make any alteration, or cause the same to be made, in any police tax receipt, shall be deemed guilty of a felony, and, on conviction thereof, shall be fined in a sum not exceeding one thousand dollars, and imprisoned in the State Prison for a period not exceeding two years; and the police tax receipt so sold, with blank date, or which shall not be signed and dated, and blanks filled with ink, as aforesaid, or which shall have been altered, shall be received in evidence in any Court of competent jurisdiction.

SEC. 7. Any person or company who shall hire persons liable to pay the Chinese police tax shall be held responsible for the payment of the tax due from each person so hired; and no employer shall be released from this liability on the ground that the employee is indebted to him (the employer), and the Collector may proceed against any such employer in the same manner as he might against the original party owing the taxes. The Collector shall have power to require any person or company believed to be indebted to, or to have any money, gold dust, or property of any kind, belonging to any person liable for police taxes, or in which such person is interested, in his or their possession, or under his or their control, to answer, under oath, as to such indebtedness, or the possession of such money, gold dust, or other property. In case a party is indebted, or has possession or control of any moneys, gold dust, or other property, as aforesaid, of such person liable for police taxes, he may collect from such party the amount of such taxes, and may require the delivery of such money, gold dust, or other property, as aforesaid; and in all cases the receipt of the Collector to said party shall be a complete bar to any demand made against said party, or his legal representatives, for the amounts of money, gold dust, or property, embraced therein.

SEC. 8. The Collector shall receive for his service, in collecting police taxes, twenty percent of all moneys which he shall collect from persons owing such taxes. And of the residue, after deducting the percentage of the Collector, forty percent shall be paid into the County Treasury, for the use of the State, forty percent into the general County Fund, for the use of the County, and the remaining twenty percent into the School Fund, for the benefit of schools within the County; *provided*, That in counties where the Tax Collector receives a specific salary, he shall not be required to pay the percentage allowed for collecting the police tax into the County Treasury, but shall be allowed to retain the same for his own use and benefit; *provided*, That where he shall collect the police tax by Deputy, the percentage shall go to the Deputy.

SEC. 9. All tax receipts required by this Act shall be issued from the Controller of State's office, and shall be numbered consecutively, commencing with number one, on the first Monday of May, eighteen hundred and sixty-two, and running to the second Monday of November, eighteen hundred and sixty-two; and they shall commence with number one, on the second Monday of November in the year one thousand eight hundred and sixty-two, and on the second Monday of November in each year thereafter, and all such tax receipts shall be signed by the Controller of State, or by a Deputy.

SEC. 10. It is hereby made the duty of the various officers charged with the execution of the provisions of this Act, to carry out said provisions by themselves or Deputies; and for the faithful performance of their duties in the premises, they shall be liable on their official bonds, respectively. The Treasurers of the respective counties shall make their statements and settlements under this Act with the Controller of State, at the same times and in the same manner they make their settlements under the general Revenue Act.

SEC. 11. This Act shall take effect and be in force from and after the first day of May, next ensuing.

From California Statutes, 1862

California's Immigrant Tax (1855)

An Act to Discourage the Immigration to This State of Persons Who Cannot Become Citizens Thereof.
[Approved April 28, 1855]

The People of the State of California, represented in Senate and Assembly, do enact as follows:

SECTION 1. The master, owner, or consignee of any vessel, arriving in any of the ports of this State from any foreign State, country, or territory, having on board any persons who are incompetent by the laws of the United States or the laws and constitution of this State to become citizens thereof are hereby required to pay a tax, for each such person, of fifty dollars.

SEC. 2. It shall be the duty of the Commissioner of Emigrants of the City of San Francisco, or the Mayor or other chief municipal officer of any town or city in other parts of this State, to visit all such vessels immediately upon their arrival in any of said ports, and whenever the said Commissioner, Mayor, or other chief municipal officer shall be satisfied by personal inspection, or otherwise, of the number of passengers referred to in the first section of this Act, on board of said vessel, he shall demand and receive of the master, owner, or consignee of such vessel, the sum of fifty dollars for each such passenger so disqualified from becoming a citizen of the United States.

SEC. 3. In the event of the nonpayment of said tax within three days after the arrival of said vessel, or within three days after demand for said tax, said Commissioner, Mayor, or chief officer of any city, town, or village, shall commence suit in the name of the State against the master, owner, or consignee, or all of them for said tax before any court of competent jurisdiction in said town or city; and the commencing of said suit shall constitute a lien upon such vessel for the amount of said tax, and it shall be forever liable for the same.

SEC. 4. The Commissioner of Emigrants of San Francisco is hereby required to pay over on the first Monday of every month to the Treasurer of State, for the use of the Hospital Fund, all moneys collected under the provisions of this Act, reserving to himself first five percent of the amount so collected as compensation under this Act.

SEC. 5. The said Commissioner of Emigrants is required, before entering upon the duties of this Act, to enter into a bond to the State of California in the sum of thirty thousand dollars, with good and sufficient security to be approved by the Governor, conditioned that he will well and truly discharge all the duties required of him by this Act, which said bond shall be filed in the office of the Secretary of State.

SEC. 6. This Act shall take effect from and after the first day of September next.

From *California Statutes*, 1855

Chinese Barred From California (1858)
An Act to Prevent the Further Immigration of Chinese or Mongolians to This State.
[Approved April 26, 1858]

SECTION 1. On and after the first day of October, anno Domini, eighteen hundred and eighty-five, any person, or persons, of the Chinese or Mongolian races, shall not be permitted to enter this State, or land therein, at any port or part thereof, and it shall be unlawful for any man, or persons, whether captain or commander, or other person, in charge of, or interested in, or employed on board of, or passengers upon, any vessel, or vessels of any nature or description whatsoever, to knowingly allow, or permit, any Chinese or Mongolian, on and after such time, to enter any of the ports of this

State, to land therein, or at any place, or places, within the border of this State, and any person or persons violating any of the provisions of this Act, shall be held and deemed guilty of a misdemeanor, and upon conviction thereof shall be subject to a fine in any sum not less than four hundred dollars, nor more than six hundred dollars, for each and every offense, or imprisonment in the County Jail of the County in which the said offense was committed, for a period of not less than three months, nor more than one year, or by both such fine and imprisonment.

SEC. 2. The landing of each and every Chinese or Mongolian person, or persons, shall be deemed and held as a distinct and separate offense, and punished accordingly.

From *California Statutes,* 1858

Restrictions on Chinese Female Immigrants (1870)

An Act to Prevent the Kidnapping and Importation of Mongolian, Chinese, and Japanese Females, for Criminal or Demoralizing Purposes.
[Approved March 18, 1870]

WHEREAS, The business of importing into this State Chinese women for criminal and demoralizing purposes has been carried on extensively during the past year, to the scandal and injury of the people of this State, and in defiance of public decency; and whereas, many of the class referred to are kidnapped in China, and deported at a tender age, without their consent and against their will; therefore, in exercise of the police power appertaining to every State of the Union, for the purpose of remedying the evils above referred to and preventing further wrongs of the same character:

The People of the State of California, represented in Senate and Assembly, do enact as follows:

SECTION 1. It shall not be lawful, from and after the time when this Act takes effect, to bring, or land from any ship, boat, or vessel, into this State, any Mongolian, Chinese, or Japanese females, born either in the Empire of China or Japan, or in any of the islands adjacent to the Empire of China, without first presenting to the Commissioner of Immigration evidence satisfactory to him that such female desires voluntarily to come into this State, and is a person of correct habits and good character, and thereupon obtaining from such Commissioner of Immigration a license or permit particularly describing such female and authorizing her importation or immigration.

SEC. 2. Any master, officer, owner or part owner of any steamship, sailing or other vessel, or any other person violating any of the provisions of this Act, shall be deemed guilty of a misdemeanor, and shall be punished by a fine of not less than one thousand dollars nor more than five thousand dollars, or imprisonment for a term not less than two nor more than twelve months, or by both such fine and imprisonment.

SEC. 3. Every individual person of the class hereinbefore referred to, transported into this State contrary to the provisions of this Act, shall render the person so transporting liable to a separate prosecution and penalty, and the transportation of each one as aforesaid shall create a separate and distinct offense, and render the person offending liable to the pains and penalties herein provided.

SEC. 4. The Commissioner of Immigration shall reside and keep his office in the City of San Francisco, and perform all the duties assigned to him by this Act, and also all such duties and functions as may devolve upon such Commissioner under the laws now in force. He shall hold his office for the term of four years, and shall be subject to removal by the Governor. Before entering upon his duties, the Commissioner shall take and subscribe the constitutional oath of office, and file in the office of the Secretary of State a bond in the sum of twenty-five thousand dollars, with sufficient sureties, to be approved by the Governor, conditioned for the faithful performance of his duties. The office of Commissioner of Immigration, as it now exists, is hereby declared vacant.

SEC. 5. All fees and commissions collected or received by the Commissioner of Immigration shall, less twenty percent retained as his fees and commissions, be paid by him into the State Treasury each month, and a detailed statement of the same, verified by oath, shall be, at the time of each payment, filed by him in the office of the Controller of State. Such stationery as he may require shall be furnished to him by the Secretary of State.

SEC. 6. The County Courts throughout the State shall each have jurisdiction of prosecutions for offenses against the provisions of this Act.

SEC. 7. All Acts and parts of Acts, so far as they may be in conflict with the provisions of this Act, are hereby repealed.

SEC. 8. This Act shall take effect and be in force from and after its passage.

From *California Statutes*, 1869–1870

Further Restrictions on Chinese Immigrants (1870)

An Act to Prevent the Importation of Chinese Criminals and to Prevent the Establishment of Coolie Slavery.
[Approved March 18, 1870]

WHEREAS, Criminals and malefactors are being constantly imported from Chinese seaports, whose depredations upon property entail burdensome expense upon the administration of criminal justice in this State; and whereas, by the importation of such persons a species of slavery is established and maintained which is degrading to the laborer and at war with the spirit of the age; now, therefore, in the exercise of the police powers appertaining to this State,

The People of the State of California, represented in Senate and Assembly, do enact as follows:

SECTION 1. It shall not be lawful, from and after the time when this Act takes effect, to bring or to land from any ship, boat or vessel, into this State, any Chinese or Mongolian, born either in the Empire of China or Japan, or in any of the islands adjacent to the Empire of China, without first presenting to the Commissioner of Immigration evidence satisfactory to him that such Chinaman or Mongolian desires voluntarily to come into this State, and is a person of correct habits and good character, and thereupon obtaining from such Commissioner of Immigration a license or permit, particularly describing such Chinaman or Mongolian and authorizing his importation or immigration.

SEC. 2. Any master, officer, owner or part owner of any steamship, sailing or other vessel, or any other person, violating any of the provisions of this Act, or assisting in such violation, shall be deemed guilty of a misdemeanor, and shall be punished by a fine of not less than one thousand dollars nor more than five thousand dollars, or by imprisonment for a term of not less than two nor more than twelve months, or by both such fine and imprisonment.

SEC. 3. Every individual person of the class hereinbefore referred to, transported into this State contrary to the provisions of this Act, shall render the person so transporting liable to a separate prosecution and penalty, and the transportation of each one, as aforesaid, shall create a separate and distinct offense, and render the person so offending liable to the pains and penalties herein provided.

SEC. 4. The several County Courts throughout the State shall each have jurisdiction of prosecutions for offenses against the provisions of this Act.

SEC. 5. This Act shall take effect and be in force from and after the first day of July, anno Domini, eighteen hundred and seventy.

From *California Statutes*, 1869–1870

Chinese May Not Testify Against White Men in Court (1854)

THE PEOPLE, Respondent, *v.* GEORGE W. HALL, Appellant.

Mr. Ch. J. Murray delivered the opinion of the Court. Mr. J. Heydenfeldt concurred.

The appellant, a free white citizen of this State, was convicted of murder upon the testimony of Chinese witnesses.

The point involved in this case is the admissibility of such evidence.

The 394th section of the Act Concerning Civil Cases provides that no Indian or Negro shall be allowed to testify as a witness in any action or proceeding in which a white person is a party.

The 14th section of the Act of April 16th, 1850, regulating Criminal Proceedings, provides that "No black or mulatto person, or Indian, shall be allowed to give evidence in favor of, or against a white man."

The true point at which we are anxious to arrive is, the legal signification of the words, "black, mulatto, Indian, and white person," and whether the Legislature adopted them as generic terms, or intended to limit their application to specific types of the human species.

Before considering this question, it is proper to remark the difference between the two sections of our statute, already quoted, the latter being more broad and comprehensive in its exclusion, by use of the word "black," instead of Negro.

Conceding, however, for the present, that the word "black," as used in the 14th section, and "Negro," in 394th, are convertible terms, and that the former was intended to include the latter, let us proceed to inquire who are excluded from testifying as witnesses under the term "Indian."

When Columbus first landed upon the shores of this continent, in his attempt to discover a western passage to the Indies, he imagined that he had accomplished the object of his expedition, and that the Island of San Salvador was one of those Islands of the Chinese Sea, lying near the extremity of India, which had been described by navigators.

Acting upon this hypothesis, and also perhaps from the similarity of features and physical conformation, he gave to the Islanders the name of Indians, which appellation was universally adopted, and extended to the aboriginals of the New World, as well as of Asia.

From that time, down to a very recent period, the American Indians and the Mongolian, or Asiatic, were regarded as the same type of the human species.

In order to arrive at a correct understanding of the intention of our Legislature, it will be necessary to go back to the early history of legislation on this subject, our statute being only a transcript of those of older States.

At the period from which this legislation dates, those portions of Asia which include India proper, the Eastern Archipelago, and the countries washed by the Chinese waters as far as then known, were denominated the Indies, from which the inhabitants had derived the generic name of Indians.

Ethnology, at that time, was unknown as a distinct science, or if known, had not reached that high point of perfection which it has since attained by the scientific inquiries and discoveries of the masterminds of the last half century. Few speculations had been made with regard to the moral or physical differences between the different races of mankind. These were general in their character, and limited to those visible and palpable variations which could not escape the attention of the most common observer.

The general, or perhaps universal opinion of that day was, that there were but three distinct types of the human species which, in their turn, were subdivided into varieties of tribes. This opinion is still held by many scientific writers, and is supported by Cuvier, one of the most eminent naturalists of modern times.

Many ingenious speculations have been resorted to for the purpose of sustaining this opinion. It has been supposed, and not without plausibility, that this continent was first peopled by Asiatics, who crossed Behring's Straits, and from thence found their way down to the more fruitful climates of Mexico and South America. Almost every tribe has some tradition of coming from the North, and many of them, that their ancestors came from some remote country beyond the ocean.

From the eastern portions of Kamtschatka, the Aleutian Islands form a long and continuous group, extending eastward to that portion of the North American Continent inhabited by the Esquimaux. They appear to be a continuation of the lofty volcanic ranges which traverse the two continents, and are inhabited by a race who resemble, in a remarkable degree, in language and appearance, both the inhabitants of Kamtschatka (who are admitted to be of the Mongolian type), and the Esquimaux, who again, in turn, resemble other tribes of American Indians. The similarity of the skull and pelvis, and the general configuration of the two races; the remarkable resemblance in eyes, beard, hair, and other peculiarities, together with the contiguity of the two continents, might well have led to the belief that this country was first peopled by the Asiatics, and that the difference between the different tribes and the parent stock was such as would necessarily arise from the circumstances of climate, pursuits, and other physical causes, and was no greater than that existing between the Arab and the European, both of whom were supposed to belong to the Caucasian race.

Although the discoveries of eminent archeologists, and the researches of modern geologists, have given to this continent an antiquity of thousands of years anterior to the evidence of man's existence, and the light of modern science may have shown conclusively that it was not peopled by the inhabitants of Asia, but that the Aborigines are a distinct type, and as such claim a distinct origin, still, this would not in any degree alter the meaning of the term, and render that specific which was before generic.

We have adverted to these speculations for the purpose of showing that the name of Indian, from the time of Columbus to the present day, has been used to designate, not alone the North American Indian, but the whole of the Mongolian race, and that the name, though first applied probably through mistake, was afterward continued as appropriate on account of the supposed common origin.

That this was the common opinion in the early history of American legislation cannot be disputed, and, therefore, all legislation upon the subject must have borne relation to that opinion.

Can, then, the use of the word "Indian," because at the

present day it may be sometimes regarded as a specific, and not as a generic term, alter this conclusion? We think not; because at the origin of the legislation we are considering, it was used and admitted in its common and ordinary acceptation, as a generic term, distinguishing the great Mongolian race, and as such, its meaning then became fixed by law, and in construing statutes the legal meaning of words must be preserved.

Again: the words of the Act must be construed in *pari materia*. It will not be disputed that "white" and "Negro" are generic terms, and refer to two of the great types of mankind. If these, as well as the word "Indian," are not to be regarded as generic terms, including the two great races which they were intended to designate, but only specific, and applying to those whites and Negroes who were inhabitants of this continent at the time of the passage of the Act, the most anomalous consequences would ensue. The European white man who comes here would not be shielded from the testimony of the degraded and demoralized caste, while the Negro, fresh from the coast of Africa, or the Indian of Patagonia, the Kanaka, South Sea Islander, or New Hollander, would be admitted, upon their arrival, to testify against white citizens in our courts of law.

To argue such a proposition would be an insult to the good sense of the Legislature.

The evident intention of the Act was to throw around the citizen a protection for life and property, which could only be secured by removing him above the corrupting influences of degraded castes.

It can hardly be supposed that any Legislature would attempt this by excluding domestic Negroes and Indians, who not unfrequently have correct notions of their obligations to society, and turning loose upon the community the more degraded tribes of the same species, who have nothing in common with us, in language, country, or laws.

We have, thus far, considered this subject on the hypothesis that the 14th section of the Act Regulating Criminal Proceedings and the 394th section of the Practice Act were the same.

As before remarked, there is a wide difference between the two. The word "black" may include all Negroes, but the term "Negro" does not include all black persons.

By the use of this term in this connection, we understand it to mean the opposite of "white," and that it should be taken as contradistinguished from all white persons.

In using the words "no black or mulatto person, or Indian shall be allowed to give evidence for or against a white person," the Legislature, if any intention can be ascribed to it, adopted the most comprehensive terms to embrace every known class or shade of color, as the apparent design was to protect the white person from the influence of all testimony other than that of persons of the same caste. The use of these terms must, by every sound rule of construction, exclude everyone who is not of white blood.

The Act of Congress, in defining what description of aliens may become naturalized citizens, provides that every "free white citizen," etc., etc. In speaking of this subject, Chancellor Kent says that "the Act confines the description to 'white' citizens, and that it is a matter of doubt, whether, under this provision, any of the tawny races of Asia can be admitted to citizenship." (2 Kent's Com. 72.)

We are not disposed to leave this question in any doubt. The word "white" has a distinct signification, which *ex vi termini*, excludes black, yellow, and all other colors. It will be observed, by reference to the first section of the second Article of the Constitution of this State, that none but white males can become electors, except in the case of Indians, who may be admitted by special Act of the Legislature. On examination of the constitutional debates, it will be found that not a little difficulty existed in selecting these precise words, which were finally agreed upon as the most comprehensive that could be suggested to exclude all inferior races.

If the term "white," as used in the Constitution, was not understood in its generic sense as including the Caucasian race, and necessarily excluding all others, where was the necessity of providing for the admission of Indians to the privilege of voting, by special legislation?

We are of the opinion that the words "white," "Negro," "mulatto," "Indian," and "black person," wherever they occur in our Constitution and laws, must be taken in their generic sense, and that, even admitting the Indian of this continent is not of the Mongolian type, that the words "black person," in the 14th section, must be taken as contradistinguished from white, and necessarily excludes all races other than the Caucasian.

We have carefully considered all the consequences resulting from a different rule of construction, and are satisfied that even in a doubtful case, we would be impelled to this decision on grounds of public policy.

The same rule which would admit them to testify, would admit them to all the equal rights of citizenship, and we might soon see them at the polls, in the jury box, upon the bench, and in our legislative halls.

This is not a speculation which exists in the excited and overheated imagination of the patriot and statesman, but it is an actual and present danger.

The anomalous spectacle of a distinct people, living in our community, recognizing no laws of this State, except through necessity, bringing with them their prejudices and national feuds, in which they indulge in open violation of law; whose mendacity is proverbial; a race of people whom nature has marked as inferior, and who are incapable of progress or intellectual development beyond a certain point, as their history has shown; differing in language, opinions, color, and physical conformation; between whom and ourselves nature has placed an impassable difference, is now presented, and for them is claimed, not only the right to swear away the life of a citizen, but the further privilege of participating with us in administering the affairs of our Government.

These facts were before the Legislature that framed this Act, and have been known as matters of public history to every subsequent Legislature.

There can be no doubt as to the intention of the Legislature, and that if it had ever been anticipated that this class of people were not embraced in the prohibition, then such specific words would have been employed as would have put the matter beyond any possible controversy.

For these reasons, we are of opinion that the testimony was inadmissible.

The judgment is reversed and the cause remanded.

> From *Reports of Cases Argued and Determined in the Supreme Court of the State of California, 1854*

The Exclusion of Chinese Witnesses Reaffirmed (1871)

THE PEOPLE OF THE STATE OF CALIFORNIA, Respondents, *v.* JAMES BRADY, Appellant.

Appeal from the County Court of the City and County of San Francisco.

The defendant appealed.

The other facts are stated in the opinion.

Hall & Dudley, for Appellant.

Jo Hamilton, Attorney-General, for Respondent.
Darwin & Murphy, of Counsel.

The statutes of this State say, "Chinese shall not be witnesses in an action or proceeding wherein a white person is a party." And again: "No Chinese shall be permitted to give evidence in favor of or against any white person." These provisions are in force, unless in whole or in part repealed by a clause in the Fourteenth Amendment to the National Constitution, which provides: "Nor shall any State deprive any person of life, liberty or property, without due process of law, nor deny to any person within its jurisdiction the equal protection of the laws." Now, if the denial of the power to testify, found in our statutes, amounts to a denial of an equal State protection, then such denial by our State law is made void by the superior force of the Fourteenth Amendment. Or, let us put it this way: The United States Constitution, in its Fourteenth Amendment, provides that no State shall deny to any person within its borders any legal protection which it accords to another—that its laws shall be so impersonal as to afford an equal protection to each. Now if our State, by excluding Chinamen from testifying in cases where white men are suffered to do so, deprives them of an equal legal protection, then such deprivation is in contravention of the higher law—that of the National Constitution, and should be judicially disregarded. The question then to be answered is, whether a person who is deprived of the power of testifying is less protected than one, who amid the same surroundings, enjoys that power.

It is true that there are many cases in which the power of testifying is neither an object of desire, nor in any sense a right. Cases wherein it is but a burden, such are those in which the witness having no personal concern is summoned by another to illustrate that other's cause. But there are cases in which the dearest interests of the witness are involved, and must stand or not stand as the witness can stand or not stand in the tribunal which passes upon them. As to these I shall insist, that if the law allows one man to become a witness in his own cause, it is an unequal law, and distributes an unequal protection, unless it allows every other man the same right. Were it not for the wonderful force of human prejudice, no argument would be needed to establish this proposition. Certainly to any number of which men similarly disfavored, the inequality would seem clear—would arouse the liveliest concern for their rights, and inflame just and instant resistance. Suppose one white man, unaided by other than his own proof, could bring down the law upon his injurer, and thus punish a past and avert a future aggression, while another must stagger under repeated aggressions and could only invoke a tardy redress through the oath of one who might very much hesitate to be just and generous enough to incur the odium of seeming to take his part. The supposal in the case of white men would be the strongest argument. Nor is it true, as urged by the objector, that to afford an equal protection by the laws means that the State shall stop in making an equal menace against the criminal, whether his victim be a white or a Chinaman. This the State has done. It means more. It demands that such other laws as shall be passed in aid of the menace shall also apply equally. The menace may be a flaming sword for the protection of one because he can take and wield it, and it may sleep upon the wall within its sheath as to another, because he has been forbidden to take it down. To have equal protection of the laws means to have equal protection of all the laws which contribute directly toward it. The State secures that protection by means of, first, a menace against the wrongdoer; second, the enactment of means adequate to his discovery and conviction; and, third, the infliction of the menaced penalty. To constitute an equal protection to a Chinaman and white man, there must be an equality in each of these elements that go to afford it; and to deny equality in any one of these is to deny an equal protection. The State must not only utter an equal menace against and inflict an equal pain upon his aggressor, but it must also provide equal facilities and appliances for his conviction.

The deliberating aggressor is dissuaded, not by the menace, but by considerations touching the certainty of its execution. If this certainty is as great in the case of a Chinaman injured by a white man as it is in that of a white man injured by a Chinaman, then the restraining influences of the laws in each case are also equal; and if this certainty be not as great in the case of the Chinaman, then the protection afforded him is not that equal protection demanded by the Fourteenth Amendment. If a man is kept at a disadvantage in the means of conviction, he cannot make equal avail either of the menace or its infliction. For *his* protection the menace bears less intimidation and its infliction a diminished assurance.

Equality of protection, demanding equality in the means of conviction, therefore, also demands that whether a Chinaman or a white man be concerned, the modes of judicial investigation shall be the same. There shall be an equal right to the same instruments of proof; the same power to compel their attendance; the same sanctions to insure their veracity; the same right for the party concerned, if he be cognizant of the facts to put himself and his oath into the judicial balance.

It is true that when the law shall have announced equal opportunities in each of these means of self-protection, individual and national likings and loathings will yet, nevertheless, advance the conviction in one case and retard it in another, and an equality of protection will not be exactly attained. But this failure will not be the fault of the law. The State will have done its duty. The law will have ceased to lend its support to the unfair denial. And until the law shall have done that, it will stand in conflict with the National Constitution. The natural consequence of the excluding law is that more crimes against Chinamen than against white men go unwhipped of justice. The menace of the law is void, so far as regards all those injuries of which some friendly white man is not also cognizant. If a white man having malice enough, have also sufficient prescience, he may strike a Chinaman with every crime in the statute, without legal risk. True, a white man may also be struck at under conditions precluding discovery. But in his case the impunity is accidental—is in spite of the law, and no law could prevent it. While in the case of a Chinaman, if not suggested by, it flows from, a defect in the law. The law does not equally mean to prevent it. It does not intend an equal protection. Let us emphasize the statement that there can be no equal protection unless there be equal facilities in making the legal menace productive of it; an equal power of pointing out the criminal, and of charging home his guilt. The Chinaman is mainly at the mercy of another for such protection as he receives from the laws. The white man bears about with him his own protection. He cannot get beyond the reach of it. He is everywhere attended by a power which intimidates aggression by the menace of discovery. He himself is the accredited messenger of the State to bear to its tribunals the story of his own wrongs, and may become their swift-winged avenger.

If it be conceded then, that one, denied the power of testifying against his aggressor, is less protected that one permitted to do so, it must also be conceded that the law of the State, which allows the white man to bear witness against his aggressor and denies a Chinaman the same right, in doing so, comes in conflict with the National Constitution, and to that extent is discharged of its force and becomes void. And our statutory exclusion of Chinamen in this sort of a case should be legally held for nought; and in all those cases where white men may protest life or liberty or property by their own testimony, Chinamen should enjoy the same right.

It is objected that to be protected is a right, but to be a witness is not a right but a privilege, which the State may confer or not.

1st. If to be protected be a right, then to be a witness is also a right, if being a witness be necessary to protection.

2d. To be a witness, generally, may be a privilege or rather a duty which the officer conducting the prosecution may impose or not, in his discretion, under the law; but to be a witness in case of injury to one's self, against the aggressor, is not subject to such discretion, but a legal right of the injured party, if he claim to exercise it. Section 1416, Hittell's Digest, makes the injured party competent, and, I claim, confers the right to enjoy the competency. Sections 1694 and 2195, the only ones on accusations or complaints, and Section 1740, seem to sustain this view.

But, no matter how that may be, it is practically true that whatever discretion the State Attorney possesses, he commonly uses it in favor of obtaining all the testimony he can, including that of the injured party, and that while he can, with or without right, decline to use a white party injured, he cannot in that discretion use a Chinaman, if a white man be the aggressor. So that even the presumed discretion does not help the objector's case; for that discretion does not and cannot operate an equal protection. The deliberating aggressor, who agrees with the objector as to this discretion knows, at most, that the prosecutor, in an unusual exercise of power, may decline to testify the sufferer, even though a white man; but he also knows that the prosecutor cannot, in any contingency, testify him if a Chinaman. The fact remains that in one case the injured party may be used, and in the other he cannot; and if power to testify is power to protect, there is higher protection where it may be, than where it cannot be exercised.

Again, it is argued that as those of our criminal laws which prohibit are impersonal and general, that is all that is required by the amendment.

I have said that the mere utterance of a prohibition under a penalty is but a small part of the legal machinery used in protecting from crime, and all that machinery must be applied, as well to the protection of the Chinaman as to that of the white man, else he has not equal protection. Suppose, while the menace of the law against robbery stood as now, it was declared that a Chinaman should not accuse, nor make complaint, nor have warrant, nor subpena, nor his witnesses sworn, nor the aid of an officer, nor of the State's Attorney. That the defendant should not be convicted save on the testimony of a dozen witnesses, nor even put upon his defense if he denied the accusation on oath. That, in case of his conviction, his punishment should be much smaller than if he had injured a white man. There are none but in such a case would see that the Chinaman had not equal protection, and also see that the protection does not come from the menace, but from the combined group of laws which bring it down upon the spoiler.

But among the group of protective laws—protective because conducing to conviction—there is none of so much direct value as that suffering the party injured to be a witness.

But the objector says the testimony of the injured party does not secure conviction and so is no sure protection. It often does; it often aids it; is often the sole testimony to a technical point, which point has been made morally certain, but not been legally proved by other testimony. But it always tends, *a priori*, to make the conviction more likely, and so is a dissuading element in the mind of him who deliberates a crime. He can more safely strike a man legally dumb than one legally voiceful, and he prefers the former as a victim. The accident of nonpunishment will always be possible, but in the one case it is reduced to a minimum, and in the other not. Only where this accident in both classes of cases possesses the same legal likelihood will the protection be equal.

But the Chinaman would not be believed, for the law is only a popular conception of his unveracity, which would guide the jury were the law repealed.

Answer: The law is not a popular expression of his unveracity, as much as of our prejudice. If we held him unworthy of belief, we would not admit him as a witness in any case; but we do so when another Chinaman is concerned, and holding him credible when a Chinaman is concerned, we can only exclude him when a white man is, on the ground of prejudice. We really let him tell the truth, in case it hurts only a Chinaman, but not if it hurts a white man. To hold him capable of truly presenting his observations, in case of a Chinaman as actor and not in case of a white man, is an absurdity which can only be explained by prejudice.

The fact may be and probably is, that the Chinese, as a race, are not as credible as the whites, as a race. But there is no race absolutely credible, and their lower grade of credibility is no reason for refusing the degree they possess. Then again, it is not the race but an individual that testifies, and we can apply to him, of whatsoever race, the same *experimentum crucis*, the same methods of verification we do in the case of a white witness. Credence is no more compulsory in the one than in the other case. Indeed, prejudice apart, the laws of belief are quite independent of person, and dependent only on logic and conformity with known truths, and are the same in all cases.

Some white men, not generally credible, are believed, in the particular case, because undoubted truths endorse them; we test their testimony by fixed canons and established likelihoods; we doubt or disbelieve in the case of disconformity.

Submit the Chinaman to the same tests; the unveracious Chinaman is no more likely than the unveracious white man to steal away our faculties or misdirect our judgment.

But these considerations are rather on the reason of the law excluding, than to the effect of the amendment; and the logical answer is that, if the Chinaman testify, he may be more or less believed, and that chance of being believed, no matter how small, is a chance which might to that extent augment his protection by augmenting the risk of injuring him with impunity. If he is denied the value of that chance, be it ever so small, he has not as much protection as the white man who enjoys the chance. The law which denies him ever so small a chance of protecting himself by his testimony protects him less than it does the white man, to whom it accords the chance denied to him. It denies him thereby an equal protection.

The case of *People* v. *Washington* (36 Cal. 658) was decided on the strength of the Civil Rights bill, but it decided a point or two which go in support of my argument. It decided (before the Fourteenth Amendment) that a white man in this State had the security of not being testified against by a Chinaman, and that the Negro had the same right by virtue of the Civil Rights bill. Now, if exemption from being testified against be a security, or protection, capacity to testify in one's own behalf is also a security or protection. For testimony is decided to be a power to help or hurt, and its denial is the denial of a security or protection. Again, the Civil Rights bill guaranteed to Negroes "the full and equal benefit of all laws and proceedings for the security of person," etc., and the Court (in 36 Cal. 667) said, "That in order to secure this, the rules of evidence must apply equally to all alike." Again (on page 670) the Court says: "The statutes of the State, regulating the competency of witnesses, are made applicable to all alike."

Now, if this all follows from the terms of the Civil Rights bill, it quite as strenuously follows from those of the Fourteenth Amendment.

While citing this Washington case, I will add, that while we conceive the case in hand securely anchored on the Fourteenth Amendment, we yet, in the spirit of the suggestions of that case, urge that we are also sustained, and the Chinaman's admissibility is supported by Sections 1, 11, and 17 of our own State Constitution. (See Cooley, Const. Lim. p. 355 and note, and pp. 392, 393, 369; *James* v. *Reynolds*, 2 Texas 251; 2 Yerger 269, 554; 44 Barb. 472; Cooley pp. 368, 369.)

'TEMPLE, J., delivered the opinion of the Court, WALLACE, J., and SPRAGUE, J., concurring:

The defendant, a white man, was convicted of the crime of robbery, committed upon Hing Kee, a Chinaman, who was permitted to testify against the defendant on the trial.

The ruling of the Court admitting this testimony against the defendant's objections is assigned as error, and is the only question raised on this appeal.

Section 14 of the Act of this State concerning crimes and punishments, as amended in 1863, reads as follows: "No Indian or person having one half or more Indian blood or Mongolian or Chinese, shall be permitted to give evidence in favor of, or against, any white man."

This section is in full force, unless it is rendered inoperative in whole or in part by a clause in the Fourteenth Amendment to the Federal Constitution, which amendment, so far as material to this inquiry, reads as follows: "All persons born or naturalized in the United States, and subject to the jurisdiction thereof, are citizens of the United States and of the State wherein they reside. No State shall make or enforce any law which shall abridge the privileges or immunities of citizens of the United States. Nor shall any State deprive any person of life, liberty or property without due process of law, nor deny to any within its jurisdiction the equal protection of the laws."

It is claimed that the statute which denies to the Chinaman the right to testify against a white man is in conflict with this amendment, because it deprives the Chinaman of some degree of legal protection which it accords to the white man. That is to say, the ability to testify is a protection, because it tends to deter from crime against the person, by adding to the probability of conviction and punishment.

It is not charged that the law discriminates against the Chinaman in affording a remedy to the white man for an injury, which upon the same state of facts is not afforded to the Chinaman. The facts being proven, the law pronounces the same judgment upon one as upon the other. The same facts being made to appear, the law provides for the Chinaman the same protection against threatened violence as for the white man. The protection of the whole police power of the State is afforded to them under the same circumstances, in the same way, and on precisely the same terms as to any other class of inhabitants. If a crime be committed against the person or property of a Chinaman, the same punishment is meted out to the criminal, when convicted, as though the crime had been committed upon a white man. But not only do the same consequences follow upon the same state of facts being proven, whether they affect Chinese or white men, but the law affords the Chinaman every means of bringing the facts to the knowledge of the Court for judicial action that is afforded to the white man. If a Chinaman be robbed, the commission of the crime may be proven by the same means as though he were a white man. If a white man be robbed by a white man, the fact cannot be established by Chinese testimony; and yet it may frequently happen that the fact cannot be proven in any other way. The same is true of a robbery committed upon a Chinaman by a white man. If a white man be robbed by a Chinaman, the fact may be proved by the evidence of white men or Chinese; and this is true as to a robbery committed upon a Chinaman by a Chinaman.

It is plain, therefore, that a crime is punished in the same way and may be proven by the same means in all cases whether a white man or a Chinaman be the injured party. But it is said that if the general disqualification of Chinese to testify for or against a white man prevents them from testifying when a crime is committed upon them, the law is to that extent unequal and therefore void; that the right of the injured party to testify stands upon a very different footing from the right to call other witnesses. He may have a right to the use of the same species of evidence, but if he be the party concerned, he should also have the same right to offer himself as a witness. A crime may be committed under such circumstances that the party against whom it is committed is the only person by whom it can be proven. If the injured party be a white man, his testimony alone may be sufficient to cause the punishment of the wrongdoer, and by punishing a past wrong prevent a future wrong, and the Chinaman not being able to do this, is less protected. That although the law threatens the same punishment for a crime committed upon the person of a Chinaman as when committed upon the person of a white man, the certainty of the punishment, and therefore the amount of protection afforded, is necessarily lessened by his exclusion as a witness.

I confess myself unable to see the force of this position, notwithstanding the confidence with which it is relied upon by the ingenious counsel who has made an interesting and able argument in the case on the part of the people. The white man is not permitted to testify because he is the injured party, but because he is a competent witness on other grounds. The Chinaman is not excluded because he is the injured party and also a Chinaman, but because on other grounds he is an incompetent witness. The fact that he is the injured party is an immaterial circumstance in this discussion. His disadvantage is one shared, in a greater or lesser degree, by all who are so circumstanced as not to be surrounded by persons competent to testify. The fact that his countrymen, who are more likely to be his associates, are excluded, may be said to have an effect, in some degree, in the same direction. But this is not owing to the inequality of the law. That affords to all the same instruments of proof. All general laws operate more or less unequally—not on account of the partial provisions of the law, but from the various circumstances in which those upon whom they operate are placed. The white man who employs Chinese as workmen upon his estate is less likely to be able to prove offenses against his property than one who employs other laborers. He may, therefore, be said to be less protected; but this is the accident of his circumstances, and not the partiality of the law. He happens to be isolated from those who are competent to testify.

But it is contended that, although another may be so circumstanced as to be deprived of the equal protection of the laws, this is always accidental and not the necessary consequences of the provisions of law.

As to them the law is impersonal, and deprives them of no advantages afforded to others under the same circumstances; but the law excludes Mongolians, as a class, and itself creates the circumstance which places them at a disadvantage.

I think I have shown that there is no difference in principle —that the law does not cause them to be isolated from those competent to testify, although the fact of their exclusion may increase the chances that they will be so isolated. But if the position be admitted, then the question resolves itself into this: Has the Legislature the power to declare classes of persons such as Indians and Mongolians incompetent to testify? That it may rightfully do so independently of the Fourteenth Amendment cannot be questioned. The Legislature of every State in the Union, so far as I know, and certainly of nearly every one, has continuously asserted and exercised this power during its entire history. To declare who shall be competent to testify and to regulate the production of evidence has always been considered a proper exercise of legislative power. It has excluded persons for nonconformity of religious belief, for inability to understand the nature of an oath, for having been convicted of an infamous crime, for having Negro blood, for being an Indian or a Mongolian, and I am not aware that the power of the Legislature to pass such laws as ever been questioned.

Now, in passing these laws, the Legislature does not act arbitrarily. It does not exclude a person because of his unbelief in popular theogical dogmas, nor the Mongolian for being a Mongolian merely. The theory of the law and the idea upon which these laws are based is, that every person shall be permitted to testify who can aid the Court in coming to a correct conclusion as to the facts upon which it is to adjudicate. The reason why the testimony of such persons would be valueless in judicial investigations may be that they are incapable of testifying intelligently; that they are too unreliable to be of any service; that their admission would probably defeat justice by producing false testimony, or that they have particular prejudices against certain classes which would cause their evidence likely to do harm where the rights of such persons are concerned; such evidence, it is presumed, would impede rather than advance the cause of justice. It would not tend to protect any, but might cause the conviction of the innocent, or the acquittal of the guilty. Could counsel be convinced that Chinese testimony could never have any weight, or that it would be more likely to cause the escape of the guilty than their punishment, and as likely to cause the conviction of the innocent as the guilty, he would not think their exclusion deprived them of any degree of protection to which they are fairly entitled; and yet this is what the Legislature has decided, and had a right to decide, in enacting the law. I am not called upon to defend such legislation, or to deny that a more reasonable rule would be to allow the Courts to seek information from such sources as may be available, and to give to testimony such weight as it may deem it entitled to. The power of the Legislature to pass such laws is too well established to be called in question at this late day. (*Duffy* v. *Holson*, October Term, 1870.)

If I am correct in the proposition that this is a proper subject to be regulated by legislative action, and that the ground upon which the Legislature acts is that such evidence could not aid the Courts in their investigations, but would tend to defeat rather than promote the ends of justice, then it seems to me it must follow that the Fourteenth Amendment to the Federal Constitution can have no bearing upon the subject. It cannot be intended to compel the Courts to occupy their time in listening to evidence which cannot influence their judgment, or to deprive the State of the power to make such regulations as the cause of justice may absolutely require.

I am not called upon to say what should be the ruling if it

were to appear that, under the pretense of regulating the production of evidence, the State has really deprived any person within its jurisdiction of any substantial means of protection afforded to others by its laws. There is no reason to suppose that the law in question was not passed in good faith, and with the honest purpose of promoting the cause of justice, even if that could be called in question here. The relation between the States and the Federal Government would forbid any such suspicion upon the motives of a State Legislature on the part of the Federal Government, and certainly this Court, a coordinate branch of the Government, cannot impugn their motives. And, independently of the comity which should exist between the departments of the Government, we can hardly conceive it possible that a legislative body in a Christian country would deliberately deprive its Courts and police of any proper means for the detection and prevention of crime; that it would willingly leave any class unprotected, so far as the commission of crimes against them are concerned; this would directly encourage crime, and lead inevitably to the demoralization of society, and consequently the insecurity of all. To withdraw from any class the protection of the police laws, through prejudice or from a desire to discourage their presence, would be inhuman and barbarous. We cannot attribute any such motives to a coordinate department of the Government, and we must conclude that the provisions of the law under consideration were supposed by the Legislature to provide every means for the detection and punishment of crime consistent with justice and the safety of the community.

At the time the amendment was adopted similar laws existed in nearly every State of the Union. They had never been regarded as depriving anyone of any degree of protection which the law afforded to others, or depriving the Courts of any proper assistance they could otherwise have had in their investigations. They were sustained on the ground that they were necessary that the guilty might be punished and the innocent escape. The amendment did not render such laws less appropriate or less necessary, and there is nothing in the principle established by it which conflicts with the theory of such laws. It cannot be supposed, therefore, that in adopting the amendment it was intended to deprive the State Legislature of their power over the subject.

I think I have shown that there is no inequality in the protective laws of this State; that the law interposes the same shield for the protection of the Chinaman as for the white man, and that it imposes the same punishment when he has been injured; that upon the same facts it pronounces the same judgment, without regard to the person upon whom it may fall; that it dispenses equal justice to all; and further, that in the rules of evidence established by the Legislature there is no inequality, or, if there is, it is made in furtherance of justice, and is unavoidable; that in excluding Chinamen the Legislature exercises a discretion properly entrusted to it, and that a proper exercise of it in the interests of justice, although it may exclude a Chinaman where another is allowed to testify, is not a violation of the Fourteenth Amendment. I cannot think, however, that this last inquiry was necessary in this case. The inquiry should stop when it is ascertained that upon the same state of facts the same legal consequences follow to all. If the laws themselves are equal, imposing the same burdens upon and affording the same remedies to all, under the same ascertained circumstances, the requirement of equality is satisfied.

Limitations upon the powers of the State Governments are appropriate in the Federal Constitution. It may be necessary to restrain the powers of the State that it may not interfere with the General Government in the exercise of the powers granted to it, or that a State may not, by its individual action, defeat any of the purposes for which the General Government exists. To the extent, however, of the powers not granted to the General Government or denied to the States, the power of the State is supreme. It enacts laws of its own right and should be allowed to execute them in its own way. The Federal Government cannot supervise its exercise of the powers it undoubtedly possesses. It is no part of purpose for which that Government was created, to stand guard over the States to see that they execute their laws in a manner not to oppress those who are subject to them. The State Government is complete in itself, so far as matters of internal government are concerned, and contains in its own Constitution every necessary safeguard against improper use of its powers, and every protection to individual rights, which the people thought necessary.

Rules of evidence are a part of the contrivance by means of which the State executes its laws. They are always the means to an end, and if the law be one the State has a right to pass, I cannot think it was intended to interfere with the means the State may adopt to enforce it.

This view is sustained by a consideration of the particular purpose the amendment was designed to accomplish. Its chief purpose undoubtedly was to protect Negroes in those States where slavery recently existed. Under those laws it sometimes happened that the law pronounced a different judgment upon a Negro from that it pronounced upon a white man upon the same state of facts. The law provided a different punishment to the Negro when convicted of crime from that which was provided for a white man when convicted of the same crime, and in other respects the law discriminated against the Negro. The amendment was evidently intended to prevent these inequalities. It could not have been intended to authorize the Federal Government to supervise the State in the exercise of its undoubted powers. Such a construction would reduce a State to condition of a mere municipality, exercising its meager powers by sufferance, and render meaningless that clause of the Constitution which recognizes the possession of reserved powers by the States.

The counsel for the People cites the case of *The People* v. *George Washington* (36 Cal. 658) as supporting his views, and it must be admitted that some of the positions taken in that case are inconsistent with the views I have expressed in this case. That case presented for consideration the constitutionality of the Act of Congress commonly called the Civil Rights bill, and its effect upon the fourteenth section of the Act of this State, concerning crimes and punishments, cited above. The Court decided the Act of Congress constitutional; that it was authorized by the Thirteenth Amendment to the Federal Constitution, which provides that "neither slavery nor involuntary servitude, except as a punishment for crime, whereof the party shall have been duly convicted, shall exist within the United States, or any place subject to their jurisdiction"; and also in the second section, that Congress may enforce the amendment by appropriate legislation.

I dissent, both from the reasoning used and conclusions arrived at in that case, for the reasons given by Mr. Justice Crockett in his dissenting opinion, and for reasons which will readily suggest themselves from what I have already stated. If I am correct as to the theory upon which legislation concerning the competency of evidence is based, it seems to me it must follow that the positions taken by the Court in that case are wrong. There is one reason why I disapprove of that case, however, which, as it has a direct bearing upon this case and differs a little from positions taken by Judge Crockett in that, and is, withal, an important matter, I propose to state.

It is stated in the opinion of the Court, in that case, that the object of the first section of the Thirteenth Amendment is not only to abolish slavery, but to deprive Congress and the States of the power to reduce any person within the jurisdiction of the United States to a state of slavery. That is to say, so far as its future operation is concerned it is a mere limitation upon the legislative power of the States and of the United States. That the second section confers upon Congress the power, by appropriate legislation, to secure all persons in the United States in the full enjoyment of that liberty contemplated by the first section; "or, in other words, the Thirteenth Amendment was at least intended to make all men born in the United States, without reference to race or color, equal before the law in respect to *personal liberty—*

one of the absolute rights of man—and to give Congress power to pass any and all laws necessary and proper to accomplish that end."

The first section is said by the Court, and I think corrrectly, to be simply a limitation upon the power of the State to establish slavery or reduce any one to a state of slavery or involuntary servitude; and I cannot think that the second section, which simply empowers Congress to enforce this limitation upon the legislative power of the State, confers upon Congress any power to establish a police system for the internal government of the State, or by its laws to annul the laws of a State, or to control their operation in any way whatever.

There is nothing in the language used in the first section of the amendment which can be construed into a grant of power. It is a restriction, and not an enlargement of the powers of the General Government, if it applies to the General Government at all. It is a limitation upon the States, depriving them of the power to establish slavery. If it were within the province of the Federal Government to establish a system of police laws for the protection of individuals within the States, the language is inappropriate to confer any power over the subject matter of the section. The apparent purpose of the amendment was not to prevent the illegal duress of individuals. It was aimed exclusively at the institution of slavery as established by the laws of the States. It was directed to the States in their sovereign capacity as lawmakers, and was not intended to afford relief to individuals *unlawfully* deprived of their liberty. Its purpose is satisfied when such restraint is rendered illegal. The right to personal liberty is secured by the amendment itself, and it is not necessary that Congress should pass laws upon the subject, much less give to anyone political rights which may add to their importance and enable them to maintain their state of freedom. This is absolutely secured by the Constitution itself, which renders void all laws for their enslavement. They are not to be armed that they may resist State laws, or given importance that they may influence State legislation.

The second section of the amendment certainly contains no substantive grant of power. It merely authorizes Congress to enforce the amendment by appropriate legislation. Its scope is limited by the first section. That is a mere limitation upon the powers of the States. It authorizes Congress, therefore, to pass such laws as under our system of Government would be appropriate to enforce a limitation upon the legislative power of a State, and no other. It is not an affirmative grant of power before which State legislation must give way, like the power to establish uniform laws upon the subject of bankruptcy. The laws of the State must be tried by the language of the Constitutional inhibition and not by the laws of Congress. The power to enforce a limitation upon the power of a State cannot be construed to authorize Congress to enlarge the limitation if necessary to render it effectual. The State law in question ought, therefore, to have been tested by the language of the Constitution and not by the Civil Rights bill.

Nor is it appropriate legislation for Congress to nullify a law of the State, either directly or by preventing its execution. It could only do so when the law is unconstitutional, and to determine that question is the province of the judiciary. It would compel the people unnecessarily to sustain two police systems—one to execute the laws, and the other to control and, in certain cases, to prevent their execution. It would interfere with efficiency of the police system of the State, and almost inevitably lead to conflicts between the two Governments. The two Governments, however, are not antagonistical, either in theory or interest. They are parts of one system, supplementary to each other, together supplying all the governmental wants of the people. They are both under the control of the people, but in their operation should be independent of and, therefore, a check upon each other.

Ever since the Federal Government has been in operation it has been the practice to test the constitutionality of State laws, and enforce the limitations upon the powers of the

States by judicial decisions. The claim on the part of the Supreme Court of the United States of the right to pass upon these questions, even when arising in the State Courts, though not always conceded, has been generally acquiesced in. Constitutional limitations, so far as they affect individual rights, have always under our system been enforced by judicial action, and I have no doubt a proper construction of the second section of the Thirteenth Amendment would confine legislation on the part of Congress to laws providing for judicial action in the premises.

But the claim on the part of Congress of the right to interfere with or control the operation of State laws is utterly repugnant to our system of Government. "The genius and character of the whole Government seem to be," said Chief Justice Marshall, in *Gibbons* v. *Ogden* (9 Wheaton 195), "that its action is to be applied to all the external concerns of the nation and to those internal concerns which affect the States generally, but not to those which are completely within a particular State, which do not affect other States, and with which it is not necessary to interfere, for the purpose of executing some of the general powers of the Government." The division of powers between the State and Federal Governments, and the independence of the States within the sphere of their reserved powers, and their exclusive right of legislation as to most of the objects for which Governments exist, has always been considered the principal and most valuable safeguard for civil liberty afforded by our system. The right of local legislation for each Colony is said by Mr. Madison to have been the fundamental idea of the Revolution. That the Colonies were with each other and with Great Britain coordinate members of one empire, under a common executive or sovereign, but not united by a legislative sovereign. The legislative power was maintained to be as complete in each American as in the British Parliament (Madison's Virginia Report).

The States, said Mr. Hamilton, can never lose their powers, till the whole people of America have lost their liberties.

When the Federal Constitution was formed, no idea was more fixed than that the States should continue independent of Federal control as to all reserved powers, which were to include entire control over all matters exclusively appertaining to a particular State. The Colonies, with their local Legislatures, had been the nurseries of civil liberty, and to the States, their legitimate successors, was entrusted the duty of maintaining it. Chiefly to secure the continued existence of the States, to uphold and maintain them as independent States, and *thereby* to secure to the people and their posterity the blessings of liberty, the Constitution and the Union were formed.

At that time no writer was more popular with American statesmen than Montesquieu. From him was derived the idea of dividing the Government into three departments—the executive, legislative, and judicial—as an essential security for the liberties of the people. Another idea advanced by him, which was very popular at that time, and often quoted, was that small States naturally gravitate to a republican form of Government; larger States to a monarchical, and vast empires to a despotic Government. The first was most favorable to individual liberty; the last, to national power. They claimed to have secured the advantages of the first by assuring the independence of the States, and the last by establishing the Federal Government as a common agent, which, in the exercise of certain limited powers, should be supreme over all.

It was more efficient than the Confederacy it displaced, for it executes its own laws. To it was entrusted the control of the foreign relations of all the States. It could declare war, and, to carry it on, wield the entire military power of the Union. As to all the world, at least, except its own members, it presented us as one nation. Within the sphere of its limited authority it wielded the power of a vast empire with all the efficiency of the most despotic Government, and yet it was supposed that it could not be dangerous to the liberties of the people, for its powers were limited and well defined, and could be used but for a few purposes, and those in which all the States had a common interest. The great mass of governmental powers were still reserved to the States. The absolute right of uncontrolled local legislation upon all subjects most intimately connected with individual rights and most essential to the maintenance of personal liberty was reserved.

The Federal Government was created by the compact of sovereign States, and their continued existence in the uncontrolled exercise of their powers is an essential element of the system. This is doubtless what Hamilton meant when he said that for the General Government to supersede or destroy the State Governments would be to commit suicide. It rests upon them as the dome rests upon and yet upholds the columns which support it.

We cannot conclude from any doubtful language that it was intended to strike from the Constitution the fundamental idea upon which the Union was constructed—to rob the Government of its crowning glory and most beneficent principle; and had such been its apparent meaning, we ought to be diligent to find out some construction which would be less pernicious in its consequences; we should regard it as we would a law apparently legalizing murder or robbery; we could not conclude such a purpose was intended unless it is expressed in unmistakable language.

In this case, however, we are not forced to any such extremity. The most obvious construction is that which is most in accord with the principles of our Government, and which preserves its beneficent features.

The judgment reversed and a new trial ordered.

BY CROCKETT, J.: I concur in the judgment and in the opinion of Justice Temple, except in so far as it dissents from or questions the correctness of certain views expressed by me in the case of *The People* v. *Washington.*

BY RHODES, C. J.: I dissent. My views upon the questions involved in this case were to some extent expressed in *The People* v. *George Washington* (36 Cal. 658); and I will hereafter, should time permit, more fully state the reasons which lead me to the conclusion that Section 14 of the Act concerning crimes and punishments was abrogated by the Fourteenth Amendment to the Constitution.

> From *Reports of Cases Argued and Determined in the Supreme Court of the State of California*, 1854

The "Cubic Air" Ordinance (1870)
Regulating Lodging Houses
[Approved July 29, 1870]

SECTION 1. Every house, room, or apartment within the limits of the City and County of San Francisco, except such public prisons and hospitals as may have been already erected, which shall be used or occupied as lodging house, room, or apartment, and every building, house, room, or apartment in which persons live or sleep, shall contain within the walls of such houses, rooms, or apartments, at least five hundred cubic feet for each adult person dwelling or sleeping therein: and every owner or tenant of any house, room, or apartment, who shall lodge, or permit to be lodged, in such house, room, or apartment more than one person to each five hundred cubic feet of air in such house, room, or apartment, shall be deemed guilty of a misdemeanor, and for every offense shall be fined not less than ten nor more than five hundred dollars, or imprisoned in the city prisons not less than five days nor more than three months, or both such fines and imprisonment.

SEC. 2. No person or persons shall lodge, dwell, sleep, or have their abode in any room, house, building, or apartment which shall not contain at least five hundred cubic feet of air each, and every person lodging, dwelling, sleeping, or having their place of abode therein: and any person or persons who shall violate any provision of this Section shall be deemed guilty of a misdemeanor and punished as provided in the first section of this Order.

SEC. 3. It shall be the duty of the Chief of Police to detail a competent and qualified officer of the regular police force to examine into and arrest for all violations of any of the provisions of this Order all persons who may be guilty thereof.

San Francisco Board of Supervisors, Order No. 939

Removing the Chinese Pigtail: The Queue Ordinance (1876)

... Each and every male prisoner incarcerated or imprisoned in the County Jail of the City and County under or pursuant to a judgment or convictions, had by any Court having jurisdiction of criminal cases in this City and County, shall, immediately upon their arrival at said County Jail, under and pursuant to a judgment, or sentenced as aforesaid, have the hair of their head cut or clipped to a uniform length of one inch from the scalp thereof. It shall be, and is hereby, made the duty of the Sheriff to have enforced the provision of this order.

City and County of San Francisco, Order No. 1294

No "Special Police" for the Chinese (1878)

An Act to Liable the Board of Supervisors of the City and County of San Francisco to Increase the Police Force of said City and County, and Provide for the Appointment, Regulation, and Payment Thereof.
[Approved April 1, 1878]

SEC. 3. The system of "special police" officers as heretofore practiced in said City and County, is hereby abolished and prohibited, and no special officer shall be appointed except as herein provided for. It shall be lawful for the Police Commissioner to appoint a special officer when the same is petitioned for by any persons, firms, or corporations so petitioning. . . .

SEC. 4. No special police officer shall ever be appointed in that portion of said City and County known as the Chinese quarter, the boundaries of which shall be established from time to time by police commissioners. It shall be the duty of the Chief of Police to change the police officers of the regular force stationed in the Chinese quarter, and to substitute others in their places, so that the whole force, in their turn, shall regularly be assigned for duty in the said quarter, in regular and continuous rotation.

From *California Statutes*, 1877–1878

Provisions in the Article on the Chinese of the Constitution of California (1879)

SECTION 1. The Legislature shall prescribe all necessary regulations for the protection of the State, and the counties, cities, and towns thereof, from the burdens and evils arising from the presence of aliens, who are or may become vagrants, paupers, mendicants, criminals, or invalids afflicted with contagious or infectious diseases, and from aliens otherwise dangerous or detrimental to the well being or peace of the State, and to impose conditions upon which such persons may reside in the State, and to provide the means and mode of their removal from the State upon failure or refusal to comply with such conditions; *provided,* That nothing contained in this section shall be construed to impair or limit the power of the Legislature to pass such police laws or other regulations as it may deem necessary.

SEC. 2. No corporation now existing or hereafter formed under the laws ot this State shall, after the adoption of this Constitution, employ, directly or indirectly, in any capacity, any Chinese or Mongolian. The Legislature shall pass such laws as may be necessary to enforce this provision.

SEC. 3. No Chinese shall be employed on any State, County, municipal, or other public work, except in punishment for crime.

SEC. 4. The presence of foreigners ineligible to become citizens of the United States is declared to be dangerous to the well being of the State, and the Legislature shall discourage their immigration by all the means within its power. Asiatic coolieism is a form of human slavery, and is forever prohibited in this State; and all contracts for coolie labor shall be void. All companies or corporations, whether formed in this country or any foreign country, for the importation of such labor, shall be subject to such penalties as the Legislature may prescribe. The Legislature shall delegate all necessary power to the incorporated cities and towns of this State for the removal of Chinese without the limits of such cities and towns, or for their location within prescribed portions of those limits; and it shall also provide the necessary legislation to prohibit the introduction into this State of Chinese after the adoption of this Constitution. This section shall be enforced by appropriate legislation.

The constitution contained two other discriminations against the Chinese. By silence, natives of China were denied the right to own and inherit land.

Foreigners of the white race, or of African descent, eligible to become citizens of the United States under the naturalization laws thereof, while bona fide residents of this State, shall have the same rights in respect to the acquisition, possession, enjoyment, transmissions, and inheritance of property as native-born citizens.

In this section an object which had been defeated in connection with the article on the Chinese was achieved by indirect statement. The other discrimination was contained in the provision that natives of China, along with idiots, insane persons, and persons convicted of infamous crimes or of the embezzlement of public money, should never exercise the privileges of electors in the State.

From *The Anti-Chinese Movement in California*, by Elmer C. Sandmeyer

A Misdemeanor to Employ Chinese Workers (1880)

178. Any officer, director, manager, member, stockholder, clerk, agent, servant, attorney, employee, assignee, or contractor of any corporation now existing, or hereafter formed under the laws of this State, who shall employ in any manner or capacity, upon any work or business of such corporation, any Chinese or Mongolian, is guilty of a misdemeanor, and is punishable by a fine of not less than one hundred, nor more than one thousand dollars, or by imprisonment in the County Jail of not less than fifty nor more than five hundred days, or by both such fine and imprisonment; *provided,* That no director of a corporation shall be deemed guilty under this section who refuses to assent to such employment, and has such dissent recorded in the minutes of the board of directors.

1. Every person who, having been convicted for violating the provisions of this section, commits any subsequent violation thereof, after such conviction, is punishable as follows:

2. For each subsequent conviction, such person shall be fined not less than five hundred, nor more than five thousand dollars, or by imprisonment not less than two hundred and fifty days nor more than two years, or by both such fine and imprisonment.

179. Any corporation now existing or hereafter formed under the laws of this State, that shall employ, directly or indirectly, in any capacity, any Chinese or Mongolian, shall be guilty of a misdemeanor, and upon conviction thereof shall, for the first offense, be fined not less than five hundred nor more than five thousand dollars, and upon the second conviction shall, in addition to said penalty, forfeit its charter and franchise, and all its corporate rights and privileges, and it shall be the duty of the Attorney-General to take the necessary steps to enforce such forfeiture.

From *Criminal Laws and Practice of California* (A. L. Bancroft & Co., 1881)

The U.S. Congress Enacts the Exclusion Law (1882)

An Act to Execute Certain Treaty Stipulations Relating to Chinese.
[Approved May 6, 1882]

WHEREAS, In the opinion of the Government of the United States, the coming of Chinese laborers to this country endangers the good order of certain localities within the territory thereof: Therefore,

Be it enacted by the Senate and House of Representatives of the United States of America in Congress assembled, That from and after the expiration of ninety days next after the passage of this Act, and until the expiration of ten years next after the passage of this Act, the coming of Chinese laborers to the United States be, and the same is hereby, suspended; and during such suspension it shall not be lawful for any Chinese laborer to come, or, having so come after the expiration of said ninety days, to remain within the United States.

SEC. 2. That the master of any vessel who shall knowingly bring within the United States on such vessel, and land or permit to be landed, any Chinese laborer, from any foreign port or place, shall be deemed guilty of a misdemeanor, and on conviction thereof shall be punished by a fine of not more than five hundred dollars for each and every such Chinese laborer so brought, and may be also imprisoned for a term not exceeding one year.

SEC 3. That the two foregoing sections shall not apply to Chinese laborers who were in the United States on the seventeenth day of November, eighteen hundred and eighty, or who shall have come into the same before the expiration of ninety days next after the passage of this Act, and who shall produce to such master before going on board such vessel, and shall produce to the Collector of the port in the United States at which such vessel shall arrive, the evidence hereinafter in this Act required of his being one of the laborers in this section mentioned; nor shall the two foregoing sections apply to the case of any master, whose vessel, being bound to a port not within the United States, shall come within the jurisdiction of the United States by reason of being in distress or in stress of weather, or touching at any port of the United States on its voyage to any foreign port or place: *Provided,* That all Chinese laborers brought on such vessel shall depart with the vessel on leaving port.

*SEC. 4. That for the purpose of properly identifying Chinese laborers who were in the United States on the seventeenth day of November, eighteen hundred and eighty, or who shall have come into the same before the expiration of ninety days next after the passage of this Act, and in order to furnish them with the proper evidence of their right to go from and come to the United States of their free will and accord, as provided by the treaty between the United States and China dated November seventeenth, eighteen hundred and eighty, the Collector of Customs of the district from which any such Chinese laborer shall depart from the United States shall, in person or by Deputy, go on board each vessel having on board any such Chinese laborer and cleared or about to sail from his district for a foreign port, and on such vessel make a list of all such Chinese laborers, which shall be entered in registry books to be kept for that purpose, in which shall be stated the name, age, occupation, last place of residence, physical marks or peculiarities, and all facts necessary for the identification of each of such Chinese laborers, which books shall be safely kept in the custom house; and every such Chinese laborer so departing from the United States shall be entitled to, and shall receive, free of any charge or cost upon application therefor, from the Collector or his Deputy, at the time such list is taken, a certificate, signed by the Collector or his Deputy and attested by his seal of office, in such form as the Secretary of the Treasury shall prescribe, which certificate shall contain a statement of the name, age, occupation, last place of residence, personal de-

*See act approved October 1, 1888, which prohibits the issuance of certificates of identity of Chinese laborers and declares void such certificates therefore issued.

scription, and facts of identification of the Chinese laborer to whom the certificate is issued, corresponding with the said list and registry in all particulars. In case any Chinese laborer after having received such certificate shall leave such vessel before her departure he shall deliver his certificate to the master of the vessel, and if such Chinese laborer shall fail to return to such vessel before her departure from port the certificate shall be delivered by the master to the Collector of Customs for cancellation. The certificate herein provided for shall entitle the Chinese laborer to whom the same is issued to return to and reenter the United States upon producing and delivering the same to the Collector of Customs of the district at which such Chinese laborer shall seek to reenter; and upon delivery of such certificate by such Chinese laborer to the Collector of Customs at the time of reentry in the United States, said Collector shall cause the same to be filed in the custom house and duly canceled.

*SEC. 5. That any Chinese laborer mentioned in Section 4 of this Act being in the United States, and desiring to depart from the United States by land, shall have the right to demand and receive, free of charge or cost, a certificate of identification similar to that provided for in Section 4 of this Act to be issued to such Chinese laborers as may desire to leave the United States by water; and it is hereby made the duty of the Collector of Customs of the district next adjoining the foreign country to which said Chinese laborer desires to go to issue such certificate, free of charge or cost, upon application by such Chinese laborer, and to enter the same upon registry books to be kept by him for the purpose, as provided for in Section 4 of this Act.

SEC. 6. That in order to the faithful execution of Articles 1 and 2 of the treaty in this Act before mentioned, every Chinese person other than a laborer who may be entitled by said treaty and this Act to come within the United States, and

*See act approved October 1, 1888, which prohibits the issuance of certificates of identity of Chinese laborers and declares void such certificates therefore issued.

who shall be about to come to the United States, shall be identified as so entitled by the Chinese Government in each case, such identity to be evidenced by a certificate issued under the authority of said Government, which certificate shall be in the English language or (if not English language) accompanied by a translation into English, stating such right to come, and which certificate shall state the name, title, or official rank, if any, the age, height, and all physical peculiarities, former and present occupation or profession, and place of residence in China of the person to whom the certificate is issued and that such person is entitled conformably to the treaty in this Act mentioned to come within the United States. Such certificate shall be *prima facie* evidence of the fact set forth therein, and shall be produced to the Collector of Customs, or his deputy, of the port in the district in the United States at which the person named therein shall arrive.

SEC. 7. That any person who shall knowingly and falsely alter or substitute any name for the name written in such certificate or forge any such certificate, or knowingly utter any forged or fraudulent certificate, or falsely personate any person named in any such certificate, shall be deemed guilty of a misdemeanor; and upon conviction thereof shall be fined in a sum not exceeding one thousand dollars, and imprisoned in a penitentiary for a term of not more than five years.

SEC. 8. That the master of any vessel arriving in the United States from any foreign port or place shall, at the same time he delivers a manifest of the cargo, and if there be no cargo, then at the time of making a report of the entry of the vessel pursuant of law, in addition to the other matter required to be reported, and before landing, or permitting to land, any Chinese passengers, deliver and report to the Collector of Customs of the district in which such vessel shall have arrived a separate list of all Chinese passengers taken on board his vessel at any foreign port or place, and all such passengers on board the vessel at that time. Such lists shall show the names of such passengers (and if accredited officers of the Chinese Government traveling on the business of that Government, or their servants, with a note of such facts), and the names and other particulars, as shown by their respective certificates; and such list shall be sworn to by the master in the manner required by law in relation to the manifest of the cargo. Any willful refusal or neglect of any such master to comply with the provisions of this section shall incur the same penalties and forfeiture as are provided for a refusal or neglect to report and deliver a manifest of the cargo.

SEC. 9. That before any Chinese passengers are landed from any such vessel, the Collector or his Deputy shall proceed to examine such passengers, comparing the certificates with the list and with the passengers; and no passenger shall be allowed to land in the United States from such vessel in violation of law.

SEC. 10. That every vessel whose master shall knowingly violate any of the provisions of this Act shall be deemed forfeited to the United States, and shall be liable to seizure and condemnation in any district of the United States into which such vessel may enter or in which she may be found.

SEC. 11. That any person who shall knowingly bring into or cause to be brought into the United States by land, or who shall knowingly aid or abet the same, or aid or abet the landing in the United States from any vessel of any Chinese person not lawfully entitled to enter the United States, shall be deemed guilty of a misdemeanor, and shall, on conviction thereof, be fined in a sum not exceeding one thousand dollars, and imprisoned for a term not exceeding one year.

SEC. 12. That no Chinese person shall be permitted to enter the United States by land without producing to the proper officer of customs, the certificate in this act required of Chinese persons seeking to land from a vessel. And any Chinese person found unlawfully within the United States shall be caused to be removed therefrom to the country from whence he came, by direction of the President of the United States, and at the cost of the United States, after being brought before some justice, judge, or commissioner of a Court of the United States and found to be one not lawfully entitled to be or remain in the United States.

SEC. 13. That this Act shall not apply to diplomatic and

other officers of the Chinese Government traveling upon the business of that Government, whose credentials shall be taken as equivalent to the certificate in this Act mentioned, and shall exempt them and their body and household servants from the provisions of this Act as to other Chinese persons.

SEC. 14. That hereafter no State Court or Court of the United States shall admit Chinese to citizenship; and all laws in conflict with this Act are hereby repealed.

SEC. 15. That the words "Chinese laborers," wherever used in this Act, shall be construed to mean both skilled and unskilled laborers and Chinese employed in mining.

> From "Enforcement of the Geary Law, 1893," House Executive Documents 9 and 10, 53rd Congr., 1st sess., 1893

The Exclusion Law Amended (1884)

An Act to Amend an Act Entitled "An Act to Execute Certain Treaty Stipulations Relating to Chinese," approved May sixth, eighteen hundred and eighty-two.
[Approved July 5, 1884]

Be it enacted by the Senate and House of Representatives of the United States of America in Congress assembled, That Section 1 of the Act entitled "An Act to Execute Certain Treaty Stipulations Relating to Chinese," approved May sixth, eighteen hundred and eighty-two, is hereby amended so as to read as follows:

WHEREAS, In the opinion of the Government of the United States the coming of Chinese laborers to this country endangers the good order of certain localities within the territory thereof: Therefore

"Be it enacted by the Senate and House of Representatives of the United States of America in Congress assembled, That from and after the passage of this Act, and until the expiration of ten years next after the passage of this Act, the coming of Chinese laborers to the United States be, and the same is

hereby, suspended, and during such suspension it shall not be lawful for any Chinese laborer to come from any foreign port or place, or having so come to remain within the United States."

Section 2 of said Act is hereby amended so as to read as follows:

"SEC. 2. That the master of any vessel who shall knowingly bring within the United States on such vessel, and land, or attempt to land, or permit to be landed any Chinese laborer, from any foreign port or place, shall be deemed guilty of a misdemeanor, and, on conviction thereof, shall be punished by a fine of not more than five hundred dollars for each and every such Chinese laborer so brought, and may also be imprisoned for a term not exceeding one year."

Section 3 of said Act is hereby amended so as to read as follows:

"SEC. 3. That the two foregoing sections shall not apply to Chinese laborers who were in the United States on the seventeenth day of November, eighteen hundred and eighty, or who shall have come into the same before the expiration of ninety days next after the passage of the Act to which this Act is amendatory, nor shall said sections apply to Chinese laborers who shall produce to such master before going on board such vessel, and shall produce to the Collector of the port in the United States at which such vessel shall arrive, the evidence hereinafter in this act required of his being one of the laborers in this section mentioned; nor shall the two foregoing sections apply to the case of any master whose vessel, being bound to a port not within the United States, shall come within the jurisdiction of the United States by reason of being in distress or in stress of weather, or touching at any port of the United States on its voyage to any foreign port or place: *Provided,* That all Chinese laborers brought on such vessel shall not be permitted to land except in case of absolute necessity, and must depart with the vessel on leaving port."

Section 4 of said Act is hereby amended so as to read as follows:

*"SEC. 4. That for the purpose of properly identifying Chinese laborers who were in the United States on the seventeenth day of November, eighteen hundred and eighty, or who shall have come into the same before the expiration to ninety days next after the passage of the Act to which this Act is amendatory, and in order to furnish them with the proper evidence of their right to go from and come to the United States as provided by the said Act and the treaty between the United States and China dated November seventeenth, eighteen hundred and eighty, the Collector of Customs of the district from which any such Chinese laborer shall depart from the United States shall, in person or by Deputy, go on board each vessel having on board any such Chinese laborer, and cleared or about to sail from his district for a foreign port, and on such vessel make a list of all such Chinese laborers which shall be entered in registry books to be kept for that purpose, in which shall be stated the individual, family, and tribal name in full, the age, occupation, when and where followed, last place of residence, physical marks or peculiarities, and all facts necessary for the identification of each such Chinese laborers, which books shall be safely kept in the custom house; and every such Chinese laborer so departing from the United States shall be entitled to and shall receive, free of any charge or cost upon application therefor, from the Collector or his Deputy, in the name of said Collector and attested by said Collector's seal of office, at the time such list is taken, a certificate, signed by the Collector or his Deputy and attested by his seal or office, in such form as the Secretary of the Treasury shall prescribe, which certificate shall contain a statement of the individual, family, and tribal name in full; age, occupation, when and where followed, of the Chinese laborer to whom the certificate is issued, corresponding with the said list and registry in all particulars. In case any Chinese laborer, after having received such certificate, shall

*See act approved October 1, 1888, which prohibits the issuance of certificates of identity of Chinese laborers and declares void such certificates theretofore issued.

leave such vessel before her departure, he shall deliver his certificate to the master of the vessel; and if such Chinese laborer shall fail to return to such vessel before her departure from port, the certificate shall be delivered by the master to the Collector of Customs for cancellation. The certificate herein provided for shall entitle the Chinese laborer to whom the same is issued to return to and reenter the United States upon producing and delivering the same to the Collector of Customs of the district at which such Chinese laborer shall seek to reenter, and said certificate shall be the only evidence permissible to establish his right of reentry; and upon delivering of such certificate by such Chinese laborer to the Collector of Customs at the time of reentry in the United States, said Collector shall cause the same to be filed in the custom house and duly canceled."

Section 6 of said Act is hereby amended so as to read as follows:

"SEC. 6. That in order to the faithful execution of the provisions of this Act, every Chinese person other than a laborer, who may be entitled by said treaty or this Act to come within the United States, and who shall be about to come to the United States, shall obtain the permission of and be identified as so entitled by the Chinese Government, or of such other foreign government of which at the time such Chinese person shall be a subject, in each case to be evidenced by a certificate issued by such government, which certificate shall be in the English language and shall show such permission, with the name of the permitted person in his or her proper signature, and which certificate shall state the individual, family, and tribal name in full, title or official rank, if any, the age, height, and all physical peculiarities, former and present occupation or profession, when and where and how long pursued, and place of residence of the person to whom the certificate is issued, and that such person is entitled by this Act to come within the United States. If the person so applying for a certificate shall be a merchant, said certificate shall, in addition to above requirements, state the nature, character, and estimated value of the business carried on by him prior to and at the same time of his application as aforesaid: *Provided,* That nothing in this Act nor in said treaty shall be construed as embracing within the meaning of the word 'merchant' hucksters, peddlers, or those engaged in taking, drying, or otherwise preserving shell or other fish for home consumption or exportation. If the certificate be sought for the purpose of travel for curiosity, it shall also state whether the applicant intends to pass through or travel within the United States, together with his financial standing in the country from which such certificate is desired. The certificate provided for in this Act, and the identity of the person named therein, shall, before such person goes on board any vessel to proceed to the United States, be viséd by the endorsement of the diplomatic representative, or of the consular representative of the United States at the port or place from which the person named in the certificate is about to depart; and such diplomatic representative or consular representative whose endorsement is so required is hereby empowered, and it shall be his duty, before endorsing such certificate as aforesaid, to examine into the truth of the statement set forth in said certificate, and if he shall find upon examination that said or any of the statements therein contained are untrue it shall be his duty to refuse to endorse the same. Such certificate viséd as aforesaid shall be *prima facie* evidence of the facts set forth therein, and shall be produced to the Collector of Customs of the port in the district in the United States at which the person named therein shall arrive, and afterward produced to the proper authorities of the United States whenever lawfully demanded, and shall be the sole evidence permissible on the part of the person so producing the same to establish a right of entry into the United States; but said certificate may be controverted and the facts therein disproved by the United States authorities."

Section 8 of said Act is hereby amended so as to read as follows:

"SEC. 8. That the master of any vessel arriving in the United States from any foreign port or place shall, at the same time he delivers a manifest of the cargo, and if there be no cargo, then at the time of making a report of the entry of the vessel pursuant to law in addition to the other matter required to be reported, and before landing, or permitting to land, any Chinese passengers, deliver and report to the Collector of Customs of the district in which such vessel shall have arrived a separate list of all Chinese passengers taken on board his vessel at any foreign port or place, and all such passengers on board the vessel at that time. Such list shall show the names of such passengers (and if accredited officers of the Chinese or of any other foreign government, traveling on the business of that government, or their servants, with a note of such facts) and the names and other particulars as shown by their respective certificates; and such list shall be sworn to by the master in the manner required by law in relation to the manifest of the cargo. Any refusal or willful neglect of any such master to comply with the provisions of this section shall incur the same penalties and forfeiture as are provided for a refusal or neglect to report and deliver a manifest of the cargo."

Section 10 of said Act is hereby amended so as to read as follows:

"SEC. 10. That every vessel whose master shall knowingly violate any of the provisions of this Act shall be deemed forfeited to the United States, and shall be liable to seizure and condemnation in any district of the United States into which such vessel may enter or in which she may be found."

Section 11 of said Act is hereby amended so as to read as follows:

"SEC. 11. That any person who shall knowingly bring into or cause to be brought into the United States by land, or who shall aid or abet the same, or aid or abet the landing in the United States from any vessel, of any Chinese person not lawfully entitled to enter the United States, shall be deemed guilty of a misdemeanor, and shall, on conviction thereof, be fined in a sum not exceeding one thousand dollars, and imprisoned for a term not exceeding one year."

Section 12 of said Act is hereby amended so as to read as follows:

"SEC. 12. That no Chinese person shall be permitted to enter the United States by land without producing to the proper officer of customs the certificate in this Act required of Chinese persons seeking to land from a vessel; and any Chinese person found unlawfully within the United States shall be caused to be removed therefrom to the country from whence he came, and at the cost of the United States, after being brought before some justice, judge, or commissioner of a Court of the United States and found to be one not lawfully entitled to be or to remain in the United States; and in all such cases the person who brought or aided in bringing such person to the United States shall be liable to the Government of the United States for all necessary expenses incurred in such investigation and removal; and all peace officers of the several States and Territories of the United States are hereby invested with the same authority as a marshal or United States marshal in reference to carrying out the provisions of this Act or the Act of which this is amendatory, as a marshal or deputy marshal of the United States, and shall be entitled to like compensation to be audited and paid by the same officers; and the United States shall pay all costs and charges for the maintenance and return of any Chinese person having the certificate prescribed by law as entitling such Chinese person to come into the United States who may not have been permitted to land from any vessel by reason of any of the provisions of this Act."

Section 13 of said Act is hereby amended so as to read as follows:

"SEC. 13. That this Act shall not apply to diplomatic and other officers of the Chinese or other governments traveling upon the business of that government, whose credentials shall be taken as equivalent to the certificate in this Act mentioned, and shall exempt them and their body and household servants from the provisions of this Act as to other Chinese persons."

Section 15 of said Act is hereby amended so as to read as follows:

"SEC. 15. That the provisions of this Act shall apply to all subjects of China and Chinese, whether subjects of China or any other foreign power, and the words Chinese laborers, wherever used in this Act, shall be construed to mean both skilled and unskilled laborers and Chinese employed in mining."

SEC. 16. That any violation of any of the provisions of this Act, or of the Act of which this is amendatory, the punishment of which is not otherwise herein provided for, shall be deemed a misdemeanor, and shall be punishable by a fine not exceeding one thousand dollars, or by imprisonment for not more than one year, or both such fine and imprisonment.

SEC. 17. That nothing contained in this Act shall be construed to affect any prosecution or other proceeding, criminal or civil, begun under the Act of which this is amendatory; but such prosecution or other proceeding, criminal or civil, shall proceed as if this Act had not been passed.

From "Enforcement of the Geary Law, 1893"

Congress Reaffirms the Exclusion of Chinese Workers (1888)

An Act to Prohibit the Coming of Chinese Laborers to the United States.

Be it enacted by the Senate and House of Representatives of the United States of America in Congress assembled, That from and after the date of the exchange of ratifications of the pending treaty between the United States of America and His Imperial Majesty the Emperor of China, signed on the twelfth day of March, anno Domini eighteen hundred and eighty-eight, it shall be unlawful for any Chinese person, whether a subject of China or of any other power, to enter the United States, except as hereinafter provided.

SEC. 2. That Chinese officials, teachers, students, merchants, or travelers for pleasure or curiosity, shall be permitted to enter the United States, but in order to entitle themselves to do so, they shall first obtain the permission of the Chinese Government, or other Government of which they may at the time be citizens or subjects. Such permission and also their personal identity shall in such case be evidenced by a certificate to be made out by the diplomatic representative of the United States in the country, or of the consular representative of the United States at the port or place from which the person named therein comes. The certificate shall contain a full description of such person, of his age, height, and general physical features, and shall state his former and present occupation or profession and place of residence, and shall be made out in duplicate. One copy shall be delivered open to the person named and described, and the other copy shall be sealed up and delivered by the diplomatic or consular officer as aforesaid to the captain of the vessel on which the person named in the certificate sets sail for the United States, together with the sealed certificate, which shall be addressed to the Collector of Customs at the port where such person is to land. There shall be delivered to the aforesaid captain a letter from the consular officer addressed to the Collector of Customs aforesaid, and stating that said consular officer has on a certain day delivered to the said captain a certificate of the right of the person named therein to enter the United States as a Chinese official, or other exempted person, as the case may be. And any captain who lands or attempts to land a Chinese person in the United States, without having in his possession a sealed certificate, as required in this section, shall be liable to the penalties prescribed in Section 9 of this Act.

SEC. 3. That the provisions of this Act shall apply to all persons of the Chinese race, whether subjects of China or other foreign power, excepting Chinese diplomatic or consular officers and their attendants; and the words "Chinese laborers," whenever used in this Act, shall be construed to mean both skilled and unskilled laborers and Chinese employed in mining.

SEC. 4. That the master of any vessel arriving in the United States from any foreign port or place with any Chinese passengers on board shall, when he delivers his manifest of cargo, and if there be no cargo, when he makes legal entry of his vessel, and before landing or permitting to land any

Chinese person (unless a diplomatic or consular officer, or attendant of such officer), deliver to the Collector of Customs of the district in which the vessel shall have arrived the sealed certificates and letters as aforesaid, and a separate list of all Chinese persons taken on board of his vessel at any foreign port or place, and of all such persons on board at the time of arrival as aforesaid. Such list shall show the names of such persons and other particulars as shown by their open certificates, or other evidences required by this Act, and such list shall be sworn to by the master in the manner required by law in relation to the manifest of the cargo.

The master of any vessel as aforesaid shall not permit any Chinese diplomatic or consular officer or attendant of such officer to land without having first been informed by the Collector of Customs of the official character of such officer or attendant. Any refusal or willful neglect of the master of any vessel to comply with the provisions of this section shall incur the same penalties and forfeitures as are provided for a refusal or neglect to report and deliver a manifest of the cargo.

SEC. 5. That from and after the passage of this Act, no Chinese laborer in the United States shall be permitted, after having left, to return thereto, except under the conditions stated in the following sections.

SEC. 6. That no Chinese laborer within the purview of the preceding section shall be permitted to return to the United States unless he has a lawful wife, child, or parent in the United States, or property therein of the value of one thousand dollars, or debts of like amount due him and pending settlement. The marriage to such wife must have taken place at least a year prior to the application of the laborer for a permit to return to the United States, and must have been followed by the continuous cohabitation of the parties as man and wife.

If the right to return be claimed on the ground of property or of debts, it must appear that the property is bona fide and not colorably acquired for the purpose of evading this Act, or that the debts are unascertained and unsettled, and not promissory notes or other similar acknowledgments of ascertained liability.

SEC. 7. That a Chinese person claiming the right to be permitted to leave the United States and return thereto on any of the grounds stated in the foregoing section, shall apply to the Collector of Customs of the district from which he wishes to depart at least a month prior to the time of his departure, and shall make on oath before the said Collector a full statement descriptive of his family, or property, or debts, as the case may be, and shall furnish to said Collector such proofs of the facts entitling him to return as shall be required by the rules and regulations prescribed from time to time by the Secretary of the Treasury, and for any false swearing in relation thereto he shall incur the penalties of perjury. He shall also permit the Collector to take a full description of his person, which description the Collector shall retain and mark with a number. And if the Collector, after hearing the proofs and investigating all the circumstances of the case, shall decide to issue a certificate of return, he shall at such time and place as he may designate, sign and give to the person applying a certificate containing the number of the description last aforesaid, which shall be the sole evidence given to such person of his right to return. If this last named certificate be transferred, it shall become void, and the person to whom it was given shall forfeit his right to return to the United States. . . .

Enacted by the 50th Congr., 1st sess., 1888

Chinese Denied Readmission to the United States (1893)

An Act to Supplement an Act entitled "An Act to Execute Certain Treaty Stipulations Relating to Chinese," approved the sixth day of May, eighteen hundred and eighty-two.
[Approved October 1, 1888]

Be it enacted by the Senate and House of Representatives of the United States of America in Congress assembled, That from and after the passage of this Act, it shall be unlawful for any Chinese laborer who shall at any time heretofore have been, or who may now or hereafter be, a resident within the United States, and who shall have departed, or shall depart, therefrom, and shall not have returned before the passage of this Act, to return to, or remain in, the United States.

SEC. 2. That no certificates of identity provided for in the fourth and fifth sections of the Act of which this is a supplement shall hereafter be issued; and every certificate heretofore issued in pursuance thereof is hereby declared void and of no effect, and the Chinese laborer claiming admission by virtue thereof shall not be permitted to enter the United States.

SEC. 3. That all the duties prescribed, liabilities, penalties, and forfeitures imposed, and the powers conferred by the second, tenth, eleventh, and twelfth sections of the Act to which this is a supplement are hereby extended and made applicable to the provision of this Act.

SEC. 4. That all such part or parts of the Act to which this is a supplement as are inconsistent herewith are hereby repealed.

From "Enforcement of the Geary Law, 1893"

Congress Again Prohibits Chinese Immigration (1892)

An Act to Prohibit the Coming of Chinese Persons into the United States.
[Approved May 5, 1892]

Be it enacted by the Senate and House of Representatives of the United States of America in Congress assembled, That all laws now in force prohibiting and regulating the coming into this country of Chinese persons and persons of Chinese descent are hereby continued in force for a period of ten years from the passage of this Act.

SEC. 2. That any Chinese person or person of Chinese descent, when convicted and adjudged under any of said laws to be not lawfully entitled to be or remain in the United States, shall be removed from the United States to China, unless he or they shall make it appear to the justice, judge, or commissioner before whom he or they are tried that he or they are subjects or citizens of some other country, in which case he or they shall be removed from the United States to such country: *Provided,* That in any case where such other country of which such Chinese person shall claim to be a citizen or subject shall demand any tax as a condition of the removal of such person to that country, he or she shall be removed to China.

SEC. 3. That any Chinese person or person of Chinese descent arrested under the provisions of this Act or the Acts hereby extended shall be adjudged to be unlawfully within the United States unless such person shall establish, by affirmative proof, to the satisfaction of such justice, judge, or commissioner, his lawful right to remain in the United States.

SEC. 4. That any such Chinese person or person of Chinese descent convicted and adjudged to be not lawfully entitled to be or remain in the United States shall be imprisoned at hard labor for a period of not exceeding one year and thereafter removed from the United States, as hereinbefore provided.

SEC. 5. That after the passage of this Act, on an application to any judge, or Court of the United States in the first instance for a writ of habeas corpus, by a Chinese person seeking to land in the United States, to whom that privilege has been denied, no bail shall be allowed, and such application shall be heard and determined promptly without unnecessary delay.

SEC. 6. And it shall be the duty of all Chinese laborers within the limits of the United States at the time of the passage of this Act, and who are entitled to remain in the United States, to apply to the Collector of Internal Revenue of their respective districts, within one year after the passage of this Act, for a certificate of residence, and any Chinese laborer within the limits of the United States who shall neglect, fail, or refuse to comply with the provisions of this Act, or who, after one year from the passage hereof, shall be found within the jurisdiction of the United States without such certificate of residence, shall be deemed and adjudged to be unlawfully within the United States, and may be arrested by any United States customs official, Collector of Internal Revenue or his Deputies, United States Marshal or his Deputies, and taken before a United States Judge, whose duty it shall be to order that he be deported from the United States as hereinbefore provided, unless he shall establish clearly to the satisfaction of said Judge that by reason of accident, sickness, or other unavoidable cause, he has been unable to procure his certificate, and to the satisfaction of the Court, and by at least one credible white witness, that he was a resident of the United States at the time of the passage of this Act; and if upon the hearing it shall appear that he is so entitled to a certificate, it shall be granted upon his paying the cost. Should it appear that said Chinaman had procured a certificate which has been lost or destroyed, he shall be detained and judgment suspended a reasonable time to enable him to procure a duplicate from the officer granting it, and in such cases the cost of said arrest and trial shall be in the discretion of the Court. And any Chinese person, other than a Chinese laborer, having a right to be and remain in the United States, desiring such certificates as evidence of such right, may apply for and receive the same without charge.

SEC. 7. That immediately after the passage of this Act the Secretary of the Treasury shall make such rules and regulations as may be necessary for the efficient execution of this Act, and shall prescribe the necessary forms and furnish the necessary blanks to enable Collectors of Internal Revenue to issue the certificates required hereby, and make such provisions that certificates may be procured in localities convenient to the applicants. Such certificates shall be issued without charge to the applicant, and shall contain the name, age, local residence, and occupation of the applicant, and such other description of the applicant as shall be prescribed by the Secretary of the Treasury, and a duplicate thereof shall be filed in the office of the Collector of Internal Revenue for the district within which such Chinaman makes applications.

SEC. 8. That any person who shall knowingly and falsely alter or substitute any name for the name written in such certificate or forged certificate, or knowingly utter any forged or fraudulent certificate, or falsely personate any person named in such certificate, shall be guilty of a misdemeanor, and upon conviction thereof shall be fined in a sum not exceeding one thousand dollars or imprisoned in the penitentiary for a term of not more than five years.

SEC. 9. The Secretary of the Treasury may authorize the payment of such compensation in the nature of fees to the Collectors of Internal Revenue, for services performed under the provisions of this Act, in addition to salaries now allowed by law, as he shall deem necessary, not exceeding the sum of one dollar for each certificate issued.

From "Enforcement of the Geary Law, 1893"

Regulations for the Issue of Certificates of Residence to Chinese (1892)

Treasury Department, Office of the Secretary, Washington, D.C., July 7, 1892

Section 7 of the Act of Congress approved May 5, 1892, entitled "An Act to Prohibit the Coming of Chinese Persons into the United States," provides "that immediately after the passage of this Act the Secretary of the Treasury shall make such rules and regulations as may be necessary for the efficient execution of this Act, and shall prescribe the necessary forms and furnish the necessary blanks to enable the Collectors of Internal Revenue to issue the certificates required hereby, and make such provision that certificates may be procured in localities convenient to the applicants," etc.

In accordance with the foregoing authority, the following

rules and regulations are prescribed for the purposes therein indicated, to wit:

APPLICATIONS FOR CERTIFICATES OF RESIDENCE

Collectors of Internal Revenue will receive applications on the following form, at their own offices, from such Chinese as are conveniently located thereto, and will cause their deputies to proceed to the towns or cities in their respective divisions where any considerable number of Chinese are residing, for the purpose of receiving applications.

No.———
Application of Chinese laborer (or Chinese person other than laborer) for certificate of residence under Act of May 5, 1892

I, ——— ———, a Chinese, ——— hereby make application to the Collector of Internal Revenue for the ——— district of ——— for a certificate of residence under the provisions of the Act of Congress approved May 5, 1892, and state that I arrived in the United States on the ——— day of ———, 18———, at the port of ———, per———

From "Enforcement of the Geary Law, 1893"

Congress Extends Anti-Chinese Legislation to Hawaii (1898)

Joint Resolution of July 7, 1898.

There shall be no further immigration of Chinese into the Hawaiian Islands, except upon such conditions as are now or may hereafter be allowed by the laws of the United States; and no Chinese, by reason of anything herein contained, shall be allowed to enter the United States from the Hawaiian Islands.

From "Treaty, Laws and Regulations Governing the Admission of Chinese," a report of a Special Committee on Chinese Immigration

Hawaiian Chinese Excluded from Citizenship (1900)

An Act to Provide a Government for the Territory of Hawaii.
[Approved April 30, 1900]

SEC. 4. That all persons who were citizens of the Republic of Hawaii on August 12, 1898, are hereby declared to be citizens of the United States and citizens of the Territory of Hawaii.

SEC. 101. That Chinese in the Hawaiian Islands when this Act has taken effect may within one year thereafter obtain certificates of residence as required by "An Act to Prohibit the Coming of Chinese Persons into the United States," approved November 3, 1893, entitled "An Act to Amend an Act Entitled 'An Act to Prohibit the Coming of Chinese Persons into the United States,' " approved May 5, 1892, and until the expiration of said year shall not be deemed to be unlawfully in the United States if found therein without such certificates. *Provided*, however, That no Chinese laborer, whether he shall hold such certificate or not, shall be allowed to enter any State, Territory, or District of the United States from the Hawaiian Islands.

From "Treaty, Laws and Regulations Governing the Admission of Chinese"

Congress Again Reaffirms the Exclusion Law (1902)

An Act to Prohibit the Coming into and to Regulate the Residence Within the United States, its Territories and all Territory Under its Jurisdiction, and the District of Columbia, of Chinese and Persons of Chinese Descent.
[Approved April 29, 1902]

Be it enacted by the Senate and House of Representatives of the United States of America in Congress assembled, That all laws now in force prohibiting and regulating the coming of Chinese persons, and persons therein, including Sections five, six, seven, eight, nine, ten, eleven, thirteen, and fourteen of the Act entitled "An Act to Prohibit the Coming of

Chinese Laborers into the United States," approved September thirteenth, eighteen hundred and eighty-eight, be, and the same are hereby, reenacted, extended, and continued so far as the same are not inconsistent with treaty obligations, until otherwise provided by law, and said laws shall also apply to the island territory under the jurisdiction of the United States, and prohibit the immigration of Chinese laborers, not citizens of the United States, from such island territory to the mainland territory of the United States, whether in such island territory at the time of cession or not, and from one portion of the island territory of the United States to another portion of said island territory: *Provided,* however, That said laws shall not apply to the transit of Chinese laborers from one island to another island of the same group; and any islands within the jurisdiction of any State or the District of Alaska shall be considered a part of the mainland under this section.

SEC. 2. That the Secretary of the Treasury is hereby authorized and empowered to make and prescribe, and from time to time to change, such rules and regulations not inconsistent with the laws of the land as he may deem necessary and proper to execute the provisions of this Act and of the Acts hereby extended and continued and of the treaty of December eight, eighteen hundred and ninety-four, between the United States and China, and with the approval of the President to appoint such agents as he may deem necessary for the efficient execution of said treaty and said Acts.

SEC. 3. That nothing in the provisions of this Act or any other Act shall be construed to prevent, hinder, or restrict any foreign exhibitor, representative, or citizen of any foreign nation, or the holder, who is a citizen of any foreign nation, of any concession or privilege from any fair or exposition authorized by Act of Congress from bringing into the United States, under contract, such mechanics, artisans, agents, or other employees, natives of their respective foreign countries, as they or any of them may deem necessary for the purpose of making preparation for installing or conducting their exhibits or of preparing for installing or conducting any business authorized or permitted under or by virtue of or pertaining to any concession or privilege which may have been or may be granted by any said fair or exposition in connection with such exposition, under such rules and regulations as the Secretary of the Treasury may prescribe, both as to the admission and return of such person or persons.

SEC. 4. That it shall be the duty of every Chinese laborer, other than a citizen, rightfully in, and entitled to remain in any of the insular territory of the United States (Hawaii excepted) at the time of the passage of this Act, to obtain within one year thereafter a certificate of residence in the insular territory wherein he resides, which certificate shall entitle him to residence therein, and upon failure to obtain such certificate as herein provided he shall be deported from such insular territory; and the Philippine Commission is authorized and required to make all regulations and provisions necessary for the enforcement of this section in the Philippine Islands, including the form and substance of the certificate of residence so that the same shall clearly and sufficiently identify the holder thereof and enable officials to prevent fraud in the transfer of the same: *Provided*, however, That if said Philippine Commission shall find that it is impossible to complete the registration herein provided for within one year from the passage of this Act, said Commission is hereby authorized and empowered to extend the time for such registration for a further period not exceeding one year.

Enacted by the 57th Congr., 1st sess.

U.S. Regulations Extended to the Philippines (1904)

Government of the Philippine Islands, Executive Bureau, Manila, P.I., September 23, 1904.
Executive Order 38

WHEREAS, The Department of Commerce and Labor of the U.S. has, under date of July twenty-seventh, 1903, issued a certain rule to regulate the admission of Chinese persons from the Philippine Islands into the mainland territory of the United States and into the possession of the United States other than the Philippine Islands, which said rule is as follows:

"Rule 61. (Since the issuance of this order this rule has been amended; reference should therefore be had to Rule 38). In view of the provisions of Section 1 of the Act approved April 29, 1902, it will be necessary for Chinese persons of the classes mentioned in Article 3 of the Convention of December 8, 1894, who are resident in (citizen of) the insular territory of the United States, to comply with the terms of Section 6 of the Act approved July 5, 1884, and for this purpose the permission of such persons to go from one insular territory to another of the United States, or from such insular territory to the mainland territory of the United States, shall be granted by an officer designated for that purpose by the chief executives of said insular territories, respectively, and the duties imposed by Section 6 of the Act approved July 5, 1884, upon U.S. diplomatic and consular officers in foreign countries in relation to Chinese persons of said classes shall be discharged by the chief officers in charge of the enforcement of the Chinese Exclusion Acts at the ports, respectively, from which any members of such expected classes intend to depart from any insular territory of the United States."

And whereas it is the desire of the Government of the Philippine Islands to afford to such eligible Chinese persons, residents of these Islands, as desire to depart out of the same for other parts or possessions of the United States, the privilege so to do and to give evidence of such permission and of the status of each person so permitted in the manner now required by law in the case of Chinese persons departing out of a foreign country as nearly as may be: Now, therefore, W. Morgan Shuster, Collector of Customs for the Philippine Islands, is hereby designated to grant such permission in the name of the Government of the Philippine Islands, to all such Chinese persons as shall have duly established to his satisfaction their eligibility under the law to enter the mainland territory of the United States, or any other of its insular possessions.

This permission and the *prima facie* establishment of the facts showing eligibility shall be evidenced by a certificate required by Section 6 of the Act of Congress of July 5, 1884, and referred to in Rule 61, above quoted.

It is further ordered that in the case of Chinese persons coming from the other insular possessions of the United States to the Philippine Islands, bearing certificates issued in pursuance of said Rule 61 above mentioned, they shall be accorded at the ports of the Philippine Islands the same rights of entry as they would have did they come possessed of similar certificate issued by a foreign Government.

LUKE E. WRIGHT, Civil Governor

From "Treaty, Laws and Regulations Governing the Admission of Chinese"

Regulations for the Interrogation of Chinese Entering the United States (1907)

"Regulations Governing the Admission of Chinese." [Approved February 26, 1907]

Rule 3. Chinese aliens shall be examined as to their right to admission to the United States under the provision of the law regulating immigration as well as under the laws relating to the exclusion of Chinese. As the immigration acts relate to aliens in general, the status of Chinese applying for admission must first be determined in accordance with the terms of that law and of the regulation drawn in pursuance thereof; then, if found admissible under such laws and regulations, their status under the Chinese exclusion laws and regulations shall be determined. In order to avoid inconvenience, delay, or annoyance to Chinese applicants arising through misunderstanding, and in the interest of good administration, examination under both sets of laws and regulations shall be made, in the order stated, duly at the ports named in Rule 4 hereof.

Rule 5. Immediately upon arrival of Chinese persons at any port mentioned in Rule 4, it shall be the duty of the officer in charge of the administration of the Chinese exclusion laws to have said Chinese persons examined promptly, as by law provided, touching their right to admission; and to permit to land those proving such right: *Provided,* That nothing contained in these regulations shall be construed to authorize the boarding of vessels of foreign navies arriving at ports of the United States for the purpose of enforcing the provisions of the Chinese exclusion laws.

Rule 6. The examination prescribed in Rule 5 shall be separate and apart from the public, in the presence of Government officials and such other witnesses only as the examining officers shall designate; and all witnesses presenting themselves on behalf of any Chinese applicants shall be fully heard. If upon the conclusion of the hearing the Chinese applicant, if adjudged to be inadmissible, he shall be advised of his right to appeal by a notice written or printed in Chinese language, and his counsel shall be permitted, after notice of appeal has been duly filed, to examine and make copies of the evidence upon which the excluding decision is based. If there is a consular officer of China at port where examination is held, he also shall be notified in writing that the said Chinese applicant has been refused a landing, and shall be permitted to examine the record.

Rule 7. Every Chinese person permitted to land from a vessel for examination at some designated port, or for immediate hospital treatment as provided in Rule 1, shall be considered as still on shipboard until finally and lawfully landed, so far as relates to the responsibility of the master, agents, or owner of such vessel for his safeguarding, maintenance, and hospital expenses.

Rule 9. Every Chinese person refused admission to the United States, being actually or constructively on the vessel or other conveyance by which he was brought to a port of entry, must be returned to the country whence he came, at the expense of the transportation agency owning such vessels or conveyance.

Rule 12. Every Chinese person refused admission under

the provisions of the exclusion laws by the decision of the officer in charge at the port of entry may take an appeal to the Secretary of Commerce and Labor by giving written notice thereof to the officer in charge within two days, exclusive of Sundays and legal holidays, after such decision is rendered.

From "Treaty, Laws and Regulations
Governing the Admission of Chinese"

Excerpts from the Interrogation of a Young Chinese Traveler (c. 1910)

Applicant reminded that he is still under oath.
QUESTION. *What is your name?*
ANSWER. Leong Sem.
Q. *Has your house in China two outside doors?*
A. Yes.
Q. *Who lives opposite the big door?*
A. No house opposite.
Q. *Who lives opposite the small door?*
A. Leon Doo Wui, a farmer in the village; he lives with his wife, no one else.
Q. *Describe his wife.*
A. Chin Shee, natural feet.
Q. *Didn't that man ever have any children?*
A. No.
Q. *How old a man is he?*
A. About thirty.
Q. *Who lives in the first house in your row?*
A. Leong Yik Fook, farmer in the village; he lives with his wife, no one else.
Q. *Describe his wife.*
A. Wong Shee, bound feet.
Q. *Didn't that man ever have any children?*
A. I don't know.
Q. *How many houses in your row?*
A. Two.

Q. Who lives in the first house, first row from the head?
A. Yik Haw, I don't know what clan he belongs to.
Q. Why don't you know what clan he belongs to?
A. I never heard his family name.
Q. Do you expect us to believe that you lived in that village if you don't know the clan names of the people living there?
A. He never told us his family name.
Q. How long has he lived in the village?
A. For a long time.
Q. What is his occupation?
A. A farmer in the village.
Q. What family has he?
A. A wife and one son, his wife's name I don't know, released feet.
Q. Who is his son?
A. Ah Yin, eleven or twelve years old.
Q. Is there a house on the second lot in the first row?
A. No.
Q. Who lives in the first house, third row?
A. Leong Yik Gah; he is away somewhere; he has a wife, one son and a daughter living in that house.
Q. Describe his wife.
A. Lui Shee, natural feet; his son is Wing Lok, eleven or twelve; his daughter is Suey Heon, about fifteen or sixteen years old.
Q. Who lives in the second house in the third row?
A. There is no house there.
Q. Isn't the second house in the third row opposite one of your doors?
A. The house opposite my door is in the second row.
Q. Didn't you say your house was second house, second row?
A. I have been counting from the front of the village, the house opposite my door is the third row, second house.
Q. Who lives in that house?
A. Leong Doo Gui.
Q. How many houses in the fourth row in the village?
A. No homes in that row.

Q. *How many houses in the fifth row?*
A. No houses.
Q. *How many houses in the sixth row?*
A. No houses.
Q. *How many houses in the seventh row?*
A. No houses.
Q. *According to your testimony today there are only five houses in the village and yesterday you said there were nine.*
A. There are nine houses.
Q. *Where are the other four?*
A. There is Doo Chin's house, first house, sixth row.
Q. *What is the occupation of Leong Doo Chin?*
A. He has no occupation; he has a wife, no children.
Q. *Describe his wife.*
A. Ng Shee, bound feet.
Q. *Who is another of those four families you haven't mentioned?*
A. Leong Doo Sin.
Q. *Where is his house?*
A. First house, fourth row.
Q. *What is his occupation?*
A. No occupation.
Q. *What family has he?*
A. He has a wife, no children.
Q. *Describe his wife.*
A. Toy Shee, bound feet.
Q. *There are two families, who are they and where do they live?*
A. Chin Yick Dun, fifth row, third house.
Q. *What is his occupation?*
A. No occupation.
Q. *What family has he?*
A. He has a wife and a son; his wife is Chin Shee, natural feet.
Q. *Did you ever hear of a man of the Chin family marrying a Chin family woman?*
A. I made a mistake; her husband is Leong Yick Don.
Q. *What is the name and age of that son?*

A. Leong Yick Gai; his house is first house, fourth row.
Q. *You have already put Leong Doo Sin in the fourth row, first house.*
A. His house is first house, third row.
Q. *You have already put Leong Yick Gai first house, third row.*
A. I am mixed up.
(Applicant is requested to draw a diagram of the village together with the names of the people living in the village houses and does so, marked Exhibit "A," and he signs his name thereto as "Leong Dow Sem.")
Q. *Now according to your diagram the houses across the front of your village belong to the following named men:—first house, first row, Yick Haw; first house, second row, Yick Fook; first house, third row, Yick Gai; first house, fourth row, Doo Sin; first house, fifth row, Yick Gai; first house, sixth row, Yick Don; first house, seventh row, Doo Chin.*
A. Yes, that is right.
Q. *Have you named everybody now living in the Gong Ling village?*
A. Yes.
Q. *Who is the oldest man in that village?*
A. Doo Chin.
Q. *Is there a wall around that village or any part of it?*
A. No, but there is some bamboos on the back.
Q. *Is anybody crippled or lame?*
A. No.
Q. *Is anybody in that village blind?*
A. No.
Q. *Is there a shrine near that village?*
A. Yes, there is one at the tail end of the village.
Q. *What other villages are near that village?*
A. Gong Cheo village, a little way to the right side of the village.
Q. *What clan families live in there?*
A. Leong.
Q. *Is there an ancestral hall in your village or near it?*
A. No.

Q. *Is there a fish pond near that village?*
A. No.
Q. *Is there a schoolhouse in that village?*
A. No.
Q. *A fence of any kind around that village?*
A. Earth bank in front of it about two feet high.
Q. *What market does your mother patronize?*
A. Look Bow, eight lis east of the village.
Q. *Do you cross any bridges or streams of water in going to that market?*
A. You cross one small stone bridge.
Q. *Is there a temple in that market?*
A. No.
Q. *Describe your school experience.*
A. Started when I was seven to study. See Ak Hock How, located about two lis south outside of my village.
Q. *Did you eat and sleep in the schoolhouse or at home?*
A. I slept in the schoolhouse and ate at home, I studied in that school for nine years.
Q. *How old are you?*
A. Sixteen.
Q. *Who was your last teacher?*
A. There were three teachers, Leong Yo Wah, Leong Bing, and Leong Yee On.
Q. *When was the picture taken that is on your affidavit?*
A. When I was about ten years old.
Q. *Was your father in China then?*
A. No.
Q. *Was the picture on the affidavit when you received it?*
A. Yes.
Q. *How did your father get that picture?*
A. My mother sent it to him.
Q. *How long ago did she send it to him?*
A. I'm not sure.
Q. *Why are you so excessively nervous during this examination?*
A. I am not at all nervous.
Q. *How long have you had that gold tooth?*

A. About three years.
Q. *Was that tooth fixed that way while your father was last in China?*
A. I had it crowned while my father was in China.
Q. *Where was the work done?*
A. In the Ai Gong market.
Q. *Do you know how much it cost?*
A. A little over $4 Chinese money.
Q. *Who is going to testify in your behalf besides your father?*
A. Leong Seung.
Q. *Have you any changes or corrections you wish to make in your testimony?*
A. No.
Q. *Have you understood all the questions?*
A. Yes.
Q. *Is there anything more you wish to say?*
A. No.

From *Oriental Exclusion*, by R. D. McKenzie

The 1924 Immigration Act Incorporates Previous Anti-Chinese Legislation

SEC. 13(c). No alien ineligible to citizenship shall be admitted to the United States unless such alien (1) is admissable as a nonquota immigrant under the provision of subdivision (b) . . . of Section 4,—"Sec. 4 . . . (b) An immigrant previously lawfully admitted to the United States, who is returning from a temporary visit abroad, . . ."

SEC. 28. As used in this Act— . . . (c) The term "ineligible to citizenship," when used in reference to any individual, includes an individual who is debarred from becoming a citizen of the United States under Section 2169 of the Revised Statutes, or under Section 14 of the Act entitled "An Act to Execute Certain Treaty Stipulations Relating to Chinese," approved May 6, 1882, or under Sections 1996, 1997, or 1998 of the Revised Statutes, as amended, or under Section 2 of the Act entitled "An Act to Authorize the President to Increase Temporarily the Military Establishment of the United States," approved May 18, 1917, as amended, or under law amendatory of, supplementary to, or in substitution for, any such section; . . .

> From "Restriction of Immigration," House Report No. 350, 68th Congr., 1st sess.

2. Overt Agitation

The United States established a national racial discrimination law against the Chinese in 1882, when the total number of Chinese amounted to only around one hundred thousand, heavily concentrated on the West Coast. Apparently most people in this country had not yet seen a Chinese, but the majority in the Congress supported the anti-Chinese law.

In 1929, Bruno Lasker conducted a survey of racial attitudes in children and found that, among many prejudiced views, one child stated his attitude toward the Chinese as: "I don't know, but I don't like they [them], that's all." [1] This child obviously had no personal experience with nor any knowledge of the

Chinese people, but a prejudiced view passed on to him.

Later, in the 1930s, Richard La Piere, in a similar study of Americans' racial attitudes, traveled with a married Chinese couple extensively through this country and found all but one of the hotels and restaurants receptive to them. But later Mr. La Piere sent out written requests to 256 hotels and restaurants, half of which they had visited earlier, asking them to confirm whether they accept Chinese as their guests. Almost all the replies (92 percent) stated that they refused to serve Chinese.[2] Those replies were undoubtedly based on their prejudiced "image" of the Chinese.

Even as late as in 1952 when a young Chinese couple with a small son bought a house in Southwood, south San Francisco, many white residents of that locality almost started a riot against the sale of the house to a Chinese family. The young Chinese man was a graduate of a college in Indiana, and the wife was an American-born Chinese. This Chinese couple wanted to find out whether that racially discriminatory action was taken by just a few hoodlums or by the majority of the local people. They then asked the owner of the house to call a meeting of the townpeople to decide on the controversy. In a secret ballot, it came out 174 to 28 in favor of the refusal to sell the house to the Chinese family.[3]

All of these events indicate that a prejudiced image of the Chinese is deeply entrenched in the minds of many Americans. For more than a century, in public speeches or testimonies of government officials, lawmakers, and other public figures, in school textbooks, novels, and newspapers, in movies and popular magazines, there have been prejudiced attacks on the Chinese from cultural, social, economic, religious, physiological, and even biological points of view, based on falsified "evidence" and pseudoscientific studies.

Thus an average American could not help but develop a distorted image of the Chinese as "criminal," "mentally and morally inferior," "deceitful and vicious," "debased and senile," a "distinct and unassimilable people," "filthy and loathsome," "dangerous and dreaded," etc. In his early childhood, any white American may have learned to chant:

Chink, Chink, Chinaman, sitting on a rail,
Along comes a white man and cuts off his tail . . .[4]

To understand why racial prejudice against the Chinese is so widespread in America, one need only review the abundant documents and literature pertaining to the intensive overt attacks on Chinese from all fronts for a whole century since the 1850s.

In his inaugural address of 1862, California Governor Leland Stanford pledged that "the settlement among us of an inferior race is to be discouraged" (see p. 109). Echoing his predecessor, Governor Henry Haight in 1867 stressed the disastrous results of allowing minorities (specifically, "Negroes" and "Asiatics") free participation in government. "What we desire for the permanent benefit of California," Haight claimed, "is a population of white men, who will make this State their home, bring up families here, and meet the responsibilities and discharge the duties of freemen. We ought not to desire an effete population of Asiatics for a free State like ours" (see p. 109).

In 1876, a committee appointed by the California state legislature "investigated" the Chinese in the state and published their findings a year later in the form of "An Address to the People of the United States upon the Evils of Chinese Immigration." This document, distributed across the country, opened the first nationwide anti-Chinese campaign. A more or less condensed form of the address was presented to the Congress as a "Memorial" (see p. 113) and prepared the very foundation of the 1882 Exclusion Law.

In the years preceding passage of the Exclusion Law, Congress heard much testimony on the dangers of continued immigration of Chinese. Reasons given for barring the Chinese ranged from a widely held fear that they might one day be strong enough in numbers to usurp public offices from white men (see p. 123) to the prediction that the presence of slave labor, in this case "coolieism," must eventually corrupt those who live as masters (see p. 125). Senator John P. Jones of Nevada cited the absence of names of southern families in Patent Office files as "proof" that slavery had made even creative work "dishonorable" in the South and had made idlers of southern whites.

Favoring European immigrants, Jones also declared that the Chinese had "nothing spiritual" about them and would contribute to the American ideals of liberty and free institutions only "oppression," "barbarism," and "degradation" (see p. 129).

These prejudices, high-minded enough for the floors of Congress, were reflected rather more coarsely in the anti-Chinese ideas held by most Americans. In the popular press, Chinese appeared as objects of ridicule, accusation, and vulgar conjecture. The *New York Times* reported in 1874, for instance, a complaint that a certain Chinese household had cooked and served rats, disposing of the waste in a neighborhood yard (see p. 130). The story stated that "a large portion of the community believe implicitly that Chinamen love rats as Western people love poultry. . . ." Witnesses could not agree whether the animals seen were rats or cats, and an inspection of the scene by a sanitation officer and a *Times* reporter turned up no evidence of such a practice. The complaint was apparently baseless, but the damage was done. New York Chinese were angry and indignant over the slander, and Chinaphobes had one more loathsome tale to tell their children.

In the same year, a Portland, Oregon, newspaper described a local Chinese religious festival in the "sick humor" fashion characteristic of many race jokes popular in the last few decades (see p. 133).

Late in the nineteenth century, an anti-Chinese campaign in popular literature began to focus on the idea of a "Yellow Peril" about to challenge the supremacy of the "superior race" in this country. Such ideas, combined with the ignorance and misconceptions of Chinese culture already present, spread an outlandish fear of a Chinese takeover in America.

One emotional magazine article in 1878 pointed out the "mongolization of many branches of industry" in San Francisco, then predicted a swarm of 100,000,000 more Chinese arriving by the turn of the century (see p. 134). This fear was "substantiated" on many fronts, even by the scientific community (see p. 135).

Such publicity as the Chinese received in the last century set the stage for prejudice and discrimination in the present. But some of the most damaging elements of the anti-Chinese attitudes predominant today were developed by the image of Chinese presented in more recent fiction and films. Chinese have traditionally been depicted as the villains: evil, kidnapping children, sinister, eating rats, smoking opium, and so on.

One of the most vital factors in creating the stereotype of the mysterious and villainous Chinese has been a fictitious creature invented by an English writer using the pseudonym Sax Rohmer. Dr. Fu-Manchu, the insidious villain of countless novels, was designed to be the most evil, sinister, and dreaded man, complete with yellow skin and horrifying slanted eyes. The vivid image Rohmer aroused quickly became a stereotype of the Chinese as a people, as did the expressions he frequently used, for example: "the most mysterious race, the Chinese," "the yellow menace," "the enemy of the white race," and other equally slanderous phrases (see p. 136).

Sadly, Rohmer's vilifying racism was not confined to the printed page, and the Fu-Manchu stories gained their greatest popularity when they were made into motion pictures in 1929. These movies all used more or less the same devices to show their hateful image of the Chinese character and culture: "The mysterious Chinatown was suggested by a whole series of visual clichés—the ominous shadow of an Oriental figure thrown against a wall, secret panels which slide back to reveal an inscrutable Oriental face, the huge shadow of a hand with tapering fingers and long pointed fingernails poised menacingly, the raised dagger appearing suddenly and unexpectedly from between closed curtains."[5] Hollywood promotion threatened "that Fu-Manchu had menace in every twitch of his finger, a threat in every twitch of his eyebrow, terror in each split-second of his slanted eyes." The Fu-Manchu films effectively built a completely prejudiced image in the minds of many Americans, most of them, unfortunately, children.

But the films were not alone in this distortion. Even school textbooks gave the children a cruelly biased and unjust account of the Chinese (see p. 138). "They never become like us," accused one history book, and "they form a menace to our civilization." Thus the process of "brainwashing" for racial hatred or prejudice started in early childhood for most Americans. It is no wonder that they later came to hold a strong prejudice against the Chinese, though they may never have seen an Oriental person in their lives.

That the images and stereotypes expressed in these readings have taken hold is certain. The final selection (see p. 140) is a sampling of white Americans' attitudes and opinions of the Chinese. The words are not often their own, but the words of Sax Rohmer, of Governor Stanford, of comic books and films and countless newspaper descriptions of "inscrutable" Chinese. "Distrustful," "crafty," "sneaking," "devious," "unfathomable," "backward," "savage," "obsequious," "stoic," "underdogs," and the "Yellow Peril" are recurring images.

The civil rights consciousness of the last decade has done much to eliminate open discrimination, but it may take generations to correct the wrongful, hostile attitudes most Americans were taught about the Chinese.

"The Settlement Among Us of an Inferior Race Is to be Discouraged"—California Governor Stanford's Inaugural Address (1862)

While the settlement of our State is of the first importance, the character of those who shall become settlers is worthy of scarcely less consideration. To my mind it is clear that the settlement among us of an inferior race is to be discouraged by every legitimate means. Asia, with her numberless millions, sends to our shores the dregs of her population. Large numbers of this class are already here; and, unless we do something early to check their immigration, the question which of the two tides of immigration meeting upon the shores of the Pacific shall be turned back will be forced upon our consideration, when far more difficult than now of disposal. There can be no doubt but that the presence of numbers among us of a degraded and distinct people must exercise a deleterious influence upon the superior race, and, to a certain extent, repel desirable immigration. It will afford me great pleasure to confer with the Legislature in any constitutional action, having for its object the impression of the immigration of the Asiatic races. . . .

From *California State Journal*, 13th sess., 1862, p. 99

"No Principle of Justice Is Involved"—California Governor Haight's Inaugural Address (1867)

. . . It is a question not of inalienable right, but simply of expediency. The question is, whether it will be for the greatest good of the greatest number to confine the elective franchise to the whites, or to extend it to the Negroes and Chinese. A portion of those persons in this State who favor Negro suffrage hesitate to advocate Chinese suffrage, but the congressional policy makes no distinction.

On the contrary, that policy proposes to ignore all discrimination in political privileges founded on race or color. Indeed, there is no line that can be drawn, unless suffrage is confined to the white population. If it is a question of justice, as some assert, and justice requires the ballot to be given to the Negro, then it equally requires the ballot to be given to the Chinaman. If the Negro requires the ballot to protect himself, as others assert, then the Asiatic needs it to protect himself. There is, however, no truth in either statement. No principle of justice is involved any more than in the case of females or minors, or foreigners not naturalized. Nor does the Negro need the ballot to protect himself any more than either of the other classes referred to; on the contrary, it is for the good of both of those races that the elective franchise should be confined to the whites. The aid of Africans and Asiatics would be an evil and not a benefit. It would introduce the antipathy of race into our political contests, and lead to strife and bloodshed. The opposition to giving the Negro and Asiatic the ballot is not based upon prejudice or ill will against those races, but upon a conviction of the evils which would result to the whole country from corrupting the source of political power with elements so impure.

It is not a sound reason for conferring the elective franchise upon Negroes if it were true that they need more protection. Upon this theory, the more helpless and ignorant the Negro is, the more propriety there would be in admitting him to the ballot box and making him a legislator and a sovereign. Our free institutions rest upon the virtue and intelligence of the people, and upon these qualities is based the only hope of their preservation; but this doctrine of Negro suffrage, so persistently advocated by senators and representatives in Congress, proposes as a basis for republican institutions, brutal ignorance and barbarism. So far from the ballot protecting the Negroes, it would eventuate in their destruction. The effort to give it to them by military force has already created a feeling of hostility between them and the white population of the South. These inferior races have their civil rights, as all good men desire they should have. They can sue and defend in the courts; acquire and possess property; they have entire freedom of person, and can pursue any lawful occupation for a livelihood; but they will never, with the consent of the people of this State, either vote or hold office.

The foregoing views upon national affairs will, I trust, be received in the spirit by which they are prompted. The lives of individuals are brief when compared with those of nations like ours. But a few years, and we who are now bearing the responsibilities of American citizenship will have passed away, leaving to our successors a legacy of constitutional freedom, or a spirit of lawlessness and disregard of constitutional obligations which will lead to revolution and anarchy. We have a common country, whose past glories are our joint heritage, and whose destiny in the future, whether of glory or of shame, is the destiny of ourselves and of our children.

Let us treat our southern countrymen with that spirit of charity and kindness which is our especial duty, considering that we are fully as liable to err as any other of our fellow men.

The subject of immigration and labor has engaged much attention in this State since the first organization of a State Government. Our distance from the sources of emigration, and the expense and difficulty of reaching California from the East and Europe, have prevented the increase of our laboring population as rapidly as was anticipated and desired, but while the increase of population will expedite the development of the resources of the State, it would not be wise statesmanship, in my judgment, to invite an immigration of Chinese or any other Asiatic race. Those races are confessedly inferior in all high and noble qualities to the American and European. It is the dictate of wisdom to seek the best material to populate a country. This course is for the highest good of the present and future generations.

No man is worthy of the name of patriot or statesman who countenances a policy which is opposed to the interests of the free white laboring and industrial classes. They constitute the body of the people; they sustain our free institutions; they carry forward our great public enterprises; they dig our canals, they build our railroads, cultivate our fields, explore the recesses of the earth in search of the precious metals; they fight our battles in war. It was their stubborn valor and self-sacrificing patriotism which in the late war saved the Government from destruction.

Their welfare ought to be guarded with jealous care by statesmen and legislators, for it is upon them that we must rely for the preservation of the Government. An additional influx of Chinese to compete with white laboring men in all industrial departments, ought to be discouraged by all lawful means. For the sake of some supposed advantage of cheap labor, such influx would inflict a curse upon posterity for all time. It would tend to discourage that immigration of white laborers from Europe and the Eastern States which is our great need and desire. It would be a shortsighted and selfish policy on the part of men of capital.

The completion of the Pacific Railroad will afford the laboring people of Europe and the Eastern States an opportunity to remove to this coast expeditiously, at a moderate cost, and they will flock hither if the avenues of labor are not filled by Mongolians. The lack of labor will then cease to be seriously felt. What we desire for the permanent benefit of California is a population of white men, who will make this State their home, bring up families here, and meet the responsibilities and discharge the duties of freemen. We ought not to desire an effete population of Asiatics for a free State like ours.

It is urged that this class of immigration should be permitted upon philanthropic grounds; but history and experience show that it is not the dictate of true philanthrophy, or of sound policy, to locate together in one community races so radically dissimilar in physical mental and moral constitution, as the Caucasian and African, or Mongolian.

The attempt to mix these races is in contravention of natural laws. For mutual good, they should be allowed to remain separated in location. Observation proves that neither social virtue nor public order, neither Christian civilization nor true progress is promoted by mingling these races in one community. Commercial intercourse will be mutually beneficial, but all attempts to make a national composite of such elements will be disastrous.

The passage of a law making eight hours a legal day's labor, in the absence of special contract, has been demanded with great unanimity by the working classes, and a distinct pledge was given by both parties in the late canvass that such a law should be enacted. This pledge will doubtless be redeemed without delay.

From Chinese Immigration, R. O. Polkinhorn, printer, Washington, D.C., 1882

California's Anti-Chinese Memorial to Congress (1877)

Mr. Loewy made the following report:

Mr. SPEAKER:—In accordance with the instructions of the House, a memorial to Congress, on the dangers of Chinese immigration, has been prepared by the Special Committee appointed for that purpose, and is respectfully submitted to the House for its consideration.

MEMORIAL

The Legislature of the State of California, at its thirteenth session, respectfully represents to the Senate and House of Representatives in Congress assembled, as follows:

A perfect equality of political rights, and a universal cooperation of the entire people, or at least its moral capability of cooperating in the making and administering the laws, being the cornerstone of the permanence of every republic, your memorialists deem it of the most vital importance that we should not invite a national element into our midst whose social character and moral relations are so repulsive to those fundamental principles upon which our society, and indeed every civilized society, is founded, that we can neither socially amalgamate with it, nor entrust it with the prerogatives and duties of participation in the administration of our Government. It is neither a shortsighted policy of national exclusiveness, nor a lack of charity for inferior nationalities, that impels California to lift her voice against the unrestricted influx of a race in every respect more undesirable than that population, for the absolute exclusion of which, the National Administration and Congress have already manifested their willingness to cooperate with those States which desire to rid themselves of this element of national discord.

In appealing to Congress for protection against the contingency of an overwhelming immigration of Mongolians, the Legislature of California is solely actuated by the love and care for the safety and maintenance of our institutions, and the consciousness that a condition of slavery in our midst must unavoidably be the result of an unrestrained immigration of Mongolians. The Representatives of the people of California deem it a solemn duty to manifest to the National Congress the conviction that, if this immigration be not discouraged, the time is not far when degraded labor will have become as identified with the pecuniary interests of a portion of the people of this State, and as inimical to the fundamental principles of a democratic government, as Negro labor in the now rebellious States.

Even the position of the small number of free Negroes in the free States teaches us that no republican government ought to suffer the presence of a race which must, socially and politically, be always separate and distinct, and the antipathy to which is stronger in regulating its position and disabilities in society than the laws of the land. In the conviction of your memorialists, it is not alone a legalized state of slavery, which undermines the foundation of a republic, but that social relation which is the necessary consequence of the settlement in *one* community of two entirely uncongenial races, and which tends to produce, though the inferior race

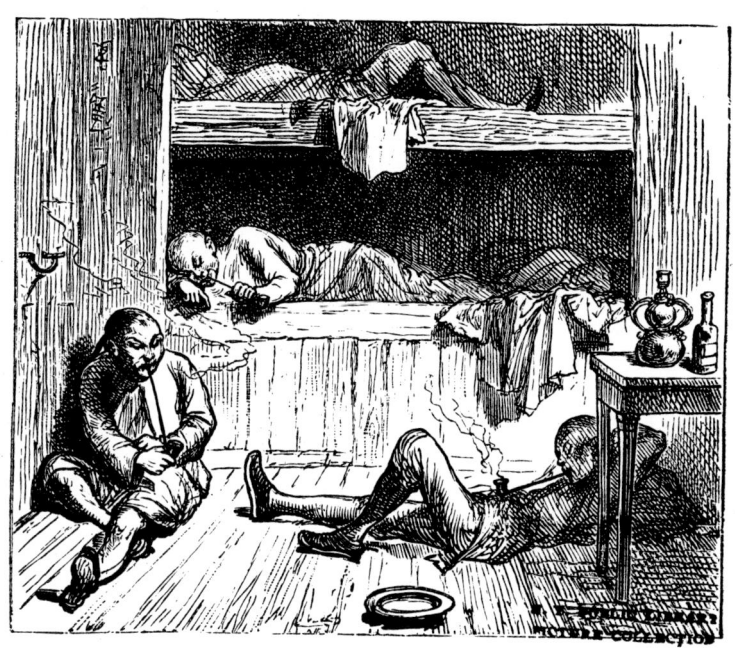

CHINESE OPIUM SMOKERS AT SAN FRANCISCO.

And he went for that heathen Chinee

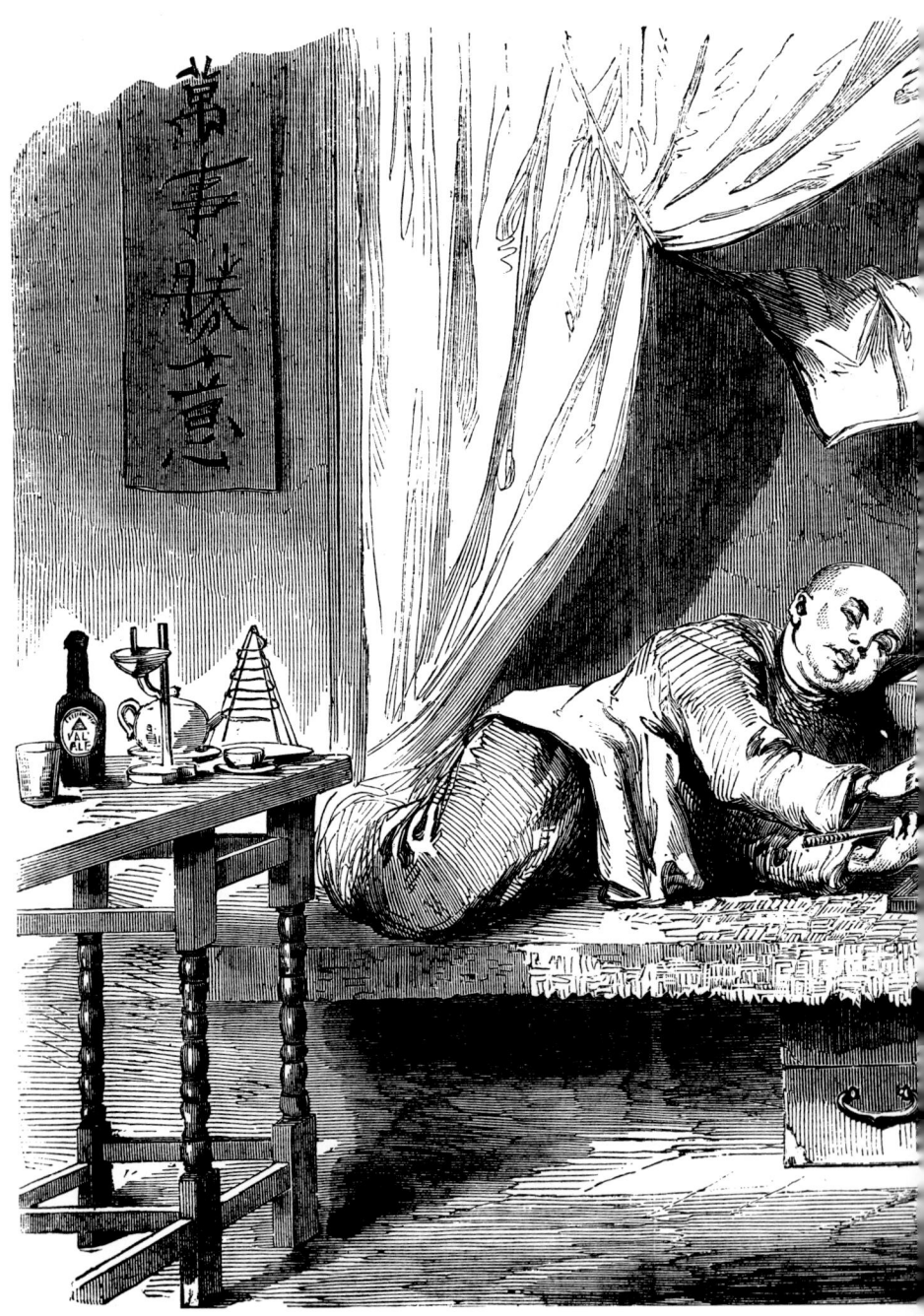

Stereotyped Chinese projected in American movie film

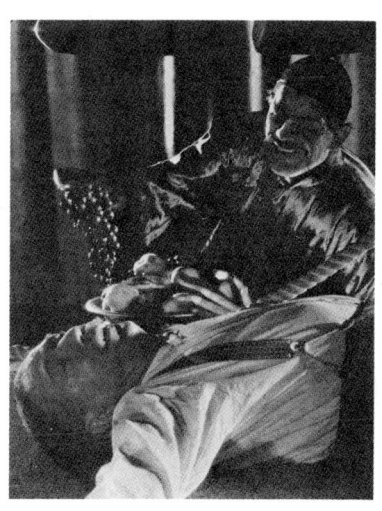

may be nominally free, the respective positions of a governing and a servile class, is just as dangerous to the permanence of republican institutions and ought to be as much guarded against as slavery itself.

Your memorialists assert that California is in a position far different from that of her sister States in regard to the settlement within the United States of races which, as long as self-respect and conservatism govern the Anglo-Saxon race in America, can never be admitted to social amalgamation or political equality. The free States in the East could only then fully appreciate the evils and complications which threaten the social system of California, if they were as much exposed to the danger of becoming colonies of free Negroes as California to the immigration of millions of Mongolians. Though the free Negro speaks our language, though he grows up among us, worships the same God as ourselves, and is accustomed to our institutions, yet the free States find the presence of a comparatively small population of this race exceedingly annoying, and fraught with dangers not only to the peace of their own community, but to the harmony between their laws and the constitutional policy of the National Legislature. What may be the difficulties and dangers which California will have to encounter, if she is not to be protected from the unlimited influx of a race which already comprises the eighth part of her entire population, which is utterly a stranger to our language, to the fundamental principles of enlightened religion, to our consciousness of moral obligations, and, with a few individual exceptions, even to a sense of the most common proprieties of life. Does it not deserve the serious consideration of the National Legislature and of the treaty-making power, that not the slightest barrier exists for the protection of California against immigration from a contiguous semicivilized empire, which counts its slaves by hundreds of millions?

The Congress of seventeen hundred and ninety and seventeen hundred and ninety-five, when no American statesman had the slightest anticipation that the domain of the Union would stretch to the Pacific Ocean, and when the people of the United States came but little into personal contact with the nations of Asia, believed sufficiently to provide against the contingency of other than congenial and desirable immigration, by excluding from the rights of citizenship all but free white aliens. It is due to the wisdom of our forefathers and to the care and foresight with which they planted institutions intended to be permanent and beyond contingencies which human sagacity might provide against, that they would have put other restrictions upon the immigration of inferior races, besides the disability of acquiring the rights of citizenship, could they have but anticipated so near a geographical relation between the United States and China, that the former would be liable to a continual and unlimited influx of population from the latter. It is, therefore, in the belief of your memorialists, no extravagant hope which California entertains, that at the present time the same Congress and the same Administration, which believe it to be their duty to offer the Federal aid to States desirous to entirely exclude Negroes from their soil, will not refuse to her the same cooperation against a race much more uncongenial to us than the other, and much more dangerous on account of the facility with which countless millions may at any time be thrust upon us by the pleasure of a barbarian potentate.

Whilst the influence of slavery is losing territory in our Eastern sister States, the unrestrained settlement of Mongolians in California is slowly but surely building up such social relations as will soon place the two races practically in the position of masters and unfree servants. A race so degraded, that it is stated by the committee of this Legislature appointed to confer with the Chinese companies at San Francisco, that according to the information from these leaders of the Chinese, there are but one hundred respectable families (i.e., married women with children) among a population of fifty thousand Chinese, a large proportion of which number consists of females—a race so devoid of a sense of truth and veracity that the testimony of ever so many individuals to the same facts has no weight upon the minds of our juries—such a race can certainly not reside long in our midst without awakening all those selfish interests which desire the introduction of cheap labor, and the immediate cultivation of articles heretofore produced by slave labor in the South, even at the cost of an irradicable system of involuntary servitude.

Degradation of labor and the impoverishment of the laboring classes are poisons which destroy the lifeblood of a republic. There are enough resources in the almost unbounded domains of the Union to support the dignity of labor for centuries, unless it is brought into competition with slave labor. Chinese labor ranks no higher in the public respect than slave labor. Its compensation is so low in proportion to the necessities of life in California that the white laborer cannot compete with the Chinaman, who needs neither a civilized abode, nor decent clothing, nor education for his children. The larger portion of the Chinese has been engaged in mining. During the early years after the discovery of gold in this State, when our population was sparse, and when there was no lack of rich surface mines, the American and European miner experienced no hardship from the presence of the Chinese; but, as in the course of time, the rich surface diggings became more and more exhausted, and the chances of generous reward for individual labor in mining claims became rare, the antipathies of our own race against the Mongolians were aroused, and grew daily stronger in proportion as the mines occupied by Mongolians became of increasing importance to American citizens or Europeans, who sought the means of a modest and toilsome subsistence for a permanent settlement upon our soil.

As a natural consequence, California has witnessed those collisions of races which are deplorable, but which will always manifest themselves between a superior and an inferior race, which are forced into permanent contact, and whose mutual antipathies are strengthened by a conflict of pecuniary interests. In many mining sections, organizations were formed for the purpose of forcibly preventing Chinese from working in places where they had not yet made their appearance, and to eject them from districts where the mineral would reward the labor of white persons. These arbitrary mining regulations were enforced by the miners, and as the Executive authorities of the State were not desirous to produce civil strife by forcibly resisting the popular will, laws have existed and still exist in this State, outside of the legal power, in restriction of the right of Chinese to work the mines.

By such treatment, and by such oppressive and tyrannical bearing, as the rude and passionate classes of a superior race will always assume towards a race residing among them, whose settlement is highly undesirable, a large portion of the Chinese in the mines was induced to resort to our towns and cities, whereby the share of the latter in the great social evil —for as such we consider the settling of the Chinese among us—has been disproportionally increased. Although the Chinese in the cities have so far not met with that spirit of persecution which discouraged their settlement in the mines, yet it is manifest that a bitter hostility against them is a marked and growing feeling among the laboring classes of our cities. This feeling is mainly due to the intrusion of the Chinese into several branches of industry, to the serious detriment of the white workingmen heretofore engaged in them. The latter, being unable to maintain a decent and civilized subsistence upon wages which afford the Chinaman a comfortable living, were compelled, in every case where Chinese competition made its appearance, to retire from their profession, and abandon its exercise to their Chinese competitors. Several of our industrial professions, which but a few years ago afforded a profitable employment to a large number of persons of our own race, and which were yearly growing in importance and in their capacity of employing white workingmen and their families, are now monopolized by Chinese, to the exclusion of our own citizens. Our working classes look, therefore, anxiously into the future, for they feel that the Chinese, with their skill for mechanical imitation, will slowly but surely push themselves into one profession after another, and reduce the value of labor to the level which it occupies in monarchies, and which makes it equivalent to pauperism and degradation. This apprehension is well founded, if the success heretofore enjoyed by Chinese competition with our working classes may be considered as a fair criterion of the position of Chinese labor to white labor in the future.

Your memorialists are aware that the Legislature of a republic ought always to encourage rather than discourage competition of labor, so long as this labor emanates from congenial or homogeneous races; but if her working classes are forced to compete with a race entirely foreign to all our moral, social, and political interests, and independent of the necessities which a civilized life imposes, then it becomes certainly the duty of the Government to shield the labor of her citizens, and to anticipate, by wise legislation, the violent collision which must be the unavoidable result of an unrestricted encroachment of an inferior race upon the self-respect, the dignity, and, above all, upon the indispensable resources of the working classes of the governing race. California needs population, but it would be far better for her future prosperity—aye, for her safety—to be content with her present population, than to increase it manifold by inviting Chinese immigration.

The Mongolian is not only by degrees diminishing the means of subsistence of our white workingmen, but he is a serious impediment in the way of the immigration of the poor and humble classes of our own race from the Eastern States and Europe. As labor is undignified and despised in the slave States, because it is performed by a race which is inferior in nature and in social standing, the unrestrained immigration of Mongolians to this State, and their intrusion into every mechanical profession, will have the same humiliating and demoralizing influence upon the working classes of our citizens. No American or European workman, even if he could work for the wages of the Mongolian, will work with him at the same workbench, in the same workshop, or, in those branches which the Chinaman does succeed in monopolizing, even in the same profession. The Chinese will infinitely more degrade labor than the Negro in the slave

States has done. The statement of the Chinese companies themselves, that there are but one hundred respectable families in the State, among fifty thousand Chinese, is a correct guide to their moral condition—if such a term can be at all applied to a people who have not the least consciousness of truth and veracity, and whose entire female population (with the exception of one hundred, according to the statement of the Chinese) are engaged in the business of prostitution.

The social habits and customs of the Chinese, if we except the merchants, are so loathsome that even the atmosphere becomes pregnant with the effluvia of their abodes, and that entire streets in which they have settled—some of which in the speedy course of California progress have become most eligible business sites—are held in disrepute, and prevent the natural growth of commercial thoroughfares and of wholesome traffic.

Such, with the exception of some respectable Chinese merchants in our larger cities, is the character of the Chinese who are in our midst and who continue to come. The Chinese population among us forms a State within a State; they are under the secret control of the five organizations which are known as companies, whose orders and decisions they implicitly obey. All indications tend to show that there exists between themselves a relation of involuntary servitude, but the slavish subjection of the Mongolian to his social system and the fear of the revenge of his superiors are so great that nothing can induce him to disclose the nature of the power which holds him to strict obedience, even against the police and judicial authorities of this State. The presence of hordes of Mongolians would at present undoubtedly be advantageous to the capitalist and the manufacturer. These classes, although very necessary to the development of a young State, are generally not as careful of the preservation of the principles of freedom and of the exclusion of every element dangerous to the maintenance and the purity of republican institutions, as they are anxious of reaping immediate and unusual profits. Better, far better, that our manufacturing interests should sleep a few years longer, until the natural decrease of the value of labor will make the employment of white laborers profitable, than to develop them by a race which we shall not be able to exclude when the time will have arrived when white workmen will gladly cooperate with the capitalists who desire to experiment in this State with the cultivation of Southern products.

But your memorialists assert that even the *present* value of the labor of our own workingmen is not in the way of the profitable development of new resources in this State. Laborers of our own race have been successfully and profitably employed in experiments of manufacture. Only, then, when a capitalist, desiring to underbid his competitors, introduced Chinese labor—only then it became impossible for others engaged in the same business to continue employing the labor of our own citizens.

It is only lately that it has become known to the people of Europe that California has all the necessary elements to become one of the richest vineyards in the world. The efforts which have been made to attract the vine-growing people of Europe to the reward which their labor and skill would reap in the southern portion of our State are just beginning to be successful. The question arises—Shall the State invite to its shores thousands of families from the wine-growing borders of the Rhine, which will be a valuable addition to the intelligent, liberty-loving, congenial population of the State, and which will, in developing the resources of our soil, build up homesteads for themselves, or shall we have hordes of Mongolians create large plantations for a few owners of immense tracts of land, and thus, in enriching a few, degrade the value and dignity of labor, and keep away from our shores the desirable working classes of Europe?

It is as well for the protection of the Chinese who reside among us, as for our own protection, that we earnestly urge the Congress to put some barrier in the way of Chinese immigration. We entreat the National Congress to consider that antipathies of races cannot be equalized or counteracted by police laws. The law has not the power of preventing the innumerable acts of brutality and violence which the lower classes of our own population exercise toward the Chinese whenever a favorable opportunity offers itself; for Chinese cannot testify against white persons, and, for fear of the revenge of their persecutors, do not dare to seek the protection of the Courts. These evils, so dangerous as well in their existing force as in their prospective consequences, call certainly for the serious consideration of the power which regulates our intercourse with foreign nations.

The Congress will in its wisdom determine whether the existing treaties interfere with such relief as California expects. If such obstacles exist, the Legislature of California begs to submit that such a revision of the treaties as would protect California from the unlimited influx of Mongolian hordes is most essential to her safety and welfare. All real advantages to be derived from a mutual intercourse of commerce with China may be enjoyed without encouraging any longer the immigration of the lowest and most degraded population of China. If the United States will henceforth admit but those Chinese who are engaged in mercantile pursuits, and either entirely exclude other Mongolians, the commercial intercourse with China, as far as it is of genuine and permanent value to California, would, in our opinion, be by no means depreciated. The Mongolians in California subsist largely on the imported products of their native country. Of our products they consume none but the most indispensable. But whatever pecuniary profits the presence of a large population of Mongolians might offer, California is willing to forego them; for she values the safety of her social and political institutions higher than the immediate cultivation upon her soil of sugar, rice, tea, and cotton.

Former Legislatures of California have also felt the greatness of the evil against which your memorialists urgently solicit the aid and cooperation of the National authorities. They repeatedly instructed their Senators and their Representatives to lay this important matter before the Congress, and invite its attention to the dangers which threaten the welfare, perhaps the existence, of the Caucasian race in the

States bordering upon the Pacific. Yet, heretofore, the wishes of California have in this respect been wholly neglected by her representatives in Congress.

Trusting in the sincerity and zeal with which our present Senators and Representatives will submit to Congress the evils but imperfectly indicated in this memorial, the State of California entertains the strong hope that the care and solicitude of Congress for the welfare of every part of the Nation will be directed to the earnest consideration of the great social danger upon the Pacific coast.

Loewy,
Campbell.

From *Chinese Immigration*, R. O. Polkinhorn, printer, Washington, D.C., 1882

Testimony at a Congressional Hearing on the Exclusion Law (1876)

QUESTION. *Why is the Italian immigration preferable to the Chinese?*

ANSWER. They are of a different race. The Italians are of the same stock that we are, and have come to their present ditch by a slow course of development for thousands of years.

Q. *They are a higher civilization?*
A. Undoubtedly.
Q. *Do you think the same objection would apply to any lower civilization as to the Chinese?*
A. Undoubtedly.
Q. *Do many of these Chinese attempt to become citizens?*
A. No, sir.
Q. *Was there not great alarm in this community at the commencement of the present Congress because the Chinese were applying to be naturalized?*
A. No, sir; I think there never was any alarm of that in this community.
Q. *What was the reason of the application to Congress at the last session to change the law?*

A. To prevent future danger.
Q. *Were there any lithographs here representing Chinese occupying the position of judges, mandarins, etc.?*
A. Yes, sir.
Q. *Were there any editorials in our papers calling attention to the danger of being governed by Chinese?*
A. Yes, sir.
Q. *Because they were all getting naturalized?*
A. No, sir; those dangers are looked on as in the future. I have not heard anybody say that there is any danger of the Chinese rushing now down to the courts and becoming naturalized.
Q. *What is your understanding in regard to Chinese students in our colleges? Do they not acquire the sciences with equal facility with white boys?*
A. I think not; I think they are like the Negroes, as I have been told; that is, up to a certain point they learn very fast, but beyond that point, it is very difficult for them to go.
Q. *Do you think the Negro also deficient in natural intelligence?*
A. So I have been told by those who have had experience in teaching them.
Q. *You think that, like the Negro, the Chinese are incapable of attaining a high state of civilization?*
A. They are incapable of attaining the state of civilization the Caucasian is capable of.
Q. *You would make the same objection to the introduction of the Negro to civilization as to the introduction of the Chinese on that ground?*
A. I would have the same objection to the introduction of the Negro as to the importation of the Chinese.
Q. *How about those who are here?*
A. The difference between the Negro and the Chinamen is that the number of Negroes in the country is fixed, while the number of Chinese may increase indefinitely.

From a Senate Report, 44th Congr., 2nd sess., 1876

"Fraught with Immense Evils"—Further Testimony to Congress (1876)

I came to California in 1849 as a minister of the gospel, to make here my permanent home; and now for more than twenty years I have been acting as traveling editor of the *Pacific,* the oldest weekly paper of the Far West. I have had, therefore, the opportunity to know fully the facts pertaining to the subject on which I write. I believe the influx of vast numbers of Chinese into our country to be fraught with immense evils to Americans in every light in which it may be viewed. This is true as to the desirable homogeneity of our population, as to our moral character, as to our political status, our military strength, our acquisition of wealth, our social relationships, and all our civil and religious institutions. Yet, to trace out the influence in these several respects would require a time and space circumstances at present forbid. But there is a line of thought, more or less comprehending the whole, which I have not seen traced out by anyone. This I wish, in short, to attempt to your honorable commission.

This line is that of a parallel and a contrast between African slavery and Chinese immigration, commonly called coolieism. First, this parallel is seen in their origin and manner of coming to this country, i.e., to America. Neither of them, excepting a very few, come of themselves; but scheming, wealthy English and American capitalists, as companies or individual adventurers, made it their object solely for the money to bring them into America. From Africa this was done by physical compulsion. From China it is done by moral compulsion, in that, by every plausible representation, they have been induced to come. The motive of the capitalists was alone that of making money—solely this, with no regard to the good of anyone. A second parallel is in the arguments used in America in favor of their coming—the African formerly, the Chinese at present: that this country is an asylum for people from all parts of the world; that it is large and needs more population; that laborers are scarce, and otherwise cannot be had; that the price of labor is high and needs to be reduced, so that we may increase our productions; that it is a benefit to the heathen that they may be elevated by our influence; that they are better off with us than in their native land; that here they can be Christianized, and go back to convert their countrymen; that there is a Providence in it for good; hence, let them come. These and other arguments used are identically the same in the two cases. But as to slavery, their fallacy is now most apparent; they may become still more so in respect to the Chinese. A third parallel is seen in their results. They both render honest labor peculiarly degrading, disreputable for our sons and daughters, a mark of inferiority to be avoided at almost any hazard. The moral and other evils of the prevalence of such a sentiment are above full description. Then, as to those who must work, the competition between them and the cheap labor of slaves and of Chinese is sure to reduce them far toward the condition of slaves and coolies in the poverty of living as a low, ignorant, despised class of "poor white trash."

They both introduce systems of heathen vice and immoralities fearfully corrupting to our youth and general population. They both come as races of men distinct from ourselves, to become permanent residents among us, with habits, customs, ideas, and prejudices different from ours, and so in conflict with us as to occasion jealousies of race and conflicts of people, fearfully distracting and dangerous to the stability of our institutions. They both constitute a class of cheap laborers, to be employed by large monopolists and landholders, excluding permanently a working white population and desirable immigrants from Christian lands, thus diminishing our wealth, weakening our military force, scattering our population, interfering with the establishing of schools, and all neighborhood social, moral, and religious institutions.

This is a rapid sketch of some of the parallels of evils between slavery and coolieism. But the *contrast* between them exhibits evils of coolieism much greater than those of slavery. Some of these contrasts are as follows:

Slavery gave the master power to destroy all the distinctive heathenism which the African brought with him, and he did destroy it. But coolieism gives the employer no such power, and he does not do it. Slavery changed the whole early acquired character of the African, leaving almost or quite nothing of his idolatrous religion, language, customs, habits, morals, tastes, and prejudices, educating him and elevating him up to a whole new character, as an American Christian citizen, in the use of the American language, with American feelings, views, and aspirations.

Coolieism, with very slight exceptions, leaves the Chinese just what they were in their native land, with all their idolatry, immorality, vice, and heathen customs, habits, dress, tastes, prejudices, and most unacquirable language—a large, distinct class of people, adverse to all that is American. Slavery rendered impossible any clanship or race combination among Africans in conflict with our interests or our Government; but coolieism gives the Chinese full opportunity to unite all their energies in any schemes they may devise in their supposed interests, to enforce and perpetuate their numerical influence, their heathen worship, their idolatrous customs, their temple ceremonies, their degrading habits, immoralities, vices, dress, prostitution, language, and every feature of abomination so common in their own country.

Already they have a perfect government among themselves distinct from our own, with their laws, their secret courts of trial, and their police, executive, and other officers, the object of which is to perpetuate their race peculiarities, their clanship interests, and their religion, with terrible sanctions of law, even the death penalty, to enforce their regulations.

They are managing a perfect and increasingly efficient *"imperium in imperio,"* to enforce obedience to their requirements, however adverse to American interests or government. They now number full 150,000 in our country, of whom about 130,000 are in California, being nearly one-sixth of our whole population. Others in large numbers are coming, amounting (when unchecked by intimidation) to 25,000 a year. Very few of these ever change in character, to become Americanized. Only about 500 in the last twenty-five years have renounced their native heathenism to profess Christianity. Thus do they remain and rapidly increase in our country, a vast united class, distinct from us in all important characteristics, tastes, habits, and language, exerting an influence adverse to our interests, soon, if unrestrained, to number 5,000,000, or even 10,000,000. It becomes inevitable that they must ultimately vote and hold office. Then wards in our cities and sections of country containing majorities of them, true already of many places, must have the administration of our laws through Chinese officers, heathen in their views, clannish in their judgment, corrupt in their decisions. The evils inevitable from a large influx of Chinese must be immensely greater than those resulting from that of the African. As to slavery, only one evil of it was greater than that of coolieism. That one evil was, it gave power and sanction to the white man to trample upon every human and divine right of the African as an intelligent being. In every other respect coolieism is the more injurious to our real interests.

I have no hesitation in expressing my strongest convictions of the immense evils sure to result from large influx of Chinese to our country. Some good men have said, "Providence will prevent all evil and bring good out of their coming. We need to have no apprehension from them." As well might "He who spake as never man spake" say to the tempter upon the pinnacle of the temple, "Providence will prevent all evil and bring good out of it. I need have no apprehension, and will let myself fall."

It is wicked presumption to be indifferent to evils and leave the results to Providence. It is false Christianity and false common sense to neglect the exercise of good human judgment and corresponding action in view of impending evil. God requires perception, reason, good judgment, and judicious, earnest action, just as though all depended alone upon ourselves, and then, after this, then and only then, trust in the divine disposal. Hence, gentlemen, I write you in the full strength of my conviction, that it is the duty of the American people and Government to look the evils of Chinese immigration into our country squarely in the face, to realize the facts and probable evil results in the case, and to put forth effectual efforts, through the treaty-making power and congressional regulations, to prevent any further large influx of Chinese into the country, and ensure a rational steady diminution of the numbers who are already here.

From a Senate Report, 44th Congr., 2nd sess., 1876, pp. 1241–1243

"A Current of Barbarians"—A U.S. Senator Speaks Out for Exclusion (1882)

Is this superior race of ours afraid of the competition with this inferior Chinese race? The main objection to the incoming of the Chinese cannot be brought against Europeans of our own race and nearly related to us. . . . Their God is our God. They are inherently lovers of liberty. When and where did the Chinese race ever make a simple declaration for liberty? When and where did they strike one single blow for freedom or free institution? What, then, I ask, has been the contribution from China? Oppression, barbarism, degradation. A civilization purely material, nothing spiritual about, everything commutable in money. . . .

The wealth of a country does not consist in the bushels of wheat, in the tons of coal and iron . . . no wealth is possible without intelligence. Let a white man go with a mountain of gold into the center of Africa and Asia and has he any considerable wealth? . . . none whatsoever. He has got to import intelligence there, without which no important accumulation of wealth can possibly be effected. Does anybody tell me that you can introduce a lower order of people into a country without affecting the higher orders? Can a current of barbarians be permitted to flow into this country without affecting its white people for the worse? You may lift up the barbarous people above their dull, dead insanity but do you not drag us down correspondingly? . . .

Look at the dearth in our Patent Office of names from the

Southern States. Why was it? Because a servile race was performing the labor of those states, making it dishonorable there; and, because few or none of the laborers of that regions belonged to this great creative race, who alone could have given the stimulus to the national development of the Southern States. . . .

The Negro possesses, in a marked degree, all the human and affectionate sympathies. He easily becomes attached to those with whom he lives and is loyal to them. He adopts our customs and is proud to imitate them instead of taking a pride, as the Chinaman does, in adhering to his own national habits. To the extent of his capacity for improvement he has a willingness and even ambition to improve himself, instead of shutting himself up as the Chinaman does, with an indomitable self-conceit within the limit of present attainments. . . .

From a speech by Senator John P. Jones
of Nevada in U.S. Senate, 1882

Do Chinese Eat Rats? (1874)

Do the Chinese eat rats? This has always been a mooted question. Geographies contain the assertion that they do, and an old woodcut of a Chinaman peddling rodents, strung by the tails to a rack which he carried over his shoulders, is a standard illustration of the common school atlases of ten years ago. A large portion of the community believe implicitly that Chinamen love rats as Western people love poultry, and the small boy from time to time gives expression to the faith that is in him by occasionally shying one of the small deer into the shop of a patient laundryman. The Chinese have always indignantly denied the charge, and now that it has been repeated by Dr. Charles Kaemmerer, of No. 20 East Thirteenth Street, they are filled with wrath toward him. The statement made by Dr. Kaemmerer is that Chinamen living at No. 5 Mott Street have killed and cooked rats and cats in the yard, and have disposed of the offal by throwing it into the yard of No. 199 Worth Street. Little groups of

Celestials were gathered together in Pell and Mott Streets yesterday, excitedly discussing the charge, and it was the all-absorbing topic of conversation in the Chinese restaurants, grocery stores, and opium joints.

The premises at No. 5 Mott Street are occupied by Chung Khe, whose real name is Mr. Wong. He is a short and slender man, has a very intelligent face, and dresses neatly. He has been here several years and is quite wealthy. He is the head of the Wong family in America, and his grocery store is their headquarters. The visiting Wongs, according to the Mongolian custom, are welcome to make his home theirs as long as they care about doing so, and some of the family have been abusing this hospitality for the past three or four years without wearing out their welcome. The second story is occupied by Mr. Wong as a storeroom and the upper floors are used for living purposes. The basement is used by Quong Hong Loung as a grocery store and living apartment. The back windows of the house open on a little courtyard in which boxes and boards are piled neatly, up to the second-story windows. The premises at No. 199 Worth Street are occupied by Mr. François Cepirio for a restaurant and saloon. The building is new and has a large back window, which faces the home of Mr. Wong and his kindred.

Dr. Kaemmerer was visited yesterday by a *Times* reporter. He is a short, stout, excitable Frenchman upward of fifty years of age, and a resident of this city for a quarter of a century. He was formerly a sanitary inspector. He said that when he was visiting his friend, Mr. Cepirio, on Saturday last, he made a sanitary inspection of the premises. Noticing a very peculiar odor arising from the courtyard, he looked into that place and saw some Chinamen standing there handling some things that looked like very small cats or very large rats. The stench prevented him from making a more thorough examination. Upon this ground he made the complaint. "I didn't see them eat the animals," said he, "but I don't know why they shouldn't do so. In Paris the Frenchmen ate rats during the siege. We eat dogs and horses, and cats are served for rabbits in almost every restaurant in Paris. I once ate part of a cat in this city, and I liked it. I thought it was French hare until several days afterward. The meat was sweet and it tasted very good."

Mr. Cepirio's story differed somewhat from Dr. Kaemmerer's. He said: "The doctor did not see the cats. My little son, who is frequently in the saloon, one day, not long ago, saw two dead cats lying on a board in the kitchen near the window. He called me and I also saw them. Later in the day I noticed that they had been removed by the Chinamen." Mr. Cepirio's son claims to have seen the Chinese cook skin the animals, cut off their heads, and chop their bodies into small pieces, and put them into a pot. After they were boiled, he says, the cook picked the meat from the bones. He did not see any of the stew eaten. Dr. Vermilye, the sanitary inspector of that district, paid a visit to the premises yesterday afternoon, accompanied by a *Times* reporter. The yard was clean. There was no offal in the yard, no cat or rat skins, and no stench. By the open window a Chinese cook was seen preparing the dinner. He was making a stew, which was composed of salted Chinese turnips, soft-shelled crabs, and pigs' ears. These and various other articles of food were washed and sliced on a huge butcher's block with a butcher's cleaver. The cook was as deft as a hotel chef, and did his work with much care and cleanliness. He shelled fresh peas, sliced a wholesome-looking cabbage head, and peeled fresh potatoes whose skins were almost white. There was nothing suggestive of rats or cats about the place, and the doctor said that he should report that there was no cause for complaint.

The reporter asked several Chinamen in the neighborhood if cat's meat was ever used for food or in the preparation of Chinese medicines. Several answered that cats and rats were never eaten, but that a nostrum was made of cat's meat. It was not made in America, but was imported from China. Wong Chin Foo, the editor of the *Chinese-American*, yesterday offered a reward of $500 for anyone who could prove that a Chinaman ate rats or cats. Chung Khe was very indignant, and told the reporter in very emphatic pidgin English that he intended to sue Dr. Kaemmerer for slander.

Wong Chin Foo said that he had traveled all over China and had never heard of a native eating a rat or a cat. They drew the line at dogs, but he had no doubt that in times of great famine they ate anything to keep from starving. He had never heard the rat story until he came to America. There was no necessity for the Chinese to eat such food here, he said, as they were all making money. Laundry hands receive $3 a day and their board, and some exceptionally good workmen get as high as $5. They can all afford to buy the best that the market affords.

From the *New York Times*, 1874

A View of Chinese Culture (1874)

Once more the Chinese of this city are engaged in their mysterious incantation on Washington Street near Second. They have secured a room near the engine house and fitted it up in a most grotesque manner at an expense of perhaps $2,000. On either side of the entrance stand two large figures, about twelve feet in height and painted in true celestial art.

The prince, or "Ah Deo" as they call them, preaches at intervals upon subjects of very little interest to the general reader, and scarcely worth mentioning. As the service will last until Saturday next, those desirous can procure a seat on the sidewalk and listen for themselves. About five minutes generally satisfies the average American. The most important feature of the proceeding is the band. He gives his entire attention to a large-size gong. In his frantic endeavors to knock a hole in it, he perfoms acrobatic feats worthy of an India-rubber man. He belabors the unfortunate instrument whose shrieks and yells tell of its terrible contest. . . . As the Chinese have a load of sins which have been accumulating for that length of time to be forgiven, they may be pardoned for taking such a lively interest in the curious proceeding.

From the Portland, Oregon, *Bulletin*,
November 18, 1874

The Yellow Peril (1878)

... political economy informs us that Chinamen will promote the growth of wealth, but where and how are we to ascertain what the effects of unrestricted Asiatic immigration will be upon the growth and distribution of the human race upon this continent?

... Will it merely furnish an addition to our industrial classes, or will it result as a substitution, as far as it goes, of Mongolian for Caucasian in the total of our population?

... [The Chinaman] has come to stay, and he has only just commenced to come. The first ripples have struck our shore. The tidal wave is now forming in interior China, which may overwhelm us.

In what numbers will they come?

In 1840, there were 8 million souls in Ireland; in 1845 the potato-famine began, which culminated in 1847. In 1855 the population had been reduced nearly one half. Two million had starved, the rest of the reduction was accomplished by emigration in spite of the well-known fecundity of the race.

China continues in round numbers 450 million inhabitants —about eleven times the population of the United States on about one fifth more ground. The famine is nearly in the same proportion of the whole as that of Ireland was. If the parallel were continued, there would be nearly 100 million deaths by starvation, and another 100 million emigrants within the next twenty years.

The swarm of Chinese in San Francisco, particularly, and their mongolization of many branches of industry, from which by their wonderful manual skill, their highly developed and intelligent imitative faculties, their tireless industry, and their abnormal frugality, they have driven out the white, bringing the latter face to face with the possibilities of the future. He needs no knowledge of the methods of scientific and philosophical reasoning to perceive the irreconcilable antagonism between himself and the newcomer.

It is another matter altogether with the free Negro. In that case, the industrious white has as great an advantage as the

Chinese has in his. The Negro is as far behind us in the art of maintaining life as we are behind the Mongol.

Is not the Mongol a thistle in our field? Shall we pluck it up as does the wise husbandman, or shall we withdraw the intelligence of artificial selection from the environment, and leave the battle to the chances of natural selection alone?

From the *North Atlantic Review*, CXXVI, 1878, pp. 506–526

A "Scientific" View of the Chinese (1876)

As white and black are apparent opposites, and science shows the white race to be superiorly developed, it is fair to presume that primitive man was black; subsequent nations, brown; their branches, red; from these sprung the yellow, and thence the white.

It is probable that no perceptible change has taken place in the Chinese race for many years, because in that time the incomplete changes of physical condition in their country have not admitted of it. Wheat found in tombs with Egyptian mummies, when brought from darkness into sunlight and planted in congenial soil, grew and produced wonderfully, but could never have developed without a change of conditions. Change is imperative to progress.

The highest type of man has been artificially advanced beyond the condition of some portion of the physical world. Miasmatic swamps are yet insufficiently reclaimed by time to permit a white man's existence, where they continue. Their present condition would involve his speedy illness and dissolution. Lower organizations, congenial to and in harmony with such conditions of physical development, may exist and flourish there; but more refined types of humanity require the most perfected physical condition for their perfect enjoyment and attainment.

Centripetal low has consolidated the Chinese into a positive and exclusive people, who delight in ignoring the centrifugal or complementary force which induces dispersions.

They have clung to unique customs and dress, resisting change or improvement. In their stereotyped form of frozen civilization, differentiation has been arrested and a peculiar type intensified. Unalterable fixedness in forms of belief and habits concreted by centuries furnish convincing evidence of great antiquity. The black race are ethnologically far less developed, and, having no fixed belief to displace, are more readily converted to any religious belief.

Neither tropical Africa nor Asia is adapted to the Anglo-Saxon constitution; every white colony there has been wasted by sickness and death; yet this is the native and natural climate of the dark races, who are there as much at home as is the polar bear on the shores of Greenland.

> "Origin of the Chinese Race," read before the California Academy of Science by Charles Wolcott Brooks, a member of the Academy

Fu-Manchu (1916)

... Dr. Fu-Manchu, the great and evil man who dreamed of Europe and America under Chinese rule ...

There I lay, fettered, in the same room with this man whose existence was a menace to the entire white race. ...

... he lay at the mercy of this enemy of the white race, of this inhuman being who himself knew no mercy, of this man whose very genius was inspired by the cool, calculated cruelty of his race, of that race which to this day disposes of hundreds, nay, thousands, of its unwanted girl-children by the simple measure of throwing them down a well specially dedicated to the purpose.

... the end of my struggle with the Fu-Manchu group —the end of the whole Yellow menace!

... *and some sensational revelations regrading the awakening of the most mysterious race, the Chinese. ...*

... *my well-grounded distrust of the Oriental character. ...*

We owe our lives, Petrie, to the national childishness of the Chinese! A race of ancestor worshipers is capable of anything. ...

... *they were informed by an intimate knowledge of the dark and secret things of the East, of that mysterious East out of which Fu-Manchu came, of that jungle of noxious things whose miasma had been wafted Westward with the implacable Chinaman.*

He [Fu-Manchu] was watching ... revealing his irregular yellow teeth—the teeth of an opium smoker—in the awful mirthless smile which I knew.

... *the filmy eyes of Dr. Fu-Manchu ...*

Either because they possessed a chatoyant quality of their own (as I had often suspected), or by reason of the light reflected through the open window, the green eyes gleamed upon me vividly like those of a giant cat. ...

He [Dr. Fu-Manchu] paused, and the weird film, which sometimes became visible in his eyes, now obscured their greenness, and lent him the appearance of a blind man.

Dr. Fu-Manchu bent forward until his face was so close to mine that I could see the innumerable lines which, an intricate network, covered his yellow skin.

... *he was dressed in the manner which I always associated with him, probably because it was thus I first saw him. He wore a plain yellow robe, and with his pointed chin resting upon his bosom, he looked down at me, revealing a great expanse of the marvelous brow with its sparse, neutral-colored hair.*

Never in my experience have I known such force to dwell in the glance of any human eye as dwelt in that of this uncanny being. His singular affliction (if affliction it were), the film or slight membrane which sometimes obscured the oblique eyes, was particularly evident at the moment that I crossed the threshold, but now, as I looked up at Dr. Fu-Manchu, it lifted—revealing the eyes in all their emerald greenness.

. . . a man whose brown body glistened, unctuously, whose shaven head was apish low, whose bloodshot eyes were the eyes of a mad dog! His teeth, upper and lower, were bared; they glistened, they gnashed, and a froth was on his lips.

Indeed, it was the unmistakable voice of the Chinaman, raised hysterically in one of those outbursts which in the past I had diagnosed as symptomatic of dangerous mania.

The voice rose to a scream, the scream of some angry animal rather than anything human. Then, chokingly it ceased. Another short sharp cry followed—but not in the voice of Fu-Manchu—a dull groan, and the sound of a fall.

From The Return of Dr. Fu-Manchu,
by Sax Rohmer

Racial Prejudice in School Textbooks and Popular Magazines

How to make these aliens of different races, languages, and ways of life into Americans is the great problem confronting us. Those who most readily adopt our customs make the best citizens. Some never become like us, coming to America only to make money, and returning to their own land when their ambitions are satisfied. The Chinese are of this sort, and they have long been considered an undesirable addition to our population. Living on only a few cents a day, they are willing to work for wages which other laborers could not accept. In cities where they have settled in any number, they congregate in a "Chinatown" in which insanitary living is combined with strange customs and low moral standards, if not crimes; it is believed that they form a menace to our civilization as well as to the industrial condition.

> From *American History for Grammar Schools*, by M. S. Dickson

In the Civics course a brief paragraph was given to other nations to show their good qualities. The glowing tribute to China was, "The Chinese eat rats." The answer of the State Commissioner of Education to a letter calling his attention to this was that the author of that textbook was "out of town."

> From *Literature for Children and Its Influence in Religious Education*, by A. J. Meyers

A long drink did not suffice the midget. He used a water tumbler, and speedily stowed away a pint of the liquid fire. In the case of white man, such indulgence might have caused sensational results. The midget, though, was Chinese, which meant that his nerves were not highly organized—that he was virtually immune to stimulants.

In the same story, the chief criminal is a Chinaman, who wades in blood, kills his partner in order to save himself, and has no other ethical code except that he honors his ancestors. There is also a petty thief who steals from the Chinese supercriminal. They are the only non-Caucasians in a story that plays in an American mining camp.

> From *Race Attitudes in Children*, by Bruno Lasker

The Chinese have dragged my darling down into the life of infamy. They have made her a white slave. . . .

... her father was later to dread the realization ... of her consistent acquaintance with the people of another race [the Chinese].

Two quotes from *The Illustrated Detective Magazine*, "Murder from Chinatown," I, no. 3, 1929, p. 59

A Miscellany of Attitudes

The following quotations are from replies of boys to a questionnaire which asked them to write down the names of any people that they did not like and to state why they did not like them (in their own spelling):

> "The Chinese and Japs are a stealing and distrustful people."
>
> "I do not like the Chinese because they are so shy. And I am afraid they will plunge a knife into me when my back is turned."
>
> "Chinese, Because they have such a bad reputation."
>
> "Chinese. I don't know, but I don't like they, that's all."
>
> "Chinese—they steal."
>
> "Chinese—to crafty."
>
> "I don't like Chinese because they stabs you with knives."
>
> "I don't like the Chinese because of the looks of the slant eyes give me a chill."
>
> "Chinese—you can never tell what they are going to do next."
>
> "Chinese—I do not like Chinese because they have a certain air about them, a sneaking, sling air."
>
> "I do not like Chinese because they are so back ward and refused to be helped—and have such aversion to help from foreigners."

Can we know how these adverse attitudes have originated in the minds of the boys?

The teacher states: "The answers suggest that the boys

had been reading stories of the Chinese which were bloodthirsty. . . ."

From Race Attitudes in Children, by
Bruno Lasker

Here is a testimony as to the effect of moving pictures on children: It occurred in Raleigh, N.C., last month. The film is called *Foreign Devils* and the story is based on the Boxers' uprising in China in 1900. It was shown on Saturday night. Next day a teacher in a Sunday school was explaining to a class that children of all countries are children of a common Father. One child responded: "I saw a movie last night, and the Chinese are terrible people."

From the Christian World Education
News Service, December 1927, p. 6

To improve his handwriting a schoolboy on vacation was asked to copy every day a page or two from whatever book he happened to be reading. This is one of the "exercises" he sent in:

> We can fix no bounds to Nature's conforming power. She has produced certain vertebrates, such as the mud turtle and the so eminently adaptive to circumstances that they are equally at home whether immersed in air, water, or mud. And there is the Chinaman, who, being of a breed that has been crowded and coerced for thousands of years, seems to have done away with nerves. He will stand all day in one position without seeming in the least distressed; he thrives amidst the most unsanitary surroundings; overcrowding and bad air are nothing to him; he does not demand quiet when he would sleep, nor even when he is sick; he can starve to death with supreme complacency.

A missionary says, "It would be easy to raise in China an army of a million men, nay, ten millions, tested by competitive examination as to their capacity to go to sleep across three wheelbarrows with head downward like a spider, mouth wide open, and a fly inside."

From *Camping and Woodcraft*, Vol. 1, by Horace Kephart, quoted in Lasker, *Race Attitudes in Children*

A Yale man was once confronted at the entrance of the dining hall by a schoolboy who was returning from his school for lunch, passing through the campus. "Are you a Jap?" "No," said the Yale man. "Then you are a Chinaman, eh? Are you just as bad or worse than a Jap?" "What do you mean?" The child answered, "You Chinamen eat snakes, dogs, and do a lot of horrible things, don't you?" "Where did you learn that?" "At school," was the swift reply. . . .

"All that I know about China," says a Harvard graduate, "is what I learned from my grammar school, and these facts I find to be far from correct; but it is very hard for me to shake off those wrong impressions; they often blur my judgment."

. . . there are those who regard the history of ancient China itself of little value. Thus writes one in his introduction: "The only historic race is the Caucasian, the others having done little worth recording."

. . . There are those who think China does not deserve a place in ancient history, because the Chinese as a race have not done much in advancing the civilization of the world: "The nations of ancient times which made the greatest contribution to this civilization were the early Egyptians, the Babylonians, the Assyrians, the Cretans, the Hittites, the Hebrews, the Greeks, the Romans, and the early Germans. Upon theirs, therefore, our study will be centered."

From *The Chinese Social and Political Science Review*, VII, no. 3, "China in American School Textbooks," by T. T. Lew

"Remember one fellow, bright and courteous, but uncommunicative. Didn't know what he thought. He spoke good English, had no difficulty communicating, but he didn't communicate much. The Chinese officials here in Washington are pretty unfathomable. I have never met a Chinaman that I felt I could know, always a barrier." (A congressman who said he had gotten an idea of the Chinese as a "savage" people from the comic strip "The Gumps.")

"I have always found the Chinese difficult, never felt that I really understood them. Maybe it is a stereotype I've had since childhood of the Chinese as mysterious people. I couldn't have got it in my home, where we almost made a fetish of tolerance of other people. Maybe it was the Fu-Manchu stories. Has the idea of 'inscrutable' attached to it. The fact is I did have the experience of dealing with Chinese and never knowing what they really had in mind." (A foundation official.)

"The common idea of 'how do you tell them apart?' People not given to showing emotion, stoic. Also geniality, from Charlie Chan, the genial sleuth. . . ." (A midwestern editor.)

"Wouldn't distinguish my views from others. . . . They include the Chinese laundryman, happy, hardworking, obsequious, overpolite. . . . The Fu-Manchu image, devious, slant-eyed Oriental schemer, though I never took this one seriously. . . ." (A professor of economics.)

"Have never seen a cross section taken on this. Would assume in most a vast ignorance. Of those with some knowledge, would expect casual contacts in restaurants, laundries, movies. Very little else. Might think the Chinese untrustworthy in business, capable of living on impossibly low wages. All hearsay and vague ideas. 'Never trust a Chink'— I heard this dozens of times in my boyhood. . . ." (A public opinion specialist.)

"I would know little of this. Assume the average thinking is based more on actual contact, laundrymen, waiters, restaurant owners, taxi drivers, Chinatowns. Rather friendly feelings so long as the underdog status remains unchanged. Suspect white Americans feel kindlier toward Negroes. Classify them comparably to Negroes but see no threat of equality or penetration." (A social scientist of European background.)

And from several people with California backgrounds:

"Idea of the 'Chinks' in California in the 1930s Yellow Peril, sea of immigration, keep them out, deviousness. . . ."

"Most Americans think of Chinese unfavorably, especially on the West Coast. They would 'rather not discuss it,' pretty much like polite people talking about Jews. A strong feeling that the Chinese are okay so long as they are in Chinatown, but not anywhere else. . . ."

"Californians think of the Chinese largely as coolies because that is what they were there, hardworking, frugal, cheaper, undersell anybody, 'undesirable,' especially as purchasers of land. Don't hear this much any more. Passage of time has changed this. Up to time of war, heard more about Japanese. The Chinese were seen as pathetic, 'poor bastards.' But now Chinese here are Americans and are accepted as such. Tension point now very low, with some exceptions. It could be aroused again.

From Scratches on Our Minds, by Harold R. Isaacs, interviews conducted by Professor Isaacs during the 1950s

3. Chinaman's Chance

The anti-Chinese legislation documented in Part 1 of this book was the product of attitudes and sentiments such as those reflected in Part 2. Almost immediately, anti-Chinese hostility manifested itself in a series of brutal—and often fatal—assaults on Chinese life and limb.

Writing in 1918, Sidney Gulick observed:

> The story would be incredible were it not overwhelmingly verified by ample documentary evidence. . . . Scores of Chinese have been murdered, hundreds wounded, and thousands robbed by anti-Asiatic mobs,

with no protection for the victims or punishment for the culprits. . . .[1]

So hopeless did the condition of the Chinese in America seem, in view of those facts, that the phrase "a Chinaman's chance" came to be used to describe a hopeless situation.

In describing the massacre of Chinese at Los Angeles in 1871, Alexander McLeod wrote: " 'The Chinaman must go!' was the watchword that night, but no Chinaman was given the chance."[2] The attack was precipitated by gunfire in connection with a feud between factions of Chinese. A mob entered Chinatown from the surrounding city, routed innocent Chinese from their homes, where they had been hiding since the beginning of violence, looted stores and residences, and lynched at least ten Chinese, "two of them mere boys" (see p. 148).

Even after the Exclusion Law was passed by the United States Congress in 1882, manifestations of anti-Chinese sentiment spread all over California, ranging from new and still more inhuman restrictions on Chinese to the burning of Chinese quarters and expulsion of the Chinese from their residential areas. Among the localities where these actions occurred were Pasadena, Santa Barbara, Santa Cruz, San Jose, Hollister, Merced, Yuba City, Petaluma, Redding, Anderson, Truckee, Lincoln, Sacramento, San Buenaventura, Napa, Gold Run, Sonoma, Vallejo, Placerville, Santa Rosa, Chico, Wheatland, Carson, Auburn, Nevada City, Dixon, and Los Angeles.[3]

Elsewhere in the country the Chinese were just as badly treated and unjustly oppressed, without a chance to alleviate their sufferings. The biggest massacre occurred in Rock Springs, Wyoming, in 1885. The mining boom had passed, and as the mines began to thin, jobs disappeared also. White miners in Rock Springs, unable to compete with the inexpensive labor the Chinese offered, drove the Chinese from their homes, cruelly killing many as they fled. Homes were burned, often with the inhabitants still hiding inside (see p. 152).

In Seattle, Chinese were taken from their quarters and boarded, without recourse, on steamships bound for San Francisco and other western ports. Violence was generally prevented by the presence of federal troops and a city government fearful that civil disorder might delay Washington's statehood. But abuse of the Chinese was rampant. Businessmen were urged to fire their Chinese employees, and most did. Shops displayed signs which declared that their goods were "made by whites." Newspapers spoke of the Chinese with epithets like "those chattering, round-mouthed lepers." Even a federal district judge admitted that the presence of the Chinese was a "real grievance" (see p. 168).

In the autumn of 1885, a camp of thirty-five Chinese in Squak Valley, Washington, was attacked at night by a group of white men and Indians. Three Chinese were killed, three were wounded, and the rest, forced into hiding for the night, left the valley the next day.

Similar outrages followed at Coal Creek, Black Diamond, and elsewhere in Washington. The cry to rid the territory of Chinese was almost unanimous among whites. One rainy night in November 1885, a band of 300 citizens of Tacoma entered the Chinese quarter and told the inhabitants they were to leave the city. Wagons were brought for provisions and for the sick and aged. The rest were marched onto the prairie carrying bundles of belongings on their backs. Some miles south of the city the wagons were unloaded and the Chinese left to survive as they could! (See p. 198.) And in 1887 the town of Tacoma banished 3,000 Chinese on twenty-four hours' notice. For decades none was permitted to return.[4]

Such vicious attitudes toward the Chinese were not at all limited to the relatively unsettled West of the late 1800s. In 1928, a Chinese boy received the highest honors at the Ruleville School in Mississippi. The white citizens, being jealous, subsequently excluded all Orientals from the school. When the Chinese fought for their rights in court, an associate justice of the Mississippi Supreme Court made the decision that "the term white race is limited to the Caucasian race, and the term colored race includes all other races." The justice further stated that the dominant purpose of the segregated school system in Mississippi was to preserve the purity and integrity of the white.[5]

In Boston, 234 Chinese were illegally imprisoned and brutally handled by the police in one case in 1902. The general public voiced criticism of the brutality of the police, and the Chinese minister to the United States complained to the federal government. But not a single officer was punished or even censured for his illegal and brutal conduct, and no reparation was obtained by the Chinese (see p. 207).

Ironically, the Chinese in America were protected by United States–China treaties as "subjects of the most favored nation." The Burlingame Treaty of 1868 and the 1880 treaty between the United States and China contained the same provisions.[6] Article III of the Treaty of 1880, for example, reads:

> *If Chinese laborers, or Chinese of any other class, now either permanently or temporarily residing in the territory of the United States, meet with ill treatment at the hands of any other persons, the Government of the United States will exert all its power to devise measures for their protection, and to secure to them the same rights, privileges, immunities, and exemptions as may be enjoyed by the citizens or subjects of the most favored nation, and to which they are entitled by treaty.*

Unfortunately those treaty rights were totally ignored. The Chinese have had no chance to live with human dignity in this country.

The Chinese Massacre at Los Angeles (1871)

The history of the Chinese massacre that occurred in this city on the night of October 24, 1871, is a recital of the most bloody and barbarous tragedies in the annals of this state. The trouble originated among the Chinese themselves. Yo Hing was the leader of one faction and Sam Yuen of another. The cause of the outbreak in the beginning was the possession of a Chinese woman named Ya Hit, young and attractive, and from a Chinese estimate of female worth, of the financial value of $2,500. This woman was stolen, or had run away, from her owner and had come into the possession of the rival company. Her owners, to regain possession of their lost chattel, brought into requisition the power of the law, and the help of the courts and its officers, by causing a warrant to be issued for the arrest of the woman on the charge of larceny of jewelry. Ya Hit was brought into court, and bail having been fixed for her appearance when needed, she was bailed out by Sam Yuen's company, who took possession of the chattel. Thus Yo Hing and his company failed to obtain possession of their stolen woman and were defeated in the attempted recovery.

Yo Hing was a well-to-do merchant of wide repute and of great authority among his countrymen, being agent of one of the great Chinese companies in this city. He was a man who in every way sustained the national reputation of his race for ways that are dark—having regard for neither habeas corpus of courts, the statutes of the state, the marital rights of his neighbors, nor, apparently, the hideous and austere countenance of even the great Joss, he communed within himself as to how he might compass his enemy, obtain lawful possession of the woman, thwart the decision of the court, and bring the influence of the law and its officers to sustain his side of the case. The scheme he devised was in keeping with the character of the man. He persuaded the woman to secretly marry him and then, coming into lawful possession of her, he had the law and the sanctity of the marriage rite to strengthen his title. The company that had thus lost the woman immediately offered a reward of $1,000 for the scalp of Yo Hing. War was at once declared between the rival companies.

On Monday morning, October 23, 1871, at nine-thirty, as Yo Hing was passing along "Nigger Alley," two shots were fired at him from a Chinese store. He immediately swore out a warrant and had Ah Choy (a brother of the woman) and Lee Tak arrested, and they in turn had Yo Hing arrested. All were bailed out. They returned to Chinatown and preparations for an open conflict between the two companies were begun. All during that and the next day the work of preparation went on. Few Chinamen were on the street. Threats and warnings were heard on every hand. Every man of the hostile factions was heavily armed. The officers of the law were warned by well-disposed Chinamen that trouble was impending.

At 5:30 P.M. Tuesday, the twenty-fourth, as Police Officer Bilderrain was near Chinatown, he heard shooting and immediately started for the scene of conflict. As he approached the Chinese quarters a Chinaman fired at him. Finding himself unable to quell the disturbance, he called for help. Sepulveda and Estaban Sanchez came to his aid. Ah Choy stood at the porch in front of the Coronel Block and emptied his pistol at the crowd, which by this time was gathering. One old man, when told to get inside the house, pulled his pistol and emptied its contents at the crowd indiscriminately. Robert Thompson, an old resident of the city, was among the first to gain the porch in answer to the cries of the police for help. He received a mortal wound from a bullet fired through the door of a Chinese store. He was taken to Wallweber's drugstore on Main Street, where he died an hour later. After some twenty-five or thirty shots had been fired, it was discovered that Bilderrain was shot in the shoulder, a boy named Juan Jose Mendible was shot in the leg, and a man by the name of Joe was shot in the hip.

The Chinese in the meantime had taken refuge in a long abode, with massive walls, heavily covered with brea. They barricaded the doors and windows and prepared for battle. The news of the fight soon spread through the city, and the people collected and surrounded the building. Don Refugio Botello, armed with a six-shooter, first ascended the roof, others following, when holes were cut through the brea, and they fired into the interior through the holes thus made.

One Chinaman attempted to leave the besieged building and escape across the street, but he was shot down before halfway over. Another one, attempting to escape into Los Angeles Street, was captured by the crowd, dragged through the street to the western gate of Tomlinson's corral, on New High Street, where he was hanged, after a second attempt, the rope breaking the first time.

Several propositions were made to burn the building, and a fire broke out in two or three places, but it was quickly extinguished. The crowd by this time had collected on the corner of Commercial and Main streets, and some advised one thing and some another, but there was no leader to direct, nor officers to control. It was then recommended that a guard be stationed round the building until daylight to await further developments, but the crowd had become furious and uncontrollable, and disregarded all expostulations and entreaties to refrain from further violence.

About nine o'clock a party battered in the eastern end of the building, and with hooting and yelling and firing of pistols, the rioters rushed in and found huddled in corners or hidden behind boxes, eight terror-stricken Chinamen, who, in vain, pleaded piteously for their lives. They were violently dragged out and turned over to the infuriated mob. One was killed by dragging him over the stones by a rope around his neck. Three were hanged to a wagon on Los Angeles Street, although they were more dead than alive from being beaten and kicked and mangled, when they reached the place of execution. Four were likewise hanged to the western gateway of Tomlinson's corral, on New High Street. Two of the victims were mere boys.

One of the victims was a Chinese doctor, an inoffensive man, respected by all the white people who knew him. He pleaded in English and in Spanish for his life, offering his captors all his wealth, some $2,000 or $3,000, but in spite of his entreaties he was hanged; then his money was stolen, and one of his fingers cut off, to obtain the rings he wore. The doctor's name was Gene Tung. It is stated that several other Chinamen were shot, a number fled to the city jail for safety, and many went into the country.

While the shooting and hanging were going on, thieves and robbers were looting the Chinese buildings. Every room in the block was thoroughly rifled and ransacked; trunks, boxes, and locked receptacles of all kinds were broken open in the search for valuables. One merchant stated he lost $4,000 in gold, and others reported losses, in sums varying from a few hundred dollars, to several thousands. It is variously estimated that the loss to the Chinese in money was from $30,000 to $70,000.

About 9:30 P.M. Sheriff Burns addressed the crowd on the corner of Spring and Temple streets, commanding all good and law-abiding citizens to follow him to Chinatown, whereupon twenty-five persons volunteered. When he arrived there he found the fighting had ceased and the mob had already commenced to disperse. He found ten men hanged on Los Angeles Street, some to a wagon, and some to an awning; he found five more at Tomlinson's corral, and that four were shot in Nigger Alley and two were wounded and had been taken to the city jail. Guards were stationed through Chinatown and around the principal buildings occupied by Chinamen.

Of all the Chinamen murdered, it is not believed that a single one of them was in any way implicated in the shooting, except Ah Choy. The leaders, Yo Hing and his gang, all fled to the country when the fight first commenced. . . .

> C. P. Dorland, read before the Historical Society of Southern California, January 7, 1894

Memorial of Chinese Laborers Resident at Rock Springs, Wyoming Territory, to the Chinese Consul at New York (1885)

We, the undersigned, have been in Rock Springs, Wyoming Territory, for periods ranging from one to fifteen years, for the purpose of working on the railroads and in the coal mines.

Up to the time of the recent troubles we had worked along with the white men, and had not had the least ill feeling against them. The officers of the companies employing us treated us and the white man kindly, placing both races on the same footing and paying the same wages.

Several times we had been approached by the white men and requested to join them in asking the companies for an increase in the wages of all, both Chinese and white men. We inquired of them what we should do if the companies refused to grant an increase. They answered that if the companies would not increase our wages we should all strike, then the companies would be obliged to increase our wages. To this we dissented, wherefore we excited their animosity against us.

During the past two years there has been in existence in "Whitemen's Town," Rock Springs, an organization composed of white miners, whose object was to bring about the expulsion of all Chinese from the Territory. To them or to their object we have paid no attention. About the month of August of this year notices were posted up, all the way from Evanston to Rock Springs, demanding the expulsion of the Chinese, &e. On the evening of September 1, 1885, the bell of the building in which said organization meets rang for a meeting. It was rumored on that night that threats had been made against the Chinese.

On the morning of September 2, a little past seven o'clock, more than ten white men, some in ordinary dress and others in mining suits, ran into Coal Pit No. 6, loudly declaring that the Chinese should not be permitted to work there. The Chinese present reasoned with them in a few words, but were attacked with murderous weapons, and three of their number wounded. The white foreman of the coal pit, hearing of the disturbance, ordered all to stop work for the time being.

After the work had stopped, all the white men in and near Coal Pit No. 6 began to assemble by the dozen. They carried firearms, and marched to Rock Springs by way of the railroad from Coal Pit No. 6, and crossing the railroad bridge, went directly to "Whitemen's Town." All this took place before 10:00 A.M. We now heard the bell ringing for a meeting at the white men's organization building. Not long after, all the white men came out of that building, most of them assembling in the barrooms, the crowds meanwhile growing larger and larger.

About two o'clock in the afternoon a mob, divided into two gangs, came toward "Chinatown," one gang coming by way of the plank bridge, and the other by way of the railroad bridge. The gang coming by way of the railroad bridge was the larger, and was subdivided into many squads, some of which did not cross the bridge, but remained standing on the side opposite to "Chinatown"; others that had already crossed the bridge stood on the right and left at the end of it. Several squads marched up the hill behind Coal Pit No. 3.

One squad remained at Coal Shed No. 3 and another at the pump house. The squad that remained at the pump house fired the first shot, and the squad that stood at Coal Shed No. 3 immediately followed their example and fired. The Chinese by name of Lor Sun Kit was the first person shot, and fell to the ground. At that time the Chinese began to realize that the mob were bent on killing. The Chinese, though greatly alarmed, did not yet begin to flee.

Soon after, the mob on the hill behind Coal Pit No. 3 came down from the hill, and joining the different squads of the mob, fired their weapons and pressed on to Chinatown.

The gang that were at the plank bridge also divided into several squads, pressing near and surrounding "Chinatown." One squad of them guarded the plank bridge in order to cut off the retreat of the Chinese.

Not long after, it was everywhere reported that a Chinese named Leo Dye Bah, who lived in the western part of "Chinatown," was killed by a bullet, and that another named Yip Ah Marn, resident in the eastern end of the town, was likewise killed. The Chinese now, to save their lives, fled in confusion in every direction, some going up the hill behind Coal Pit No. 3, others along the foot of the hill where Coal Pit No. 4 is; some from the eastern end of the town fled across Bitter Creek to the opposite hill, and others from the western end by the foot of the hill on the right of Coal Pit No. 5. The mob were now coming in the three directions, namely, the east and west sides of the town and from the wagon road.

Whenever the mob met a Chinese they stopped him and, pointing a weapon at him, asked him if he had any revolver, and then approaching him they searched his person, robbing him of his watch or any gold or silver that he might have about him, before letting him go. Some of the rioters would let a Chinese go after depriving him of all his gold and silver, while another Chinese would be beaten with the butt ends of the weapons before being let go. Some of the rioters, when they could not stop a Chinese, would shoot him dead on the spot, and then search and rob him. Some would overtake a Chinese, throw him down and search and rob him before they would let him go. Some of the rioters would not fire their weapons, but would only use the butt ends to beat the Chinese with. Some would not beat a Chinese, but rob him of whatever he had and let him go, yelling to him to go quickly. Some, who took no part either in beating or robbing the Chinese, stood by, shouting loudly and laughing and clapping their hands.

There was a gang of women that stood at the "Chinatown" end of the plank bridge and cheered; among the women, two of them each fired successive shots at the Chinese. This was done about a little past 3:00 P.M.

Most of the Chinese fled toward the eastern part of "Chinatown." Some of them ran across Bitter Creek, went up directly to the opposite hill, crossing the grassy plain. Some of them went along the foot of the hill where Coal Pit No. 4 stood, to cross the creek, and by a devious route reached the opposite hill. Some of them ran up to the hill of Coal Pit No. 3, and thence winding around the hills went to the opposite hill. A few of them fled to the foot of the hill where Coal Pit No. 5 stood, and ran across the creek, and thence by a winding course to the western end of the "Whitemen's Town." But very few did this.

The Chinese who were the first to flee mostly dispersed themselves at the back hills, on the opposite bank of the creek, and among the opposite hills. They were scattered far and near, high and low, in about one hundred places. Some were standing, or sitting, or lying hid on the grass, or stooping down on the low grounds. Every one of them was praying to Heaven or groaning with pain. They had been eyewitnesses to the shooting in "Chinatown," and had seen the whites, male and female, old and young, searching houses for money, household effects, or gold, which were carried across to "Whitemen's Town."

Some of the rioters went off toward the railroad of Coal Pit No. 6, others set fire to the Chinese houses. Between 4:00 P.M. and a little past 9:00 P.M. all the camp houses belonging to the coal company and the Chinese huts had been burned down completely, only one of the company's camp houses remaining. Several of the camp houses near Coal Pit No. 6 were also burned, and the three Chinese huts there were also burned. All the Chinese houses burned numbered seventy-nine.

Some of the Chinese were killed at the bank of Bitter Creek, some near the railroad bridge, and some in "Chinatown." After having been killed, the dead bodies of some were carried to the burning buildings and thrown into the flames. Some of the Chinese who had hid themselves in the houses were killed and their bodies burned; some, who on account of sickness could not run, were burned alive in the houses. One Chinese was killed in "Whitemen's Town" in a laundry house, and his house demolished. The whole number of Chinese killed was twenty-eight and those wounded fifteen.

The money that the Chinese lost was that which in their hurry they were unable to take with them, and consequently were obliged to leave in their houses, or that which was taken from their persons. The goods, clothing, or household effects remaining in their houses were either plundered or burned.

When the Chinese fled to the different hills they intended to come back to "Chinatown" when the riot was over, to dispose of the dead bodies and to take care of the wounded. But to their disappointment, all the houses were burned to ashes, and there was then no place of shelter for them; they were obliged to run blindly from hill to hill. Taking the railroad as their guide, they walked toward the town of Green River, some of them reaching that place in the morning, others at noon, and others not until dark. There were some who did not reach it until the fourth of September. We felt very thankful to the railroad company for having telegraphed to the conductors of all its trains to pick up such of the Chinese as were to be met with along the line of the railroad and carry them to Evanston.

On the fifth of September all the Chinese that had fled assembled at Evanston; the native citizens there threatened day and night to burn and kill the Chinese. Fortunately, United States troops had been ordered to come and protect them, and quiet was restored. On the ninth of September the

United States government instructed the troops to escort the Chinese back to Rock Springs. When they arrived there they saw only a burnt tract of ground to mark the sites of their former habitations. Some of the dead bodies had been buried by the company, while others, mangled and decomposed, were strewn on the ground and were being eaten by dogs and hogs. Some of the bodies were not found until they were dug out of the ruins of the buildings. Some had been burned beyond recognition. It was a sad and painful sight to see the son crying for the father, the brother for the brother, the uncle for the nephew, and friend for friend.

By this time most of the Chinese have abandoned the desire of resuming their mining work, but inasmuch as the riot has left them each with only the one or two torn articles of clothing they have on their persons, and as they have not a single cent in their pockets, it is a difficult matter for them to make any change in their location. Fortunately, the company promised to lend them clothing and provisions, and a number of wagons to sleep in. Although protected by government troops, their sleep is disturbed by frightful dreams, and they cannot obtain peaceful rest.

Some of the rioters who killed the Chinese and who set fire to the homes could be identified by the Chinese, and some not. Among them the two women heretofore mentioned, and who killed some Chinese, were specially recognized by many Chinese. Among the rioters who robbed and plundered were men, women, and children. Even the white woman who formerly taught English to the Chinese searched for and took handkerchiefs and other articles.

The Chinese know that the white men who worked in Coal Pit No. 1 did not join the mob, and most of them did not stop work, either. We heard that the coal company's officers had taken a list of the names of the rioters who were particularly brutal and murderous, which list numbered forty or fifty.

From a survey of all the circumstances, several causes may be assigned for the killing and wounding of so many Chinese and the destruction of so much property:

1. The Chinese had been for a long time employed at the same work as the white men. While they knew that the white men entertained ill feelings toward them, the Chinese did not take precautions to guard against this sudden outbreak, inasmuch as at no time in the past had there been any quarrel or fighting between the races.
2. On the second day of September 1885, in Coal Pit No. 6, the white men attacked the Chinese. That place being quite a distance from Rock Springs, very few Chinese were there. As we did not think that the trouble would extend to Rock Springs, we did not warn each other to prepare for flight.
3. Most of the Chinese living in Rock Springs worked during the daytime in the different coal mines, and consequently did not hear of the fight at Coal Pit No. 6, nor did they know of the armed mob that had assembled in "Whitemen's Town." When twelve o'clock came, everybody returned home from his place of work to lunch. As yet the mob had not come to attack the Chinese; a great number of the latter were returning to work without any apprehension of danger.
4. About two o'clock the mob suddenly made their appearance for the attack. The Chinese thought that they had only assembled to threaten, and that some of the company's officers would come to disperse them. Most of the Chinese, acting upon this view of the matter, did not gather up their money or clothing, and when the mob fired at them they fled precipitately. Those Chinese who were in the workshops, hearing of the riot, stopped work and fled in their working clothes, and did not have time enough to go home to change their clothes or to gather up their money. What they did leave at home was either plundered or burned.
5. None of the Chinese had firearms or any defensive weapons, nor was there any place that afforded an opportunity for the erection of a barricade that might impede the rioters in their attack. The Chinese were

all like a herd of frightened deer that let the huntsmen surround and kill them.
6. All the Chinese had, on the first of September, bought from the company a month's supply of provision and the implements necessary for the mining of coal. This loss of property was therefore larger than it would be later in the month.

We never thought that the subjects of a nation entitled by treaty to the rights and privileges of the most favored nation could, in a country so highly civilized like this, so unexpectedly suffer the cruelty and wrong of being unjustly put to death, or of being wounded and left without the means of cure, or being abandoned to poverty, hunger, and cold, and without the means to betake themselves elsewhere.

To the great President of the United States, who, hearing of the riot, sent troops to protect our lives, we are most sincerely thankful.

In behalf of those killed or wounded, or of those deprived of their property, we pray that the examining commission will ask our minister to sympathize, and to endeavor to secure the punishment of the murderers, the relief of the wounded, and compensation for those despoiled of their property, so that the living and the relatives of the dead will be grateful, and never forget his kindness for generations.

Hereinabove we have made a brief recital of the facts of this riot, and pray your honor will take them into your kind consideration.

(Here follow the signatures of 559 Chinese laborers, resident at Rock Springs, Wyoming Territory.)

LIST OF KILLED

(Investigation made by Huang Sih Chuen, Chinese consul at New York, of the Chinese Examining Commission, of Chinese laborers killed at Rock Springs, Wyoming Territory, September 2, 1885.)

The said Huang Sih Chuen submitted the following report:

I examined the dead bodies of the following Chinese laborers killed at Rock Springs:

1. The dead body of Leo Sun Tsung, found in his own hut in the native settlement, was covered with many wounds. The left jawbone was broken, evidently by a bullet. The skin and bone of the right leg below the knee were injured. I also ascertained that the deceased was fifty-one years old, and had a mother, wife, and son living at home (in China).

2. The dead body of Leo Kow Boot was found between mines No. 3 and 4, at the foot of the mountain. The neck was shot through crosswise by a bullet, cutting the windpipe in two. I also ascertained that the deceased was twenty-four years old. His family connections have not yet been clearly made known.

3. The dead body of Yii See Yen was found near the creek. The left temple was shot by a bullet, and the skull broken. The age of the deceased was thirty-six years. He had a mother living at home (in China).

4. The dead body of Leo Dye Bah was found at the side of the bridge, near the creek, shot in the middle of the chest by a bullet, breaking the breastbone. I also ascertained that the deceased was fifty-six years old, and had a wife, son, and daughter at home.

5. The dead body of Choo Bah Quot was found in the hut adjoining Camp No. 34, together with the remains of Lor Han Lung. The front part of the body was not injured, but the flesh on the back was completely gone, and the bones were scorched; the hair was also burned off. I also ascertained that the deceased was twenty-three years old, and had parents living at home.

The above five bodies were found more or less mutilated.

6. A portion of the dead body of Sia Bun Ning was found in a pile of ashes in the hut near the Chinese temple. It consisted of the head, neck, and shoulders. The two hands, together with the rest of the body below the chest, were completely burned off. I also ascertained that the deceased was thirty-seven years old, and had a mother, wife, son, and daughter living at home.

7. A portion of the dead body of Leo Lung Hong was found in a pile of ashes in a hut adjoining Camp No. 27. It consisted

of the head, neck, and breast. The two hands, together with rest of body below the waist, were burned off completely. I also ascertained that deceased was forty-five years old, and had a wife and three sons living at home.

8. A portion of the dead body of Leo Chih Ming was found in a pile of ashes in the hut of the deceased near the temple where the remains of Liang Tsun Bong and Hsu Ah Cheong were found. It consisted of the head and chest. The hands, together with the rest of the body below the waist, were burned off completely. I also ascertained that deceased was forty-nine years old, and had a mother, wife, and son living at home; also another son working with him in the coal mines.

9. A portion of the dead body of Liang Tsun Bong was found in a pile of ashes in the hut near the temple where the deceased, together with Leo Chih Ming and Hsu Ah Cheong, had lived. It consisted of the head, shoulders, and hands. The rest of the body below the chest was burned off completely. The age of the deceased was forty-two years. He had a wife and two sons living at home.

10. A portion of the dead body of Hsu Ah Cheong was found in a pile of ashes in the hut near the temple where the deceased, together with Leo Chih Ming and Liang Tsun Bong, had lived. It consisted of the skull bone, the upper and lower jawbones, and teeth. I also ascertained that the deceased was thirty-two years old, and had parents, wife, and son living at home.

11. A portion of the dead body of Lor Han Lung was found in the hut adjoining No. 34, where the remains of Choo Bah Quot was also found. It consisted of the sole and heel of the left foot. The rest of the body was completely burned. I also ascertained that the deceased was thirty-two years old, and had a mother, wife, son, and daughter, all living at home.

12. A portion of the dead body of Hoo Ah Nii was found in a pile of ashes in his own hut. It consisted of the right half of a head and the backbone. The rest of the body was completely burned. I also ascertained that the deceased was forty-three years old, and had a wife living at home.

13. A portion of the dead body of Leo Tse Wing was found in a pile of ashes in the hut adjoining Camp No. 14. It consisted of the bones of the lower half of the body, extending from hip to foot. The rest of the body was burned off completely. I also ascertained that the deceased was thirty-nine years old. His family connection has not yet been clearly made known.

The last-named eight dead bodies were found partly destroyed by fire.

The following fifteen persons were killed: Leo Jew Foo, Leo Tim Kwong, Hung Qwan Chuen, Tom He Yew, Mar Tse Choy, Leo Lung Siang, Yip Ah Marn, Leo Lung Hon, Leo Lung Hor, Leo Ah Tsun, Leang Ding, Leo Hoy Yat, Yuen Chin Sing, Hsu Ah Tseng, and Chun Quan Sing. Twelve fragments of bones, belonging to twelve of the above-named persons, were found in twelve different places in the Chinese settlement. No trace of the remaining three persons was found.

I also ascertained that the age of Leo Jew Foo was thirty-five years; he had a mother at home. Leo Tim Kwong was thirty-one years; family connection not known. Hung Quan Chuen was forty-two years; he had a father at home. Tom He Yew was thirty-four years; he had a mother, wife, and daughter at home. Mar Tse Choy was thirty-four years; he had parents, wife, and daughter at home. Leo Lung Siang was thirty-six years; he had a wife at home. Yip Hor Marn was thirty-eight years; he had a father, wife, son, and daughter at home. Leo Lung Hon was forty-one years; he had a wife, son, and daughter at home. Leo Lung Hor was forty-four years; he had a wife and two sons at home. Leo Ah Tsun was thirty-six years; he had a mother at home. Liang Ding was forty-one years; family connection not yet known. Leo Hoy Yat was twenty-five years; he had parents at home. Yuen Chun Sing was thirty-six years; he had a mother at home. Hsu Ah Tseng was twenty-six years; he had a mother at home. Chun Quan Sing was thirty-nine years; he had a mother at home. Total number of killed: 28.

LIST OF WOUNDED

(Investigation made by Huang Sih Chuen, Chinese consul at New York, of the Chinese Examining Commission, of Chinese laborers wounded at Rock Springs, Wyoming Territory, September 2, 1885.)

The said Huang Sih Chuen reported as follows: On the nineteenth and twentieth of September, 1885, I investigated and found the following Chinese laborers wounded at Rock Springs, W.T.:

1. Leo Kwong Ning was wounded in the back below his right shoulder by a bullet, causing a deep, wide wound. The bullet could not be extracted. Fatal result is feared.

2. Lee Sing Yip was wounded in the back on the right shoulder by a bullet, piercing through from the back to the front, below the shoulder. The shoulder bone was broken and the wound badly inflamed. Fatal result is feared.

3. Lee Ah Hok was wounded in the upper part of his right leg by a bullet piercing through from back to front. The bone was broken, the wound deep and wide, badly inflamed, and difficult to be healed. He was unable to stand up and the loss of the entire use of his right leg is feared.

4. Won Yin Sung was wounded below his left knee by a bullet piercing through from back to front, breaking the bone. The wound was badly inflamed and difficult to be healed. He could not walk, the left leg being entirely useless to him.

5. Lee Hok Sing was wounded in the upper part of his right leg by a bullet piercing through from right to left. The bone of the leg was fractured; the wound deep and wide; hard to be healed. The loss of the entire use of the leg is feared.

6. Lor Hong Hoon was wounded in the upper part of the left arm by a bullet piercing through from right to left. The bone was broken, the wound badly inflamed, and difficult to be healed. He was unable to move his left arm. The loss of the use of it is feared.

7. Lor Sun Kit was wounded in the right side of his backbone by a bullet, piercing from the back through the right

side. The right arm was also wounded. The bullet was extracted by a native doctor. These two wounds were not yet healed, but badly inflamed.

8. Leo Duck Yun was wounded in the right leg by a gunshot. The bullet could not be extracted.

9. Leo Yip Sun was wounded in the right shoulder by a bullet piercing through from the back to the front below the shoulder. The wound was not yet healed.

10. Leo Mun Yip was shot through in the palm of his right hand by a bullet. The wound was not yet healed.

11. Lor See Duck was wounded in the spine below the waist by a gunshot. The bullet was extracted, but the wound not yet healed.

12. Leo Lung Ming was wounded in the scalp, both sides of the forehead, the right temple, the right and left sides below the nipples, and the part below the right knee. These wounds were deep, with bones exposed. He also received a wound on the left cheekbone and one on the right thumb. All the above wounds appear to have been inflicted by iron implements. They were all being slowly healed with the exception of the right knee, which was very seriously injured.

13. Leo Kung Kwong was wounded in the right temple by iron implements. The bone was exposed, but the wound was gradually being healed.

14. Leo Gar Kwong was wounded in the left forehead apparently by a wooden cane. The wound was slowly being healed.

15. Leo Ah Go was wounded in the left cheekbone and the part below the left eye by stones. The wounds were already healed.

ESTIMATE OF PROPERTY LOSSES, MADE BY THE COMMISSION, SUSTAINED BY THE CHINESE RESIDENTS IN THEIR RESPECTIVE CAMPS AT ROCK SPRINGS, WYOMING TERRITORY, SEPTEMBER 2, 1885

Camp No. 2		Camp No. 3	
Estimated loss		Estimated loss	
1. Lin Pah Cheong	$25.00	12. Leo Lung Hop	$196.00
2. Chang Foo Mow	47.00	13. Leo Lung Yu	133.50
3. Chang Chay Sing	38.00	14. Leo Kwong Yit	139.00
4. Tung Gar Jok	43.75	15. Leo Ying Sing	114.50
5. Tom Tiu Ying	34.75	16. Leo Ah Sow	120.25
6. Leo Ah Cheong	17.00	17. Leo Hin Wing	133.50
7. Hung Quan Chuen (killed)	532.25	18. Leo Lung Hong (killed)	200.00
8. Tom Hee Yow	423.70	19. Leo Lung Ming (wounded)	243.50
9. Mar Tse Choy	115.75	20. Leo Gar Kwong (wounded)	180.70
10. Liang Tung	220.00	21. Leo Kwong Ning (wounded)	119.00
11. Property owned in common by persons in Camp No. 2	268.95	22. Property owned in common by persons of Camp No. 3	219.40
Total	1,766.15	Total	1,799.35

Camp No. 4
Estimated loss

23. LeoQuanKwong $223.40
24. Leo Hung Hoo 101.50
25. Leo Win Kwong 178.15
26. Leo Ah See 51.25
27. Leo Ah Hor 28.50
28. Leo Kwong Hoo 126.45
29. Wong Foo Teen 211.50
30. Leo Sun King 61.00
31. Leo Hin Ying 194.05
32. Leo Kwang Sung 42.45
33. Leo Won Yit 85.20
34. Property owned in common by persons of Camp No. 4   277.40
    Total   1,580.85

Camp No. 5
Estimated loss

35. Liang Ah Bing $212.65
36. Liang Ah Yun 91.35
37. Liang Ah Whay 97.20
38. Liang Ah Choy 67.25
39. Ow Ah Yii 72.25
40. Woo Ah Dye 55.75
41. Liang Ah Nung 80.50
42. Liang Day Ying 117.00
43. Liang Ah Yik 72.00
44. Liang Ah Hoon 92.85
45. Low Hing Kwang 109.75
46. Cheng Ah Sum 101.50
47. Property owned in common by persons of Camp No. 5   221.85
    Total   1,391.90

Camp No. 6
Estimated loss

48. Leo Sun Lung $46.50
49. Leo Kway Wah 73.50
50. Leo Yeh Yung 212.15
51. Leo Sing He 34.50
52. Leo Ying Lung 251.50
53. Leo Lung Ho 198.50
54. Leo Lin Ngok 80.50
55. Leo Tsing Lung 50.00
56. Property owned in common by persons of Camp No.6   187.00
    Total   1,134.15

Camp No. 7
Estimated loss

57. Leo Chee Boo $387.80
58. Bah Ah Wong 129.50
59. Leo Wing Sung 758.80
60. Leo Duck Yun (wounded) 82.00
61. Leo Sun Oy 384.10
62. Leo Sun Tu 168.75
63. Leo Chong Kwun 114.20
64. Leo Bong Duck 227.70
65. Low Kwong Ming 160.25
66. Low Chay Heong 123.00
67. Property owned by common by persons of Camp No.7   258.20
    Total   2,794.30

"Memorial of Chinese Laborers Resident at Rock Springs, Wyoming Territory, to the Chinese Consul at New York," dated September 18, 1885

A Local Press Comment on the Rock Springs Pogrom (1885)

The return!—Three hundred soldiers protecting them—Chinatown to be rebuilt—United and determined action needed.

It was rumored Wednesday noon that the Chinese were on their way back to Rock Springs. Few believed the rumor, as it was not thought they could be induced to return.

But about two o'clock a passenger train came in bearing two hundred armed soldiers. Closely following was a freight train of twenty-two cars loaded with 650 of the hated Chinese, the latter train switching off and went toward No. 3 mine, where the Chinese disembarked, and hurried over to the ruins of their houses. They began digging in the cellars, and soon unearthed a large amount of money. Six thousand dollars in gold and silver was dug up from one cellar, and as much more from another, where it had been concealed before their flight.

Numbers of them soon came up town. Some looked bold and defiant, while others were evidently fearful of being attacked, but no demonstration was made against them. The cars were afterwards brought down the track to a point near the soldiers' camp, where the Chinamen built fires, had supper, and spent the night.

The action of the company in bringing back the Chinese means that they are to be set to work in the mines, and that American soldiers are to prevent them from again being driven out.

It means that all the white miners in Rock Springs, except those absolutely required, are to be replaced by Chinese labor.

It means that the company intend to make a "Chinatown" out of Rock Springs, as they proposed to the Almy miners last Monday.

It means that Rock Springs is killed, as far as white men are concerned, if such program is carried out.

From the Rock Springs *Independent*, September 3, 1885

The Anti-Chinese Outbreaks in Seattle
(1885–1886)

Seattle has experienced a crowded if brief history. While still a struggling town in an area restive under territorial status, it was projected into the national and international limelight. This dubious fame was attained in February of 1886 at the culmination of serious anti-Chinese agitation.

The prejudice in Seattle was not an isolated phenomenon. Centering in California in the 1870s, it spread throughout the Northwest. The year 1885 was an explosive one; September saw massacres at Rock Springs, Wyoming Territory, and Squak Valley, Washington Territory. These attacks upon the Chinese stemmed from a potent mixture of general economic unrest and racial antagonism.[1] The Seattle violence illustrates the economic difficulties of the period, the class cleavages, and the specific grievances against the Chinese which are to be found in other outbursts.

Seattle in 1885 was not a happy city. "For months the times have been bad. The peculiar industries of the region are all depressed. . . . The inevitable consequence follows. . . . Our towns are full of idle men. . . ."[2] The employment of the Chinese while whites were unwillingly idle[3] aroused intense resentment and bitterness in Seattle.[4] Consequently workingmen played the most prominent role in the agitation[5] in the belief that, if the Chinese could be driven out, more employment would be provided for white labor.[6]

The view that white workingmen were being injured by Chinese competition was widespread. Judge Roger S. Greene, a steadfast opponent of violence, referred to the "under-competitive cheapness of Chinese labor" in a charge to a grand jury.[7] John Keane, a shoemaker, who was a popular orator at anti-Chinese meetings, painted a dire picture of the economic impact upon Seattle of the Orientals, "who were impoverishing and enslaving the workingman; causing our sons to be tramps in search of work, when there is no work; driving our daughters into disrepute and houses of ill fame."[8] A leader of the Chinophobe forces from nearby Colby, Hiram Cornell, attempted to prove that Chinese gardeners, having no families to support, could sell their produce at such ruinously low prices that it was impossible for any white farmer to compete with them.[9] The workingmen did not confine their denunciation solely to the Orientals. Their leaders, like D. M. Crane, president of the Liberal League, and Keane, also blamed "monopolies" for sponsoring Chinese immigration to the coast.[10]

Racial prejudice was also a prominent cause of the anti-Chinese agitation. For example, the Seattle *Post-Intelligencer* asserted: "The civilization of the Pacific Coast cannot be half Caucasian and half Mongolian."[11] The Seattle *Call* attributed part of its antipathy to the Chinese to the belief that they were "alien and nonassimilating."[12] Naturally the Chinese were accused of a number of offenses against the American legal and ethical codes, which transgressions should serve to bar them from Seattle. One recurrent charge was that Chinese were regularly smuggled from British Columbia into Washington Territory.[13] Another grievance was the "utter disregard" of a Chinese "of an oath or affirmation in court."[14] The Orientals were also accused of exporting their earnings, of requiring protection without being available for service themselves, and of creating "race and class irritation, which is a perpetual menace to social order."[15]

With labor organizations leading the campaign, chanting "The Chinese Must Go,"[16] support for the movement was provided by the Seattle newspapers and by advertisers who owned businesses catering to the workers. Every Seattle daily, except the weak *Chronicle*,[17] participated to some extent in the attacks on the Orientals. While the *Post-Intelligencer* confined its views principally to its editorial columns, the venom of the *Call* dipped over into its news sections. For example, it published lurid articles on the unreliability of Chinese witnesses,[18] and on the overcrowding, uncleanliness, and flagrant immorality in San Francisco's Chinatown.[19] It also published anti-Chinese editorials from other newspapers,[20] and provided elaborate coverage of the anti-Chinese mass meetings. Its language was open to question. In the course of one denunciatory article, it mentioned "the two-bit conscience of a scurvy opium fiend," "the treacherous almond-eyed sons of Confucius," "chattering, round-mouthed lepers," and "those yellow rascals who have infested our western country."[21] On another occasion it referred to the "rat-eating Chinamen."[22] The *Star* also gave strong editorial support to the agitation and ample space to the anti-Chinese meetings. In addition, it published on its front page anti-Chinese editorials from other newspapers.[23]

Advertisements both demonstrated the depth of the feelings and fanned the hatred. At least seven restaurants and two laundries urged that they be patronized because they employed "white help only." D. R. Judkins, a photographer, headed his advertisement with the black-lettered slogan: "The Chinese Must Go." M. E. Eisbert, who called himself the Queen City Boot Black, announced: "The Chinese are going and we are going to black boots for ten cents." The I.X.L. clothing store shouted: "War! War! War! The Chinese must go! . . . Our goods are made exclusively by white labor. . . ."[24]

September 1885 saw the anti-Chinese agitation start along the road which led to the riots of February 1886. It was heralded by a series of mass meetings. Approximately two weeks after the Squak Valley outbreak, the Liberal League, an organization of workingmen, sponsored a meeting in Yesler's Hall to discuss the Chinese question. An overflow crowd of between seven and eight hundred people filled the room. "All and everyone evinced the popular sentiment that 'The Chinese must go.'"

Since the speakers seemingly regarded the evils of Chinese residence as self-evident, they were primarily concerned with removing the Chinese from Seattle. Various methods of eliminating the Orientals were suggested. P. P. Good, a lawyer, urged legislation against Chinese immigration. T. H. Cann, another attorney, asserted that the way to get rid of the Chinese was to deprive them of work. In addition, he scoffed at attempts to Christianize them: "You might as well try to convert a loon."

M. McMillan, a representative of the Knights of Labor, and John Keane provided glimpses into the future. McMillan announced: "I for one will go into the Chinese quarters... and lead down to the steamer two or three Chinamen, and ask them peacefully and politely 'to go!'" Keane added that prominent men like Mayor Henry L. Yesler and former mayor John Leary should inform the Chinese that they were no longer wanted in Seattle, and that they should be ready to leave on the next *Queen*. "They must go; they've got to go," he concluded. D. Cronin, an organizer of the Knights of Labor, then introduced a series of resolutions, which were adopted. The most important urged the calling of a Puget Sound Congress on September 28 to "formulate a plan of concerted and intelligent action" in regard to the Chinese. Each town, labor organization, and labor union was to elect three delegates.[25]

Apparently the temper of this meeting alarmed the "better elements" of Seattle. On September 22, 1885, Mayor Yesler issued a call for an assembly of "taxpayers and property owners," who would devise "ways and means to prevent further bloodshed and destruction of property." He emphasized the "threatening aspect of affairs over the agitation of the Chinese question."[26] In approving Yesler's announcement, the *Post-Intelligencer* said: "There has been a feeling of uneasiness throughout King County for the past two weeks.... There is unrest, disquiet, and apprehension."[27]

In response to Yelser's call, approximately one thousand people thronged Frye's House on the evening of September 23. After the audience had unanimously elected the mayor as chairman, it heard addresses by Orange Jacobs, an attorney who served on the territorial council, J. T. Ronald, former King County prosecutor, and by other prominent residents of Seattle, as well as one by Governor Watson C. Squire. Jacobs, the first speaker, set the tone for the other orators. After admitting that the "immigration of Chinese to this coast has been a curse," and describing its evils at length, he nevertheless insisted that the people of Seattle should be loyal to the American treaties stipulating that the Chinese in the United States were afforded protection similar to that extended to American citizens. In addition, he pointed out that, if violence ensued, there might be retaliation in China, and that the prospective violations of law might prevent Washington Territory from becoming a state. After other talks urging obedience to the law, James McNaught, a lawyer, stated: "The Chinese must go, but legally by the abrogation of the treaty and by legislation."

As usual, the evening was concluded by the adoption of resolutions. Introduced by Jacobs, the proposals committed the gathering to a vigorous enforcement of the restriction acts, the solution of all questions by lawful means, and the amendment of ineffectual laws. Finally, the residence of the Chinese in Seattle was deplored, and it was agreed that their removal should be obtained by legal methods.[28]

Consequently, by late September, it was obvious that Seattle possessed a reasonable unity on the evils of Chinese immigration. One faction insisted, however, that law and order were the primary considerations; the other demanded the immediate ousting of the Chinese. Apparently this difference was further accentuated by jealousies engendered by social, economic, and political factors.

The uneasiness in Seattle was not assuaged by the mass meeting held September 28. On the preceding evening, the arriving delegates were greeted with a parade, a band concert, and oratory in Occidental Square. Delegates had been sent by the towns of Colby, Black Diamond, Newcastle, Squak, Sumner, Tacoma, Whatcom, and Seattle. In addition, the following organizations were represented: Seattle Turn Verein, Seattle Typographical Union, Seattle Labor League, International Workmen's Association, and the Knights of Labor of Renton, Seattle, and Tacoma.

A preliminary session was held in the morning. At the afternoon meeting, Mayor R. Jacob Weisbach of Tacoma was chosen president of the Congress. The other officers, all from Seattle, included Good, McMillan, Walter Walker, the secretary of the Queen City Assembly, Knights of Labor, and Dr Anna E. Galloway, a "vitapathic physician."

Weisbach set the theme for the Congress: in view of the unlawful entry of the Chinese and the failure of legislation the people must safeguard themselves. In his mind the only question was what means should they utilize to protect them selves. The other speeches evinced strong anti-Chinese feeling, especially on the part of the Tacoma delegation. Its members insisted that, if nothing more than a resolution favoring a boycott was passed, they could not return to their homes.

The third session was held in the evening at Yesler's Hall, with standing room at a premium. The committee on resolutions provided a lengthy report, introducing various proposals. After declaring their "firm . . . resolution to rid our Territory . . . from the presence of Chinese slave labor," they called "upon all citizens to aid and assist us. . ." Furthermore, they asked "all citizens to immediately discharge all Chinese in their employ." The delegates were instructed to call mass meetings in their locales on October 3, for the purpose of appointing committees which would notify the Chinese to leave on or before November 1. The committees would have until November 6 to submit their reports. In conclusion, the committee said that the enforcement of these resolutions 'would eradicate the Chinese evil, and we hold ourselves not responsible for any acts of violence which may arise from the noncompliance with these resolutions." After adopting these proposals and transacting other business, the delegates listened to a number of rousing speeches.[29]

With the anti-Chinese agitation having become a major problem in Seattle,[30] gatherings of two rival factions were held October 3. The committee selected by the September 28 Congress issued a call for a mass meeting at Yesler's Hall on Saturday evening, October 3. Its purpose was "to elect a committee to wait upon the Chinese and notify them of the time set when they are requested to leave Seattle."[31] The Call applauded the announcement, urging the attendance of all who had "at heart the interests of the workingmen." It hoped to see "such action taken as will rid the city and the country once and forever of this blight on civilization."[32] The customarily large audience listened to the usual oratory, and elected a committee of fifteen members to deal with the Chinese. Its chairman was to be Sheriff John H. McGraw,[33] who promptly declined the appointment.[34]

On the same evening, a secret meeting, open only to ticket

holders, was held at Frye's Opera House. It was arranged by a number of "prominent" citizens, who were alarmed at the extreme measures hinted at by the more violent Chinophobes, and at the influx of "toughs," who "would enter into any deed of destruction for the sake of spoil." Over five hundred people assembled under the chairmanship of Mayor Yesler. After reiterating their opposition both to the Chinese and to acts of violence, the audience was transformed into deputy sheriffs by Sheriff McGraw. He divided the city into districts, and appointed captains to head them. He also gave detailed instructions to each group.[35]

The rival meetings created considerable friction in Seattle. The Labor League committee denounced the "opera house party" as the adherents of "capital and monopoly."[36] The *Call* and the *Star* sharply assailed both the "opera house party" and the *Post-Intelligencer*,[37] while the latter turned on its critics with equal vehemence.[38] Under the circumstances an attempt by the Chinophobes to effect a compromise between the two factions failed.[39] Differences over policy and factors of prestige were apparently the dominant stumbling blocks. Truly, Seattle was a "house divided."

The rising tide of agitation in Seattle did not go unnoticed in either the diplomatic or legal spheres. F. A. Bee, Chinese vice-consul at San Francisco, sent Governor Squire a telegram inquiring if the civil authorities were able to protect the Chinese. If they were not, he requested that Squire call upon the federal government for assistance. In reply, the governor assured him that the civil authorities were able to perform their duties.[40]

During the excitement a grand jury was convened in federal district court to determine whether the people implicated in the anti-Chinese agitation had acted illegally. Judge Roger S. Greene delivered the charge to the jury. In it he cast light on the state of mind of the so-called better elements. While freely admitting that the presence of the Chinese was a "real grievance," he insisted that a "resort to lawless violence to promote their removal is utterly inexcusable." He emphasized its danger to the reputation of the community, and stressed that the Chinese question was a national problem. In addition, the independent expulsion of Chinese from King County would frighten capital. In short, the "presence of the Chinese is an evil, but the project of driving them out by lawless violence is suicidal."[41]

The situation became even more threatening when the Committee of Fifteen acted on Saturday, October 10. Its members invaded the Chinese quarter of Seattle and private homes where Chinese were employed to notify the Orientals that the majority of the people of Seattle wanted them to depart. They also left circulars containing that message. The Chinese received the threat in various ways: a few did not understand its import, others became angry, and some resignedly inquired as to the deadline.[42] At the same time the Chinophobes circulated petitions pledging their signers not to employ Orientals.[43]

On October 15 leaders of Seattle's anti-Chinese movement and delegates from Tacoma met in the Seattle office of George Venable Smith, a Chinophobe lawyer. At this conference they decided to hold a "monster demonstration and parade" on October 24, to which citizens from the entire Puget Sound region would be invited. They then interviewed Yesler, McGraw, and Chief of Police Woolery, informing the officials of their plans and of their determination to prevent lawlessness during that day. Although opposed to the demonstration, the three could find no legal means of barring it.[44]

Two days later Yesler received an anonymous letter. Printed in ink on plain lined paper and mailed in a Hotel Brunswick envelope, it was semiliterate and threatening. After warning the mayor to "go slow" and "let the China biz alone," it told him of a cache of dynamite within one mile of Seattle ready to be utilized anytime after November 1. It instructed him to communicate this warning to Leary, Jacobs, and Dave Denny.[45]

The reaction of the so-called better classes to these developments was summarized editorially by the *Post-Intelligencer*. It said that the forthcoming demonstration was not relished by conservative citizens," who regarded it as most unwise . . . positively dangerous." Permeated with a distaste for Tacoma and outside interference, it denounced the attempt to introduce that neighbor's outrageous methods into Seattle. It claimed that violence and a disregard for law would lead to conflict with the authorities of the United States, which would be "worse than mad—it is suicidal." In addition, the demonstration would epitomize "utter uselessness," as the Chinese question in Seattle was rapidly settling itself. The few Chinese still employed would be discharged as soon as whites could be found to perform their tasks; then all would leave Seattle. Therefore, the citizens of Seattle should discourage the demonstration in every way.[46]

Undaunted by the disapproval of the "better elements," George Venable Smith on October 17 formally announced the scheduling of a peaceful "grand torchlight procession and anti-Chinese demonstration" at Seattle on October 24. Apparently fearful of premature violence, the committee announced its intention of providing special guards with authority to arrest "promptly anyone causing the least disturbance, either by word or deed."[47] In addition, it urged the closing of all saloons between five and nine in the evening in order to avoid trouble caused by drunken men.[48]

The anti-Chinese faction was gratified by the demonstration on Saturday evening, October 24, in which nearly 2,500 people took part. The Seattle Chinaphobes were joined by six hundred enthusiasts from Tacoma, Newcastle, Renton, Black Diamond, McAllister, and other towns in western Washington. Three bands played during the march, and the paraders carried numerous transparencies. Typical banners read "Discharge your Chinaman"; "White laundries are good enough. Less polish and more justice"; "Down with the Mongolian slave"; "Get off the fence; either for or against." Or nearly all could be seen "John, Go."

The focal point of the procession was Frye's Opera House the scene of the meeting, which was so crowded that hundreds had to be turned away. The orators reiterated three themes. One was an attack upon the "better class" as the "dog-salmon aristocracy," "the thieves who stole our timber and coal lands," and the representatives of the "ironclad monopolies." Another, of course, was the evils of the Chinese immigration. Third, all were united in a vocal determination that the Chinese must leave. The speeches were greeted with enthusiastic applause. Finally, the inevitable resolutions were adopted. After dwelling upon the "many evils of Mongolian immigration which are subversive of our institution," and the disillusionment of a hitherto patient populace, they called upon all classes of citizens to cooperate in directing public sentiment to the "laudable end of excluding the Mongolian curse from the land." Agitation, organization, and discussion were to be methods used to "preserve the law and prevent public disturbance, as well as to effectually solve the difficult Chinese problem."[49] It might be remarked that, in contrast to the rest of the proceedings, these resolutions were deceptively mild. A week later another large anti-Chinese meeting was held, this time at Tacoma. Three boatloads of Seattleites attended.[50]

Developments now intensified in speed. On November 3 the *Call*, acting as spokesman for agitators, demanded a boycott on commodities produced or served by Chinese. It insisted: "Agitation, constant agitation is the key.... Give the Chinese and their employers no peace until they go." Bloodshed and disorder should be avoided for practical reasons.[51] The next day Seattle's committee issued a call for a second anti-Chinese Congress to be held at Olympia on November 4. The purpose of this convention would be to create a permanent anti-Chinese organization and a "thorough system for further action toward excluding the Chinese from Washington territory."[52]

On the same day Governor Squire, previously the target of bitter oratory on the part of the anti-Chinese faction, issued a proclamation. After pointing out the illegality of acts of violence and intimidation, the tenseness of the Seattle situation, and the concern of the Department of State, he warned the citizens against participating in a riot or breach of peace. He called upon the sheriff to protect the Chinese, and upon the citizenry to aid the sheriff. Following an impassioned plea to the people to uphold the law, he concluded: "If you do not protect yourselves, you have only to look to the step beyond; which is, simply, the fate of Wyoming and the speedy interference of the United States troops."⁵³ He also secretly ordered McGraw to perfect his military organization.⁵⁴

Early the following afternoon an important conference was held in ex-mayor Leary's office. It was caused by the appointment by the Knights of Labor of three men to confer with civic leaders on the subject of Chinese expulsion, and to request them to use their influence to secure a peaceful exodus. B. F. Day, J. T. Jordan, and A. Amunds were the delegates of the Knights, while Leary, Bailey Gatzert, and Yesler represented the "better class." Also in attendance were five of the leading Chinese "bosses." After the Knights had expressed their views, Leary and Gatzert told the Chinese that they would have to leave Seattle. They explained that the lives and property of the Orientals were endangered by uncontrollable elements. They advised the Chinese leaders to send away immediately all their laborers, to dispose of all property, and to leave as soon as possible themselves. If they stayed, there would be serious trouble. Faced with these unpalatable but well-meant opinions, the Chinese agreed to depart as soon as possible. They asked only for reasonable patience to enable them to dispose of their property, pack, and leave.⁵⁵

Late on the same afternoon it was decided to hold a mass meeting that very evening.⁵⁶ Sponsored by the Knights of Labor, it was to consider the current status of the Chinese problem and feasible measures for preserving the peace of Seattle without the intervention of federal troops.⁵⁷ In spite of the lack of advance notice, about seven hundred men and women, principally of the laboring class,⁵⁸ crowded into Fyre's Opera House to hear speeches by representatives of both the "law and order" and the anti-Chinese groups. The gathering was so acrimonious that proposed compromise resolutions did not receive consideration, and the meeting adjourned with "feelings of disgust on both sides."⁵⁹ Intense bitterness was evinced by the Chinophobes.⁶⁰

The Chinese section of Seattle reflected an aura of hopelessness and defeat. Fully 150 Chinese left Seattle by boat and train during November 4, 5, and 6. The departures can be attributed to the Tacoma outbreak in early November and to the menacing situation in Seattle. The remaining Orientals indicated that they would depart as soon as they could sell their property. A few mentioned debts owed to them by whites; and others talked of the ruinous depreciation of values wrought by forced sales. Distressed countenances and tears expressed the sorrow of those unwillingly leaving their Seattle homes. It was apparent that the determination and the threats of Seattle labor were triumphing over the "better class" and the Chinese. As was remarked, "in a few weeks, or at most a few months, a Chinaman will be a curiosity in Seattle."[61] Under the circumstances the anti-Chinese mass meeting staged at Yesler's Hall, Saturday night, November 7, was virtually a victory rally. Optimism and self-congratulation were its keynotes. The Chinese problem in Seattle was almost solved.[62]

But the tension of the past weeks had created a state of alarm. Government officials entrusted with the responsibility for preserving public safety were apparently gravely disturbed by the parades, mass meetings, and incendiary threats of Seattle labor. Doubtlessly painful visions of similar anti-Chinese feeling erupting into violence in Rock Springs, Squak Valley, Tacoma, and a number of other western towns were frequently in their minds. And why should Seattle alone have the good fortune to oust the Chinese without violence?

Saturday, November 7, was the day of action. Mayor Yesler issued a proclamation enjoining the citizens to uphold the law and to refrain from action against the Chinese. He also urged everyone to remain at home unless business brought him out. In conclusion, he warned that measures had been taken to ensure "prompt arrest and punishment of all riotous violators of law."[63]

The steps adopted by the authorities were varied. First, in view of the apparent unreliability of the police,[64] the sheriff organized a company of home guards under the captaincy of George Kinnear,[65] and supplied them with arms.[66] Second, the revenue cutter *Wolcott* steamed into Seattle harbor, and lay at its wharf with guns exposed.[67] Third, as a result of the representations made by McGraw to Squire,[68] Secretary of War W. C. Endicott ordered troops dispatched immediately from Fort Vancouver to Seattle to suppress the anticipated violence.[69] The deep concern of the War Department was demonstrated by Lt. General Philip H. Sheridan, who telegraphed Major General John Pope, in command of the Pacific Division, that perhaps the Washington troubles might spread down the coast. Therefore, Pope should keep well informed and alert.[70]

Two companies of the Fourteenth Infantry left Vancouver Barracks after lunch on November 7, and traveled to Seattle by steamer and train.[71] The 350 soldiers under the command of Lt. Colonel De Russy, and accompanied by Squire, arrived at Seattle at 1:30 A.M.[72] Although the night was moonless, cold, damp, and thoroughly disagreeable, the first federal troops ever to be stationed in Seattle were greeted by approximately three hundred residents. Some had come only to gape; others, "prominent citizens," carried guns of various types.[73]

Seattle was so quiet on Sunday, November 8, that De Russy and Squire attributed the calm to the excellent moral effect of the presence of the troops.[74] Squire added that he believed that there would be no conflict, and consequently no necessity for so large a contingent. He recommended, therefore, that half be returned to Vancouver, and the rest divided between Seattle and Tacoma.[75] When General John Gibbon, in command of the Columbia Division, arrived in Seattle on the evening of November 8, he found that "everything is perfectly quiet," and ordered four companies to Tacoma to aid the United States marshal there in making arrests.[76]

Seattle apparently accepted the presence of the troops as an unusual and not unpleasant interlude in the daily routine. During Sunday and Monday, November 8 and 9, their quarters were surrounded by a large crowd, who laughed and chatted with the soldiers. While the latter behaved in exemplary fashion toward the white population, their treatment of the Chinese was not so laudable. The uniformed visitors committed a number of brutal assaults on the Orientals, of which six were formally reported. Four Chinese were beaten up in apparently unprovoked assaults; one had his queue cut off; and another was thrown into the bay.[77] In addition, according to one reporter, a group of soldiers visited the Chinese quarter on the night of November 9 to collect a "special tax" from each Oriental. This foray was supposed to have netted approximately $150.[78] After discussing these outrages, the *Call* remarked: "The chances are that the people will be called on to protect the Chinese."[79]

As Seattle continued to be quiet,[80] the remaining troops returned to Fort Vancouver November 17.[81] Whether their arrival had prevented an outbreak of violence is impossible to determine. At any rate their presence caused many Chinese to decide that they would stay,[82] thereby postponing a "solution" of the Chinese problem.

The dispatch of troops to Seattle aroused diverse opinions in the local press and the city. The *Call* proclaimed that it was a "rash" act and an "outrage." After insisting upon the peaceful nature of the anti-Chinese movement, the labor organ assailed the Chinophiles and the "politicians."[83] The *Star* also denounced the authorities.[84] On the other hand, the *Post-Intelligencer* approved the call for troops, and complimented Squire on his "wise and prudent course in a time of perplexity and danger."[85] General Pope, a dispassionate observer, believed that the government's action was unfavorably received by most of the populace.[86]

In spite of the differences of opinion regarding the wisdom of stationing troops in Seattle, the crisis apparently intensified the feeling against the Orientals. The *Post-Intelligencer* insisted that the "true way of expelling the Chinese is nonemployment, not intimidation," and urged a continuation of the boycott.[87] The *Call* remained hostile to the Chinese, of course.[88] General Gibbon summarized the situation as follows:

> Feeling here is almost universal against Chinamen but the better part of the people are opposed to any illegal action. A few demagogues taking advantage of the popular feeling are striving from selfish motives to force the Chinese out of the country.[89]

Only the Methodist Episcopal Ministers' Association of Seattle had the temerity to oppose popular sentiment. On November 12 it passed a resolution denouncing the anti-Chinese movement as "cruel, brutal, un-American, and un-Christian."[90]

While the troops were in Seattle, the legal machinery was set in motion against the anti-Chinese element. After hearing fifty-one witnesses, the grand jury, under J. C. Colman, foreman, brought in bills of indictment in District Court against seventeen residents of Seattle. They were charged with conspiring to deprive the Chinese of their rights.[91] Pleased with this action, C. H. Hanford, assistant United States attorney, informed Attorney-General A. H. Garland that it was essential to prosecute these cases with vigor, and assured him that he would make every effort to secure convictions if he were left in charge.[92] W. H. White, United States attorney, also wrote Garland that the federal government was obligated to provide Chinese on the West Coast with the protection guaranteed by treaty, and urged that "more than ordinary effort" should be exerted to obtain convictions in the Seattle cases.[93] Apparently the authorities were determined to reverse the customary outcome of anti-Chinese cases. After the usual legal maneuvers,[94] the defendants pleaded not guilty.[95] Trial was set for January 4.

Although the "Committee of Ten" countermanded the call for the second anti-Chinese Congress, scheduled for Olympia, November 24,[96] the agitation continued in a somewhat restrained manner during the following months. December and January were relatively calm, however, as the Chinophobes were still hoping that the city council and the territorial legislature would redress their grievances. They were also awaiting the outcome of the conspiracy trials.

The indictments only served to irritate further the Chinophobes. The *Call* denounced them as an "assault upon our free institutions, free speech, upon the white race, and upon civilization itself."[97] It also praised the courage of the accused.[98]

In addition, a mass meeting was held November 20 at the

Standard Theater, which was attended by an enthusiastic audience of approximately one thousand people. After a committee was appointed to solicit funds for the expenses of the indicated Chinophobes, a series of speeches was delivered. The major orator, George Venable Smith, proclaimed that he had been indicted because he had "dared to defend the rights of the workingman," and to organize labor. He also based his defense on the constitutional guarantees of free speech. In conclusion, he dwelled on the theme that "it is not a disgrace, it rather a badge of honor to be poor." Mrs. M. J. Kenworthy regaled the crowd with an analysis of the "irrepressible conflict" between capital and labor. [99] The anti-Chinese still emphasized the boycott. Various restaurants and bars were induced to replace their Chinese crews with white workers.[100] The extent of the labor turnover is questionable, however.

The decision to attempt to curb the Chinese by legal methods was apparently reached after the arrival of the federal troops in November. The *Call* opened the campaign by urging that the territorial statute permitting an alien to own property be repealed or modified.[101] It also vigorously denounced the Burlingame Treaty of 1868, insisting on its abrogation.[102] The *Post-Intelligencer* agreed that Chinese should be legally barred as landlords, and added that territorial corporations should not be allowed to employ them. It recommended that the people organize, and obtain 75,000 to 100,000 signatures on petitions.[103] In addition, it also requested revision of the Burlingame Treaty. In order to obtain popular support for its ideas, it printed a draft petition.[104] Two crowded mass meetings at the Standard Theater in December echoed the demands of the newspapers for legal action by the territorial legislature.[105]

The city council could act only on a minor scale. It passed a so-called "Cubic Air" ordinance, which went into effect December 3. This provided that each resident of Seattle was entitled to a sleeping compartment 8 × 8 × 8. Dr. Smart, the city health officer, was instructed to enforce it vigorously as a weapon against the Chinese.[106] At a meeting on December 4 the council referred to its judiciary committee a petition regarding the regulation of Chinese businesses.[107] In early February the council passed a series of measures curbing Chinese laundries and peddlers.[108]

The real drive, however, took place in the territorial legislature at Olympia. On December 15, 1885, Representative Charles F. Munday, a Democrat of King County (Seattle), introduced a resolution to have a committee of five appointed to consider petitions and bills on the Chinese question. This group was to report not later than January 15, 1886. In accordance with custom, Munday was made chairman.[109]

Almost a month later Munday introduced into the House four bills and one memorial relating to the Chinese problem. House Bill 172 provided that no alien incapable of becoming a citizen could acquire land thereafter. Furthermore, all lands then owned by such aliens should escheat to the Territory for the benefit of the common-school funds upon the deaths of the aliens. House Bill 173 conferred upon cities and towns the power to regulate and license laundries, with the proviso that such aliens be not licensed. House Bill 174 stipulated that such aliens should not be employed on public works or by municipalities. The final measure (175) stated that no private industrial or quasi-public corporation should employ such aliens after July 1886.[110] Munday also introduced a memorial—House Memorial No. 13—which was addressed to the Congress of the United States. It defended the people of the Territory against the charge of being disorderly, repeated the usual allegations against the Chinese, and requested suitable legislation to remedy the evils arising from the presence of the Chinese on the Pacific Coast.[111]

The four anti-Chinese measures were passed by the House on January 20. The land-owning bill (172) was approved unanimously; only one representative voted adversely on laundry licensing (173); four opposed ending municipal employment of Chinese (174); while seven objected to barring Chinese labor in private industry (175).[112] The memorial (13) was also approved.[113]

When Munday's bills reached the council, there apparently was a brief discussion. Orange Jacobs led the opposition. He vehemently attacked both the measures and their aims, declaring that such legislation was both useless and indiscreet. He also argued that, as the United States was a free country, it was as much the home of the Asiatic as of any other nationality.[114] The contract proposal (175) drew his hottest fire.[115] In conclusion, he expressed strongly his doubt as to the constitutionality of anti-Chinese legislation.[116] The leading defender of the measures was J. B. Reavis, Yakima Democrat. After declaring that their principles were correct, he warned against the repercussions likely to be caused by a failure to enact them.[117] The council followed Jacobs. After passing the land-owing bill (172) with amendments by a vote of 8 to 3, it defeated the proposal barring Chinese labor in private industry (175), 7 to 5, and indefinitely postponed consideration of the two remaining measures.[118] The House concurred in the amendments to the land-owning act, which became law.[119]

The reaction in Seattle to the failure of the legislature to strike at the Chinese was hostile and virtually unanimous. The *Post-Intelligencer* called the defeat of Munday's bills a calamity, the effect of which would be greater on account of its unexpectedness. It described the proposals as "wise and just," and the result of an almost universal demand. It also warned that their defeat might produce the "greatest harm."[120] Needless to say, the *Call* excoriated the council.[121] Thirty-three Seattle lawyers, including J. T. Ronald, wrote an open letter to Jacobs. Critical of his role in blocking Munday's bills by emphasizing their unconstitutionality, they said that many attorneys disagreed with him. In any event Congress and the courts could decide that question.[122] Another group of legal specialists, including the conservative Thomas Burke, G. M. Haller, and T. N. Haller, refused to express an opinion on the constitutionality of the proposals. They affirmed, however, that it would have been wiser for the legislature to have enacted the anti-Chinese laws, and then permitted the appropriate authorities to pass upon them. They added that they believed it to be everyone's duty to do all in his power to "protect American labor against the disastrous competition of the Chinese."[123]

During January, Seattle had one eye focused on the legislature at Olympia, and the other on the federal courtroom at home, where the alleged conspirators were being tried. After three days had been consumed in the selection of a jury, the testimony began January 6, and continued until January 16. The courtroom was crowded at every session. In spite of the determined efforts of the prosecution, the jury deliberated for only ten minutes before handing down a verdict of not guilty.[124]

Thus, by the first of February 1886, the situation in Seattle had become both simpler and more dangerous. While the last serious hope of eliminating the Chinese by legal action was being destroyed by Jacobs and the council, the almost indecently rapid acquittal of the alleged "conspirators" had demonstrated that violence against the Chinese would in all probability go unpunished. These factors would inevitably strengthen the hands of those who wanted to oust the Chinese, even by force, if necessary.

The intense feeling was crystallized at another anti-Chinese meeting held at the Bijou Theater Saturday evening, February 6. The speeches reflected the widespread feeling that the time for peaceful measures had ended. A. E. Turner, Mrs. Mary Kenworthy, and T. H. Cann[125] agreed that there had been enough agitation. Now was the time for action, and they suggested a boycott and nonpeaceful measures. M. P. Bulger of Tacoma then boasted that there were no Chinese in that city, and regaled the delighted audience with a narrative of the events which had occurred there on November 3. The gathering was so excited that "at the close of his remarks a man with half an eye could see that ere another day rolled by we would hear something drop."[126]

Following the speeches various proposals were adopted. The main resolution began by denouncing in lurid language "Chinese slave labor" and those who persisted in the employment and patronage of Chinese labor and products. It then recommended the appointment of another "Committee of

Fifteen" to examine the Chinese quarter in order to discover if the "Cubic Air" and other ordinances were being enforced, and to ascertain the number of Chinese remaining in Seattle and the names of their employers, which would be published. In addition, it threatened to boycott economically and socially these pro-Chinese. The report was to be delivered at the next mass meeting.[127] After the passage of the resolutions a committee was appointed, dominated by the acquitted "conspirators."[128] What transpired after the formal adjournment of the meeting is unrecorded, except in the events of the following days.

The next morning the period of agitation and oratory ended.[129] Seattle was now on the road charted by the people of Eureka and Rock Springs. At daybreak a number of five- and six-man "committees" invaded the Chinese section. The Orientals generally opened the doors of their homes without resistance. In some cases, however, doors were forced open, and windows smashed. The "committees" notified the Chinese to pack, as they were going to be sent sway on the *Queen of the Pacific* at 1:00 P.M. A few whites remained in each house to assist the frightened Orientals in their preparations for their departures. Shortly afterward a number of wagons appeared, and the "committees" loaded the Chinese and their luggage into them, and hauled them to the steamship wharf. There the Chinese were placed under an armed guard. Other groups visited homes where Chinese servants were employed, and insisted that the Orientals be entrusted to them. In virtually every instance their demand was complied with, and the servant escorted to the dock to join his compatriots. Subsequent "committees" returned to the Chinese section, and examined each house thoroughly in search of elusive Orientals who might have escaped the vigilance of the first invaders. They found about six, who were taken to the wharf immediately.

Apparently violence was at a minimum during these operations. Only a few Chinese were maltreated, and none was seriously injured. The laundrymen were not permitted to deliver the clothes in their custody, however, and property was left unprotected, although Seattle was infested by thieves.[130]

During the early hours the streets were crowded with men. The city was controlled by the adherents to the policy of removing the Chinese by force. The police, previously termed "utterly useless,"[131] insisted that they were able only to prevent abuse of the Chinese. They added that they did not intend to halt their removal. After W. H. White, United States attorney, half angrily, profanely, and unsuccessfully tried by verbal means to halt the ousting of the Chinese, the forces of "law and order" began to form. Engine house, university, and church bells were rung at 10:30 A.M. Sheriff McGraw hurriedly organized and armed deputies.

Governor Squire, who was in Seattle by chance, had to face the problems created by the lawlessness. Apparently hesitating about the adoptiion of a strong policy,[132] he issued a relatively mild proclamation, and did not declare martial law. It began with a copy of Mayor Yesler's appeal to him for assistance, based on the inadequate power of the city. After warning the lawbreakers, and urging everyone with civilian status to retire to his home, he called upon all citizens interested in the preservation of order to become deputy sheriffs, and ordered the militia companies to place themselves under arms immediately.[133] At noon Deputy United States Marshal Henry, guarded by about thirty deputies, read the proclamation from a post on the corner of Commercial and Washington streets to a good-sized crowd. It was received with jeers and derisive shouts. On their way back to the courthouse, Henry and his escort were followed; and they were hooted and hissed at in a most boisterous manner. Thoroughly alarmed now, Squire telegraphed Endicott,[134] Gibbon, and Secretary of the Interior L. Q. C. Lamar. After informing them of the activity of the "immense mob," and the formation of a *posse comitatus*, he predicted the probability of a serious conflict. Therefore, he urged that troops be immediately dispatched to Seattle.

In spite of these events in the city, the 350 Chinese on the dock had not been forgotten. Captain John Alexander, master of the *Queen of the Pacific,* agreed to transport the Chinese to San Francisco for seven dollars each. A committee was promptly formed to raise the necessary funds. At 1:30 P.M. over six hundred dollars had been obtained, which paid for tickets for eighty-nine Chinese, who promptly went aboard. They were joined by eight other Orientals, who defrayed their own fares. Before the *Queen* could lift anchor, a writ was served upon Alexander, ordering him to produce the ninety-seven Orientals in court.[135] A Chinese merchant had sworn out a writ of habeas corpus, alleging that his countrymen were unlawfully detained on board the ship.

The remainder of the Sabbath passed in tense quiet. Rumors, attempts to raise funds to provide transportation for the remaining Chinese, and militia patrols received the major attention. Late on Sunday night the anti-Chinese element, despairing of raising sufficient money to send away all the Chinese on the *Queen,* deposited $250 with the railroad company to take them to Tacoma. In view of Tacoma's outstanding Chinophobe record, the results of this maneuver would presumably have been unfortunate for the Orientals. Sheriff McGraw forestalled the anti-Chinese, however. He notified the railroad of the consequences of transporting Chinese residents unlawfully and against their will. Its alarmed agent then placed a double crew on the engine, and started the train out somewhat ahead of time.

That night, moreover, saw the first real rebuff for the mob. As so often occurs in revolutionary crises, the footweary demonstrators went home in the evening, and thus lost control of the situation. Only a skeleton guard of Knights of Labor was left on the dock to watch the Chinese, who were sleeping in a warehouse. Consequently they were helpless when McGraw dispatched the Seattle Rifles and Company D to the wharf to obtain possession of it and prevent any movement of the Chinese.[136]

At 7:15 the following morning the Chinese were escorted to the courthouse by McGraw and his deputies. Since many Chinophobes looked upon this action as a stratagem to clear the *Queen* and allow her to sail, there was a movement toward resistance. But cool heads successfully urged peace. Judge Greene informed the Chinese through an interpreter that they had a legal right to remain in Seattle, that the government was strong, and would do all in its power to protect them. He added, however, that the "general sentiment of the community is against the Chinese staying here" and that similar trouble might recur. Consequently, only sixteen of the ninety-seven expressed a desire to continue to reside in Seattle. After the court proceedings ended, the well-guarded Chinese were escorted back to the wharf.

Early the same morning warrants were sworn out in Judge Lyon's court for the arrest of eight of the leaders of the Chinophobes on a charge of riot. They were taken into custody, and marched to the city jail. News of their arrest spread rapidly, and within a few minutes bail bonds of five hundred dollars each had been provided.

The *Queen* remained in port while the anti-Chinese labored to raise money to ship all the willing Chinese on the dock. By eleven o'clock financial arrangements were completed, and the wholesale puchase of tickets began. When 196 Chinese had filed on board, Captain Alexander stated that he had his legal load of passengers. A conference between McGraw and his aides and George Venable Smith and other leading Chinophobes resulted in the agreement that the Chinese still on the wharf would be permitted to remain in Seattle until the departure of the *George W. Elder* on February 14. At noon the *Queen of the Pacific* finally sailed, almost twenty-four hours behind schedule.

The departure of the *Queen* with its large cargo of Chinese left the spectators happy and most of the remaining Orientals very disappointed. Under the guard of the deputies they started to march to their damaged houses in the Chinese quarter. Hoodlums harassed and shouted at them. News of their return from the wharf preceded them, and aroused the Chinophobes, who, ignorant of the agreement between their leaders and the sheriff, were resolved that the Chinese should not leave the dock. The determined workingmen formed in a body at the corner of Main and Commercial streets, prepared to prevent the return of the Orientals. Shortly after noon the Chinese and their guards reached this corner. The Chinophobes refused to give way, and hurled profane abuse at the deputies and the Chinese. Excitement ran high. Then the deputies attempted to arrest the "most loud-mouthed and violent." The workingmen resisted, and hand-to-hand fighting ensued. The deputies clubbed their opponents with their guns, and the irate Chinophobes struggled to gain possession of these weapons. During the melee, shots were fired, and five men fell.[137] In the meantime, the frightened Chinese deposited their packs on the ground and cowered behind them. The sight of the wounded men persuaded the crowd to fall back. Immediately the deputies, speedily reinforced by the Seattle Rifles, lined up across Commercial and Main streets, with guns prepared for action. The wounded, with the exception of James Murphy, a special officer, were placed in a wagon, and hurried to Providence Hospital.

After the casualties had been removed from the scene, the crowd commenced to regather. Within a few minutes there were thousands of men in the streets, and they arrayed themselves on both sides of the authorities. Now Company D, which had been stationed at the courthouse, came flying to the aid of the deputies. McGraw then mounted a box, and commanded the crowd to disperse. It ignored him, and the gravity of the situation was intensified. But the alarmed leaders of the workingmen strove energetically to prevent a renewal of the violence; they explained that the remaining Chinese would leave on the *Elder*, and they promised that the deputies who had done the firing would be prosecuted. Finally, the crowd dispersed; the militia and the deputies marched to the courthouse; and the Chinese took refuge in their old quarters. An uneasy silence prevailed in the city.

Governor Squire and the other officials acted rapidly. Squire immediately proclaimed the existence of a state of insurrection, declared martial law, and suspended the writ of habeas corpus.[138] Colonel Granville O. Haller was appointed adjutant general, and he issued a number of orders designed to prevent disorder.[139] For example, saloons were closed, and persons without written permission from the authorities were barred from the streets between 7:00 P.M. and 5:00 A.M. Sentinels were stationed throughout Seattle, and the city became calmer, although still a feeding ground for rumors.

There was little enthusiasm for any further violence, however. The leaders of the Knights of Labor were "now doing everything in their power for peace." Both major newspapers were in agreement. While the *Call* stressed the need for the "exercise of patience and self-control" by every citizen, the *Post-Intelligencer* said: "Recrimination, discussion, speculation must be laid aside. . . . It behooves every man to take his stand in the ranks of the law's defenders."[140]

Although the city was quiet Tuesday morning, February 9, the failure of the federal authorities to send troops to Seattle was causing considerable alarm among the so-called better element. On the other hand, the *Call* and the leaders of the Knights of Labor were already seeking the end of martial law.[141] As soon as the anti-Chinese forces had seized temporary control of Seattle Sunday morning, Squire had asked Secretary Endicott to send troops to the city,[142] but to no avail.[143] After the shootings, Judge Greene had telegraphed William M. Evarts that the regulars were needed.[144] Yet, by nine o'clock Tuesday morning, no troops had been to the scene. When this fact was laid before prominent residents, many of them sent telegrams to various senators, cabinet officers, and to C. S. Voorhees, delegate to Congress from Washington Territory. They were asked to urge upon President Cleveland the necessity for speedy action. Others telegraphed directly to Cleveland, pleading that he issue the desired order.[145]

Finally, late on February 9, Cleveland issued a proclamation, announcing a state of emergency in Seattle. He pointed out the necessity of using military force to suppress domestic violence.[146] General Gibbon was ordered to proceed at once with troops to Seattle.[147] Early Wednesday afternoon, February 10, eight companies of the Fourteenth Infantry under Lt. Colonel De Russy returned to Seattle, and marched to their quarters.[148] General Gibbon and his staff arrived that evening. Their arrival was a source of relief and joy to the militia and deputies, who had been at work with little sleep since Sunday noon.[149] They were now able to go off duty.[150]

The crisis was over, however. According to a report by Gibbon, the troops found the city perfectly quiet, and there had not been the "slightest difficulty in maintaining the most perfect order and quiet." He added that Squire's declaration of martial law had been an "absolute necessity under the circumstances." He also remarked that it would be impossible to convict any of the Chinophobes, that the feeling in Seattle was almost universal in its opposition to the presence of the Orientals, and that the "law and order" party was in a minority. After stating that he feared for the safety of the latter upon the withdrawal of the troops, he concluded: "The Chinese question has become demoralizing to our own people, and is degrading their sense of liberty, justice, and freedom."[151]

The Chinese problem approached one step nearer a temporary "solution" on February 14. That day almost two hundred Orientals huddled together in the warehouse on the dock, prepared to leave Seattle on the *George W. Elder*. The latter could take only 110 refugees, as there were eighty to ninety Chinese at Port Townsend awaiting passage.[152] The remaining Orientals once again returned to their quarters to await the next steamer.[153]

As usual, there was considerable stress beneath the surface. It existed both in official circles in Seattle and among the general populace. Apparently an administrative crisis was possible. After consultation with Gibbon, Judge Greene sent two telegrams to Evarts. In the first he inquired if Governor Squire's proclamation of martial law was to be fully ratified by President Cleveland. If not, since he had urged it, he would "probably resign." He also was anxious to know Cleveland's purposes, as he would not perform his judicial functions within military lines.[154] The next day Greene was even more alarmed. He informed Evarts that, "while superficially all is quiet in Seattle, there are deadly purposes and plottings underneath"; consequently, the withdrawal of the troops would be followed by "civil war on a small but terrible and perhaps expanding scale." Furthermore, he emphasized that the Seattle disorders were only part of the national problem, and that the federal government's attitude toward Seattle would determine the future of the Coast in regard to racial problems. He also urged the continuation of martial law. Finally, in view of the fact that he and Cleveland were of different parties, he offered to resign if Cleveland desired.[155] Evarts promptly told Greene that his conduct had been approved, and urged him not to retire from office.[156]

In spite of Greene's fears, the violence had ended February 8, and the Seattle factions now turned to legal and political channels to settle their disputes over the Chinese. On February 22, Mayor Yesler requested the restoration of civil law, and Squire immediately revoked his proclamation of February 8.[157] At the same time, however, the governor urged President Cleveland to order at least two companies of federal troops to remain in Seattle for several months. He insisted that they were "very necessary for preserving peace and forestalling disastrous contingencies otherwise probable."[158] Judge Greene echoed this opinion.[159] On February 14, General Gibbon decided to send four companies back to Fort Vancouver the next day, and keep four in Seattle.[160]

The question of holding federal troops in Seattle proved to be disturbing. On February 16 and March 11, Gibbon asked for instructions, as he did "not feel at liberty to act on my own judgment and withdraw the troops." He mentioned the availability of six militia companies, comprising 425 men, in Seattle, calling it a "sufficient force to aid the civil authorities in case of trouble." The withdrawal would save considerable money."[161] Three weeks later, Gibbon again requested instructions. He categorically stated that a "further stay there is unnecessary. As a matter of economy I advise their recall."[162] Shortly afterward he was authorized to withdraw two of the four companies in Seattle. Instructions in regard to the disposition of the remaining troops were to be sent shortly."[163]

After several more weeks had elapsed, Gibbon was instructed to ascertain from the civil authorities their opinion of the necessity of keeping troops in Seattle. He was also asked to present his own opinion.[164] Two days latter Gibbon replied. Although Squire was unaccounted for, Mayor Yesler wanted the troops to remain until after the trial in May of the alleged leaders of the February riots. Gibbon added that he disagreed with the mayor, and again strongly recommended that the soldiers be removed. He argued that the dependence on federal troops had already had a deleterious effect on Seattle by being an obstacle to that community's taking proper steps for its own protection. Furthermore, the city had reduced its police force. Therefore, if police were not essential to prevent disorder, surely the troops also were not.[165] The next day Adjutant General Drum acceded to Gibbon's repeated requests, and gave him permission to withdraw the remaining two companies from Seattle.[166] The departure of the troops was scheduled for May 5.[167]

Before the withdrawal date, however, Mayor Yesler found support from some unaccustomed allies. On April 28, McMillan, Keane, and other leaders of the Knights of Labor telegraphed Cleveland that he would receive petitions signed by thousands, urging that he countermand the order withdrawing the troops. They averred that there existed in Seattle an "armed party drilling daily and declaring loudly to carry coming elections by force, if necessary. Threatens lives and property of defenseless citizens." They urged that troops be retained in Seattle until after the city elections.[168]

Yesler and the Knights were joined on May 4 by Chang Yen Hoon, Chinese Minister to the United States. He informed Secretary of State Thomas F. Bayard that he had just received a report from the Chinese in Seattle about the planned withdrawal of federal troops and the renewed threats of the Knights of Labor. Since this news corroborated other warnings, he said that he would deem it a "great favor" if the troops remained in Seattle a few months longer.[169] The diplomatic plea succeeded. Immediately Drum telegraphed Gibbon to keep the two companies in Seattle until further notice.¹⁷⁰ And Bayard was thus able to provide Chang Yen Hoon with the desired assurances.¹⁷¹

In view of the keen interest in the Seattle problems and the diverse views on the retention of troops there, the War Department immediately ordered Gibbon to visit Seattle and prepare a report on the situation. His findings were to be confidential "for political reasons."¹⁷² Gibbon traveled from Fort Vancouver to Seattle the next day,¹⁷³ and held a series of conferences. He reported that opinion on withdrawing the troops was "very much divided." While Squire halted "between two opinions," Yesler believed that troops should be retained for the present. Greene was averse to the removal of the soldiers. He considered that the Chinese were being utilized as a pretext for Socialistic outbreaks. When the latter were ended in the east, Seattle would become quiet. The general also talked to a number of prominent citizens. Some were apprehensive; they were convinced that the removal of the soldiers "would be followed by disorders. Others stated that they were ready to meet every emergency themselves. Gibbon reiterated his previous stand; that Seattle possessed three companies of well-organized and well-armed militia, and sixty to eighty special sheriffs. These comprised a force "ample for any probable contingency."¹⁷⁴

With federal troops still stationed in Seattle, the city began to prepare for the municipal elections in July, the principal issue that of the anti-Chinese riots. Two groups entered the field: the Loyal League, and the People's Party. Colonel Samuel W. Scott, candidate of the former for chief of police, summarized the one issue of the campaign at a mass meeting:

> I believe there is but one issue in this campaign—law and order on the one side, and anarchy, disloyalty and trouble on the other, as we had on the seventh of February. I for one will stand or fall by law and order.¹⁷⁵

Other speakers¹⁷⁶ and the *Post-Intelligencer*¹⁷⁷ were in accord with this opinion. The People's Party numbered among its leaders John Keane and Mrs. Kenworthy, who had been prominent in the anti-Chinese agitation. As a further gesture, it nominated for chief of police, William Murphy,[178] who, as acting chief in February, had refused to use the police force to protect the Chinese.[179]

The People's Party won a clear-cut victory. The Loyal League lost every race except the council elections in the second and third districts.[180] If, as Richard Osborn, a leader of the Loyal League, said, the "issue is, shall we endorse the riot of February 7 and 8, or shall we condemn it,"[181] the answer of Seattle was obvious. Seattle approved the agitation against the Chinese.

The final scenes in the anti-Chinese drama were quickly played. Late in July 1886, Gibbon reopened the subject of keeping troops in Seattle. Asking if the War Department desired them to remain there any longer, he added: "They have been there now nearly six months."[182] Ordered to investigate again the situation in that city,[183] he examined carefully. He reported that, after a series of conferences with officials and private citizens, he could now discover no apprehension of any disturbances likely to follow the withdrawal of the troops.[184] The next day Gibbon was instructed to remove the soldiers from Seattle,[185] and he issued the necessary order immediately.[186]

The last echoes of the February riots were heard in the district court. On June 5, the grand jury had dismissed charges of riot against seven Chinophobes. It returned indictments for unlawful conspiracy, however, against M. McMillan, C. H. Metcalf, Louis R. Kidd, J. T. Winscott, and Junius Rochester, of Seattle, and M. P. Bulger, of Tacoma.[187] They were charged with violating Section 5519 of the Revised Statutes. The indictments stated that they had conspired to drive out of the United States through force and intimidation Chinese residents in Seattle.[188] The grand jury also attributed the anti-Chinese outbreaks to an anarchist organization.[189]

Obtaining convictions was obviously going to be difficult. W. H. White, United States attorney, was not sanguine. Although the law was clear and the facts "plain and easy of proof," he felt that "conviction depends altogether upon the character of the jury." He realized, moreover, that there existed a "strong prejudice against the prosecution arising out of the intense anti-Chinese feeling in Tacoma and Seattle."[190] After two days were spent in obtaining a jury,[191] the trial of the six alleged conspirators began September 2. The proceedings attracted little attention, however. After witnesses had paraded to the stand for almost four weeks, testimony ended on the morning of September 27. W. H. White then made his opening address to the jury, but the defense attorneys created a surprise by submitting their case without arguments. The case was placed in the hands of the jury late that afternoon. It considered the testimony for almost four hours before bringing in a verdict of not guilty.[192]

From the Pacific Northwest Quarterly,
"Anti-Chinese Outbreaks in Seattle,
1885–1886," by Jules Alexander Karlin

Anti-Chinese Riots in Washington (1885–1886)

The first Chinaman to reach and remain upon the Pacific Coast was Chum Wing in 1847, a California gold seeker.[1] Gold mining and railroad building were the chief avenues of the Chinese approach to the Pacific Coast, but they early branched out into other lines of labor such as household service and laundry work.[2] Shortly after their arrival a spirit of hostility to the yellow men developed, especially among the white laboring men, based primarily on the economic status of the Mongolian, though other elements enter into the opposition. Without question one important element was race prejudice.

In Washington we find the territorial legislature placed a tax of $24 per year on each Chinaman as early as January 1864. In 1866 the tax was reduced to $16 per head. Without question this was an attempt to discourage the coming of the Mongolians to the Territory but as such it was a failure. Large numbers of the Chinese continued to arrive, making a total of 3,276 in the census of the Territory for 1885.[3]

The coming of the Northern Pacific Railroad into Tacoma brought the yellow men with it. By the time of the riots in the fall of 1885 it is estimated that there were around 700 in Tacoma and something over 1,000 in Pierce County.[4] While opposition existed at an early date, it did not reach serious proportion until the early eighties. Due to financial distress of the period, there was considerable unemployment and consequently very much unrest among the white laboring men of the Northwest. Upon the completion of the Canadian Pacific Railroad, a number of men were thrown out of employment. Large numbers of these men drifted southward to the towns and cities on the Sound, thus increasing the number of unemployed whites and adding to the agitation against the Mongolians. It was felt among certain classes that the recent Chinese Exclusion Act was not as strictly enforced by our government as it should have been and the hostility to the Chinese was one expression of this feeling.

There was no outbreak of violence used against the Chinese until early in the fall of 1885. But during the two or three years previous to this time hostility to the Orientals increased at a very rapid rate. The "Chinese Question" was discussed in numerous meetings of all kinds and of all classes. Large parades and demonstrations were held in Seattle and Tacoma, while lesser ones took place in the smaller cities and towns. Labor was definitely hostile to the Chinese remaining on the Coast, and the financial conditions of the times urged them to action. The Northwest was not alone in this unfriendly spirit to the strangers within their midst. Conditions in parts of California, Colorado, and various points west of the Mississippi where the Chinese had located parallel to quite an extent the situation in Washington Territory. This was a situation too good for the radicals and agitators to overlook as the events of late 1885 and early 1886 will prove.

On September 4, 1885, the coal miners of Rock Springs, Wyoming, drove five hundred Chinese out of the coal mines, killing eleven of them.[5] On September 7, five white men and two Indians attacked a camp of thirty-five Chinese at the hop yard of the Wold Brothers in Squak, or Issaquah, Valley. They fired into the tents, killing three Chinamen and wounding three others. The remainder of the group escaped to the shelter of the woods for the remainder of the night. Next day they left the valley. This was but three days after the tragedy in Wyoming and probably was inspired by that event. Public sentiment against the yellow race was such that though these men were arrested and tried for murder, they could not be convicted.[6]

The Rock Springs, Wyoming, outrage intensified the situation in the coal mines of Washington Territory. On the night of September 11 the Chinese coal miners at Coal Creek were raided by a small band of masked men, ten or fifteen in number. While there was no loss of life in this incident, one Chinaman was assaulted and the Chinese quarters and clothing were burned.[7] Guns were fired to frighten them and they were told to leave the country. On September 19 the white miners drove the Chinese out of Black Diamond, injuring nine men. Through the towns and villages north of the Columbia and west of the Cascades, public meetings were held to discuss the Chinese situation and applaud the violence perpetrated on the Orientals without due regard to the laws of the land or the treaty rights of the attacked. The Chinese thus driven out elsewhere began flocking through the port cities, adding to the difficulties brewing in those cities. Already numbers of them had left by train and by boat for British Columbia and San Francisco.

It would seem that at least a fair majority of the people of the Pacific Northwest were united on the proposition that the Mongolians should leave their section of the country. This group includes quite a number of influential and prominent men as well as officials of certain cities and counties. No doubt the method for accomplishing this end was a real live issue with the agitators and radicals advocating force, where no other means than peaceful persuasion were advocated.

The radical element desired immediate action and were disposed to get this by any method available, lawful or otherwise. This group met in Seattle at the so-called Anti-Chinese

Congress on September 28. The mayor of Tacoma presided over this meeting. Delegates from all directions were in attendance. All the labor organizations and several fraternal orders were well represented. "Every socialist and anarchist who could walk or steal a ride was a self-elected but nonetheless welcome delegate. Long-haired men and short-haired women were noticeable by their numbers and their noise."[8] This body, after hearing a number of speeches, put forth a series of resolutions on the Chinese situation and proclaimed that the Chinese must leave Western Washington by November 1, 1885. It condemned the employment of the Chinese in households and factories. They planned that "ouster committees" should be selected in mass meetings in Tacoma and Seattle to notify the Chinese of these cities that they were to leave by the date set. These committees were to be fifteen in number in each case.

In Tacoma the sentiment against the Orientals was quite strong. The lawless element had the advantage of the support of the mayor of the city and a "laissez faire" attitude on the part of the officials of Pierre County. The sheriff of Pierce County believed and so expressed himself to Governor Squire that there would be no lawlessness or violence perpetrated on the Chinese in Tacoma. By this it can be inferred that he did not consider unlawful what the Anti-Chinese Congress proposed to do. On the night of October 3, after a torchlight procession, a mass meeting was held where the Tacoma "Committee of Fifteen" was selected. On November 3, in spite of the Pierce County sheriff's assurance to Governor Squire that law and order would be preserved,[9] Tacoma citizens numbering about three hundred went to the Chinese quarters and demanded that the Orientals leave the city and began routing them out of the quarters. Wagons were brought and Chinese goods together with some sick and aged were loaded into the wagons. It is claimed that no violence was used on any of the Chinese, that the latter did what they were told, but numbers of the Tacoma citizens were armed with clubs. The weather was cold and rainy. Regardless of this, the Chinese, some carrying large bundles of belongings on their backs, were marched to a place south of town on the prairie. Here the goods were dumped from the wagons and the evicted foreigners were left all night to find what shelter they could from the rain and cold. From here they eventually found their way to Portland, Oregon, by rail. On the fourth and sixth of November the buildings and stores of the Chinese standing on the Northern Pacific right-of-way were burned. The removal of the Orientals from Tacoma has been called by sponsors of the movement "peaceable expulsion." Following this action in Tacoma "peaceable expulsions" were continued in the smaller towns of Pierre, King, Kitsap, Snohomish, Skagit, and Whatcom counties.[10]

Unknown to the "Committee of Fifteen" some dissatisfied men had formed a "Committee of Nine." Each one of the nine members of this committee formed a secret circle of nine men and these, in turn, formed circles of nine on an endless chain plan. Oaths were taken and secrecy maintained. The circles did not meet and none of the circle knew who the other members of his circle were but knew only the leader. The organization was extensive but the exact extent of the membership never became known.

The "Committee of Fifteen" had notified the Chinese to leave Tacoma by November first as instructed by the "Anti-Chinese Congress" in October. Apparently this warning was not taken seriously by the foreigners. On the night of November 2 this committee met at the Tacoma Hotel and after long discussion concluded to send another warning to the Orientals. The "Committee of Nine" was also in session that night and decided on immediate action. Each member notified the men of his circle that night to be prepared at the sound of a given signal next morning. It was in reality this "Committee of Nine" that is responsible for the moving of the Chinese from Tacoma instead of the "Committee of Fifteen."[11]

During the last three months Governor Squire had been in correspondence with the Chinese consul at San Francisco, with Washington, D.C., and with the sheriffs of King and Pierce counties. On November 4 Governor Squire issued a proclamation of warning against riot, breach of the peace, or inciting others to riot, and appealed to all good citizens "to array yourselves on the side of the law. If you do not protect yourselves, you have only to look to the step beyond; which is, simply, the fate of Wyoming and the speedy interference of the U.S. troops."[12]

During October a large parade and demonstration took place in Seattle followed by a mass meeting where the Seattle "Committee of Fifteen" were named. The situation in the city became more serious and on November 6 Governor Squire called for U.S. troops for the protection of the Chinese in the city. These arrived under the command of General John Gibbon from Fort Vancouver on the eighth, remaining in the city until the seventeenth.[13] This served to make the agitators and radicals more wary of their actions and to warn them that the government intended to enforce the laws and preserve order. The fact that a number of prominent, influential men of the city were opposed to intimidation of Orientals and forceful expulsion and that the sheriff of King County, John H. McGraw, was determined to do his duty and had greatly increased his force of deputies created a situation entirely different from the situation in Tacoma.

During the month of November the Seattle "Committee of Fifteen" were placed on trial in Judge Roger S. Greene's court with C. H. Hanford as the United States attorney for the prosecution under the Civil Rights Act. The trial lasted until the middle of January 1886, but they could not be convicted. But this trial helped to keep the city quiet during this period, though the anti-Chinese faction were not satisfied.[14]

Early in February a meeting of the radicals in south Seattle was held in the Bijou Theater in which the "Committee of Fifteen" was instructed to inspect Chinatown for violations of the sanitary laws of the city. The chief of police was present with the committee when the inspection was made, the real purpose of which was the expulsion of the Orientals. The steamer, *Queen of the Pacific,* was in the harbor due to sail for San Francisco on the afternoon of February 7. The radicals planned to put the Chinese on this boat by force.[15]

Before they could be stopped by the sheriff's forces and one company of the militia called for the occasion, between three and four hundred Chinese had been marched by the radicals to the dock for the forced embarkment. Captain Alexander of the *Queen* refused to allow any Chinese aboard his ship unless the fare was paid. Eventually about one hundred were sent aboard after a collection among the crowd had been taken to pay the fare. Governor Squire, who was in Seattle at the time, issued a proclamation ordering the people to desist from lawlessness and acts of violence, but the city was in control of the mob, aided and encouraged by Acting Chief-of-Police Murphy.[16] The officers of the law under Sheriff McGraw now had the Home Guards, numbering eighty men, one company of militia, the Seattle Rifles, and the University Cadets at their command. Also the fire department under Chief Gardner Kellogg was on constant duty and watch to prevent fire and do what they could to protect the property of the city. The Seattle police force was in sympathy with the mob and was ineffective as a law enforcement body.[17] To reinforce these forces of the law Governor Squire called for Federal troops.

During the night of the seventh the mob were on guard at the dock containing the Chinese, but about midnight they attempted to put some of the Orientals on the train. The Home Guards took advantage of their absence to gain control of the dock with the Chinese, which they held with the aid of the Seattle Rifles and the University Cadets throughout the remainder of the disturbance.

Early the morning of the eighth the leading agitators and leaders of the mob were arrested and locked in jail. At eight o'clock the Chinese were marched to Judge Greene's court where they were told of their rights under the laws of the land and were asked if they wished to leave the city. All but fifteen wished to leave. They were all taken back to the dock under guard for protection. By this time the leaders of the mob were out of the jail on bail.

After the *Queen* incident, it was determined to return the remaining Chinese back to Chinatown to await the next steamer to California. This proved to be a dangerous and difficult order to carry out as the mob had been constantly increasing in numbers and in boldness. It was impossible to inform the radicals that most of the Mongolians were to leave on the next boat in a few days, and the march of the foreigners through the streets was misunderstood by the anti-Chinese forces. In addition to those living in Seattle, radicals and anti-Chinese sympathizers had collected from all parts of the Northwest to see the Chinese sent out of Seattle and were taking part in the actions of the mob.

The Chinese were formed in a column with their belongings. The Home Guards were placed in front, the University Cadets and the Seattle Rifles in the rear, with the Orientals in between the two groups of guards. The march began up Main Street with Sheriff McGraw at the head. The lawless group gathered on the streets in large numbers and at the intersection of Commercial Street (First Avenue) and Main Street succeeded in blocking the progress of the marchers. Several men attempted to seize the guns from the hands of the Home Guards. Several of the guns were discharged, wounding five men, one of whom died the next day. Shots were fired by the mob but none of the Chinese or guards were injured, although one shot passed through Sheriff McGraw's coat.[18]

Amid the confusion, shouting, and excitement of the mob, who were taken completely by surprise in finding the guns loaded, a square of the guards was formed about the foreigners, who by this time were very badly frightened. The guards stood in this formation for about an hour, unable to proceed through the mob, awaiting the arrival of Company D from the courthouse. The militia appeared from the north under the command of Captain John C. Haines and opened the ranks of the rioters. The Chinese were then returned to their former quarters in Chinatown without further incidents. The city still seemed to be in the hands of the mob, as up to that time the forces organized for law and order seemed too small in numbers to effect the control of the entire city.

Early in the afternoon of the eighth, or on the day of the

mob attack, Governor Squire declared the city to be under martial law, thus suspending the courts and all civil law enforcement bodies. The saloons were ordered to be closed, all business houses were to be closed between the hours of 7:00 P.M. and 6:00 A.M. All persons found on the streets without the written consent of the provost marshal between the hours of 7:00 P.M. and 5:00 A.M.[19] were to be arrested. Volunteers were called for military duty and were enlisted. President Cleveland confirmed Governor Squire's proclamation the next day[20] and ordered Federal troops to be sent from Fort Vancouver. Major A. Alden was appointed provost marshal. The 14th Infantry under the command of Colonel De Russy arrived on the tenth to the great relief of the local organizations, who had been on constant duty for three days and nights without sleep. Guards from these volunteer groups had been placed in all important places in the city from the eighth to the tenth.

Seattle remained under martial law until February 22, a period of two weeks. The radicals from outside quickly left the city and those from within became quiet. During this period the police force was put under the control of the Provost Marshal and additional men added to the force. Others including Chief Murphy were dismissed from the force. The next step was the recruiting of the various military volunteer units up to full strength, one hundred men per company. On the site of an old skating rink on Second Avenue these companies were drilled into excellent shape for service.[21]

The steamer *Queen* on the seventh took away nearly two hundred of the Chinese; the steamer *George W. Elder* took one hundred and ten on the fourteenth. About fifty could not be taken. "These gradually departed by train and steamer until but a handful remained."[22] Thus the Orientals for a time left the Territory of Washington, largely under compulsion and at the hands of lawless men bent on accomplishing this end regardless of treaty rights of the Chinese or the laws of the land under which they lived, while officials, who should have been enforcing law and order, either openly aided the mob or refused to interfere or suppress the rioters. Credit is due the small band of earnest citizens of Seattle, who were determined to grant justice to the strangers of foreign race and blood within their city, regardless of the cost. One wonders what the outcome would have been just three years later than these events, when the Territory of Washington applied for admission to the Union, if Seattle citizens had not taken a decided stand for law and order.

> From *The Washington Historical Quarterly*, "Anti-Chinese Riots in Washington," by W. P. Wilcox

Two Instances of Police Brutality (1902, 1903)

I do not know how I can better illustrate the kind of protection, or want of protection, extended to the Chinese, as guaranteed by the Constitution, the treaties, and the solemn promises of the government of the United States, than by recalling a notorious case which occurred, not on the sandlots of California, not under the auspices of labor agitators, but in the enlightened city of Boston and under the conduct of Federal officials. The following narrative is condensed from the newspapers of that city. At about half past seven o'clock on the evening of Sunday, October 11, 1902, a number of United States officials of Boston, New York, and other cities charged with the administration of the Chinese exclusion laws, assisted by a force of the local police, made a sudden and unexpected descent upon the Chinese quarter of Boston. The raid was timed with a refinement of cruelty which did greater credit to the shrewdness of the officials than to their humanity. It was on the day and at the hour when the Chinese of Boston and its vicinity were accustomed to congregate in the quarter named for the purpose of meeting friends and enjoying themselves after a week of steady and honest toil. The police and immigration officials fell upon their victims without giving a word of warning. The clubs, restaurants, other public places where Chinese congregated, and private houses were surrounded. Every avenue of escape was blocked. To those seized no warrant for arrest or other paper was read or shown.

Every Chinese who did not at once produce his certificate of residence was taken in charge, and the unfortunate ones were rushed off to the Federal Building without further ceremony. There was no respect of persons with the officials; they treated merchants and laborers alike. In many cases no demand was made for certificates, the captives were dragged off for imprisonment, and in some instances the demand was not made till late at night or the next morning, when the certificates were in the possession of the victims at the time of their seizure.

In the raid no mercy was shown by the government officials. The frightened Chinese who had sought to escape were dragged from their hiding places, and stowed like cattle upon wagons or other vehicles, to be conveyed to the designated place of detention. On one of those wagons or trucks from seventy to eighty persons were thrown, and soon after it moved it was overturned. A scene of indescribable confusion followed, in which the shrieks of those attempting to escape mingled with the groans of those who were injured.

The case of one old man was particularly sad. In the upsetting of the wagon two of his ribs were broken, and he was otherwise bruised and injured. The attending physician made oath that his age was such that the injury might develop pleurisy or other serious complication as the result of his injuries. The rough usage to which he was subjected was a great strain upon his feeble frame, weakened by age. When the raid burst upon the Chinese quarter, he had just come downstairs from his lodgings when he was caught in the police dragnet. He informed the officers that his certificate was in his trunk upstairs, and that he could lay his hands on it without loss of time. But he was not permitted to go to get his papers even under guard, but was thrown into the overloaded wagon. The result was that this innocent man, who under treaty had a perfect right to reside in the country free from molestation, was made to suffer untold tortures in body and mind, in order that the immigration and police officers might satisfy their thirst for sensational activity.

About 250 Chinese were thus arrested and carried off to the Federal Building. Here they were crowded into two small rooms where only standing space could be had, from eight o'clock in the evening, all through the night, and many of them till late in the afternoon of the next day. There was no sleep for any of them that night, though some of them were so exhausted that they sank to the floor where they stood. Their captors seemed to think that they had to do with animals, not human beings. Some of them were released during the night, when relatives brought their certificates or merchants were identified. But the greater part were kept till the next day, when the publicity of the press brought friends, or relief through legal proceedings.

One of the Boston journals reported that the federal judge, who had a case set for hearing in an adjoining room the next morning, had to adjourn to another part of the building because of the foul exhalations from the overcrowded prison pen. It would hardly be believed that the "Black Hole of Calcutta" could at this day have an imitation in such an enlightened community.

So strong was the indignation of the respectable citizens of Boston, that a large public meeting was held in Faneuil Hall to denounce the action of the immigration officials and the police. Prominent men who took part did not hesitate to refer to that action in the strongest terms as a brutal outrage, a disgrace to the city; and the resolutions adopted assert that the Chinese were seized without warrant of law, and, after being brutally handled, were placed in close and ignominious confinement; and they declare that the lawless acts of the officials are dangerous to liberty and in defiance of constitutional rights—arbitrary, unwarranted, and outrageous.

It was announced by the immigration officials that their raid was organized under the belief that there were a number of Chinese in Boston and its vicinity unlawfully in the United States, and this method was adopted for discovering them. The official report of the chief officer soon after the event showed that 234 Chinese were imprisoned, that 121 were released without trial or requirement of bail, and that only five had so far been deported, but that he hoped that he might secure the conviction and deportation of fifty; as a matter of fact, however, the deportations fell much below that number. But even if these men were unlawfully in the country, they were entitled to humane treatment, and, above all an orderly process and application of the law. The act of Congress prescribes "that any Chinese person . . . found unlawfully in the United States or its Territories *may be arrested upon a warrant issued upon a complaint,* under oath, filed by any party on behalf of the United States," etc. (Act of September 13, 1888).

Even as to the guilty Chinese the arrest and confinement was without warrant of law. But what justification can be offered for the arrest of the two hundred peaceable and law-abiding Chinese—the indignities, hardships, and insults to which they were subjected? Although earnest complaint was made by the Chinese minister to the government at Washington, not a single officer was punished or even censured for his illegal and brutal conduct, and no reparation was obtained by the Chinese.

The American commissioners who went to Peking expressly stated that it was only the coolie class of laborers whom their government desired to exclude, and the treaty of 1880 in terms stipulated that the restriction "shall only apply to Chinese laborers, *other classes not being included in the limitation.*" But when Congress came to legislate respecting the treaty it provided that only the five classes of merchants, teachers, students, travelers, and officials should be admitted. Under this law and the construction placed upon it by the Immigration Bureau the large majority of the upper classes of the Chinese were excluded from entry or residence in the United States.

The treaty provided that to entitle the exempt class to admission into the United States "they may produce a certificate from their government . . . viséd by the diplomatic or consular representative of the United States . . . in the port whence they depart." The plain intent of this provision was that the certificate should state that the holder thereof was a merchant, student, or whatever might be his occupation. But the laws of Congress and the bureau regulations require that the certificate, if issued to a merchant, for instance, must state the name, title, if any, description of the person and all physical peculiarities, former and present occupation, place of residence, nature, character, and value of business, and where the holder expects to locate.

But it is not held sufficient if the holder presents himself with such a certificate duly viséd by the United States consul. The applicant for admission is subjected to a most searching examination, and the strictest technicalities are applied. I illustrate some of these technicalities by a case, taken from many, given by Minister Wu in a communication which was sent to Congress and published, as follows:

> Last year several merchants came to San Francisco with a good supply of money and credit to make purchases. They were provided with the legal certificates viséd by the American consul, but it appeared that in their certificates some parts of their former career were not filled up in English, although properly filled up in Chinese. The objection was raised by the customs authorities that the certificates were defective. It was contended on their behalf that the law was complied with, as every detail was mentioned in the certificate, although some of it was only in Chinese, and it was offered to supply the omission in the English from the Chinese text, but the authorities would not allow it. The case was appealed to the Treasury Department, and the decision of the San Francisco authorities was confirmed. It was of no avail that these merchants had come ten thousand miles, that their certificates were quite sufficient as far as the Chinese text was concerned, and that the American consul who viséd the document was at fault in not seeing that all the parts were filled up in the English text. It was suggested that the merchants

be released under bonds, and that their certificates be sent back to China for correction. There was no suspicion of fraud, yet the suggestion was not heeded, and these merchants were compelled to return to China.

Tom Kim Yung, the military attaché of the Chinese Legation in Washington, was in 1903 sent to San Francisco on a temporary duty. One night, after spending the evening dining with the president of the Chinese Merchants' Association, when returning to his lodgings at the Consulate General, and near that place, he was accosted by a policeman in most indecent language and struck with gross indignity. This resulted in an encounter participated in by another policeman. The attaché was beaten and severely bruised, and finally handcuffed and tied by his queue to a fence until the arrival of a patrol wagon, into which he was forced and taken to the police station. Here he was kept for some time, until released on bail given by a Chinese merchant, about half past one o'clock at night.

He was held for trial on a charge of assaulting a police officer, and when his diplomatic character was brought to the attention of the chief of police by the consul general, that officer refused to dismiss the charge. The excuse of the policeman for his conduct was that he mistook the attaché for another Chinaman for whom he was on the lookout. The attaché, not being able to secure the dismissal of the charges or any punishment of the policeman, was greatly chagrined; he felt that he had "lost face" with his countrymen; and brooding over what he regarded as his disgrace, he committed suicide.

He was followed to the grave by thousands of his countrymen who regarded themselves as personally outraged. The secretary of state brought the subject to the attention of the governor of California, and the latter to the mayor of the city, but no redress was given or punishment inflicted.

From the *Atlantic Monthly*, 97 (January 1906), "The Chinese Boycott," by J. W. Foster

4. Have They Made It? — A Conclusion

Anti-Chinese sentiment in the United States has begun to wane as a result of several developments during the past three decades. During the late 1930s, China's victimization by Japan, and her heroic resistance, aroused widespread sympathy in the United States. After Pearl Harbor, moreover, China became an ally of the United States in the struggle against Japan, and a new and far more flattering image came to be established in the American mind.

This, in turn, began gradually to transform the image of their Chinese fellow-Americans which many whites in this country had entertained. The incredibly evil and sinister Fu-Manchu, personification of the Yellow Peril, for example, gave way to the genial Charlie Chan who, *mirabile dictu,* defended rather than conspired against the law. Best-selling books such as Pearl Buck's *Good Earth* and Carl Glick's *Shake Hands with the Dragon* also did much to dissipate white American attitudes toward both China and the Chinese in America. In 1943, the old Exclusion Acts were at last repealed (see p. 217).

But these changes should not be overestimated, welcome though they may be. Charlie Chan may have become a popular hero, but he was still depicted as an "inscrutable, mysterious, and damned clever Chinaman." The Exclusion Law may have been repealed, but in its place an immigrant quota of a mere 105 Chinese per year was established, and this to include not only immigrants from China itself but also anyone of Chinese descent (and even half-Chinese) born of families which may have lived for generations outside China. It is also true that as a result of the great legislative and popular movements of the 1960s, racism in America has sustained a sharp setback. It has been forced to assume a lower profile—among other reasons because certain expressions of it are actually illegal now. As a result, we may probably say that America has become less racist.

It would be a gross mistake, however, to assume that the battle against racism in general and against anti-Chinese prejudice in particular, has been won—the *New York Times* claim that the Chinese have now "made it" into American society notwithstanding (see p. 219). A far more plausible comment is that of James W. Chin, in discussing that article (see p. 225). "Prejudice against the Orientals in America," he writes, "is no longer gross or blatant as in the past. Nevertheless," he continues, "it is still ubiquitous although now couched in very sophisticated, subtle forms. Unfortunately, to many observers not sensitive to the new nuances of prejudice, there is the frequent misinterpretation that there is no longer any discrimination against Orientals."

Discrimination does exist. It exists in employment opportunities, education, even city services to Chinese communities. It is a persistent topic in the ethnic press (see p. 227), and it's brought up more frequently and more vocally outside the Chinese community as Chinese gain access to the established press and to radio and television. In San Francisco in December

1970, for example, the State Fair Employment Practices Commission heard complaints from the Chinese community which documented racial bias in the hiring and promotion practices of the San Francisco Civil Service Commission (see pp. 229 and 231). In September of that year, five Chinese and Japanese in the city health department had been denied promotions on the basis of oral test scores, though all had scored higher on the written examination than some of the Caucasians who were promoted ahead of them (see p. 233). Furthermore, the Orientals were all graduates of the School of Public Health of the University of California, while one of the inspectors promoted had no more than a high school diploma. Reports of intimidating interviews and manipulation of oral grades to accommodate favored candidates who had scored poorly on the written test drew a wide response from the Chinese community (see p. 236).

In a similar case in Los Angeles, the Board of Governors of the Los Angeles County Arboreta and Botanical Gardens maneuvered for more than half a year in an attempt to keep a Chinese from becoming director of Arboreta and Botanical Gardens, an appointive civil service position (see p. 238).

A survey conducted by the Human Rights Commission in San Francisco in 1969 provided statistics documenting the almost total absence of Chinese, blacks, and other minorities in the upper grades of civil service employment (see p. 241). Notably, there were few Chinese in managerial and professional positions and in the essential protective services, the police and fire departments.

Schools are also slow at ending discrimination. A Louisiana-born Chinese woman, now living in California, complained of ethnic imbalance in Sacramento schools. Remarking that her husband attended a segregated school there in the 1940s, she found "many parallels between California Chinese and southern Negroes" (see p. 247).

The largest difficulty in education of the Chinese in America lies in the area of language. The son or daughter of an immigrant family who speaks Chinese at home is not likely to gain the familiarity with English necessary to benefit from the teaching offered in public schools. Consequently, he is handicapped in examinations, class discussions, and relationships with teachers and other students.

Asian community efforts to establish tutorial programs, especially in the large cities where there are many Chinese, will help. But many feel that the school districts should provide additional support with bilingual and English-as-a-second-language classes. In a U.S. district court in San Francisco in 1970, a suit was filed on behalf of Chinese-speaking students asking the San Francisco Unified School District to provide bilingual classes for approximately 3,000 Chinese students. The suit was denied with the ruling that although "special instruction would be desirable and commendable," it is not required by law (see p. 249). The decision is being appealed.

The problems of the Chinese communities, overcrowding, poor working conditions and opportunities, insufficient education, have, until recently, been ignored or misrepresented by the news media. San Francisco Chinese, who comprise about 14 percent of that city's population, complain of racism, stereotyping, and a "white perspective" in reporting events of significance to Chinese, if they are reported at all (see p. 251).

There is an increasing number of Chinese working in the news media, but even they are victims of a very subtle discrimination. Chinese have been allowed to hold positions as artists, directors, and cameramen but are refused jobs that would put them before the public "on the air" (see p. 252).

Another area where Chinese are frequently discriminated against is in the construction trades. Qualified Chinese contractors are often given little consideration in the awarding of contracts (see p. 254), and it is still difficult for a Chinese to find employment in the trades themselves. In 1970 in the San Francisco Chinatown, a twenty-seven-story structure labeled "Chinese Culture and Trade Center" was discovered, at one point, to employ only three Chinese in its construction. Later, the building was found to be a 572-room luxury hotel with only one floor given "to provide the proper atmosphere and facilities for the development of cultural perspective, self-awareness, and community understanding and participation among Americans of Chinese ancestry." Yet no more than ten Chinese from the surrounding community, which is almost entirely Chinese, were employed at any one time in construction of the building (see pp. 257 and 259).

Chinese are subject to harassment in every conceivable form. In New York, state health authorities have tried to force

Chinese markets to remove the heads and feet from poultry, traditionally sold whole (see p. 263). In California, a federal narcotics official blamed the San Francisco Chinese for the proliferation of drugs in the area (see p. 264). Even in the armed forces, Chinese are apt to be treated as bitterly and cruelly today as their great-grandfathers were a hundred years ago (see p. 266).

In October 1905, President Theodore Roosevelt, speaking in Atlanta, Georgia, commented on the spreading boycott of American goods in China by remarking, "We cannot expect China to do us justice unless we do China justice. The chief cause in bringing about the boycott of our goods in China was undoubtedly our attitude toward the Chinese who come to this country."[1] As an analysis of relations between the two countries, Roosevelt's remarks were probably simplistic then and certainly would not suffice for our own times. Nevertheless, at a critical turning point in Sino-American history, with the visit of President Nixon to the People's Republic of China, it is surely worth pondering whether the white American's ability to sustain a constructive relationship with China is not, at least in part, a function of his ability to sustain a constructive relationship with his fellow Chinese-Americans. The contemporary record is still not encouraging.

An Act to Repeal the Chinese Exclusion Acts, to Establish Quotas, and for Other Purposes (1943)
[Approved December 17, 1943]

Be it enacted by the Senate and House of Representatives of the United States of America in Congress assembled, That the following Acts or parts of Acts relating to the exclusion or deportation of persons of the Chinese race are hereby repealed: May 6, 1882 (22 Stat. L. 58); July 5, 1884 (23 Stat. L. 115); September 13, 1888 (25 Stat. L. 476); October 1, 1888 (25 Stat. L. 504); May 5, 1892 (27 Stat. L. 25); November 3, 1893 (28 Stat. L. 7); that portion of Section 1 of the Act of July 7, 1898 (30 Stat. L. 750, 751), which reads as follows: "There shall be no further immigration of Chinese into the Hawaiian Islands except upon such conditions as are now or may hereafter be allowed by the laws of the United States; and no other Chinese, by reason of anything herein contained, shall be allowed to enter the United States from the Hawaiian Islands"; Section 101 of the Act of April 30, 1900 (31 Stat. L. 141, 161); those portions of Section 1 of the Act of June 6, 1900 (31 Stat. L. 588, 611), which read as follows: "And nothing in Section 4 of the Act of August fifth, eighteen hundred and eighty-two (Twenty-second Statutes at Large, page two hundred and twenty-five), shall be construed to prevent the Secretary of the Treasury from hereafter detailing one officer employed in the enforcement of the Chinese Exclusion Acts for duty at the Treasury Department at Washington and hereafter the Commissioner-General of Immigration, in addition to his other duties, shall have charge of the administration of the Chinese exclusion law, under the supervision and direction of the Secretary of the Treasury"; March 3, 1901 (31 Stat. L. 1093); April 29, 1902 (32 Stat. L. 176); April 27, 1904 (33 Stat. L. 428); Section 25 of the Act of March 3, 1911 (36 Stat. L. 1087, 1094); that portion of the Act of August 24, 1912 (37 Stat. L. 417, 476), which reads as follows: "*Provided,* That all charges for maintenance or return of Chinese persons applying for admission to the United States shall hereafter be paid or reimbursed to the United States by the person, company, partnership, or corporation, bringing such Chinese to a port of the United States as applicants for admission"; that portion of the Act of June 23, 1913 (38 Stat. L. 4, 65), which reads as follows: "*Provided,* That from and after July first, nineteen hundred and thirteen, all Chinese persons ordered deported under judicial writs shall be delivered by the Marshal of the district or his Deputy into the custody of any officer designated for that purpose by the Secretary of Commerce and Labor, for conveyance to the frontier or seaboard for deportation in the same manner as aliens deported under the immigration laws."

SEC. 2. With the exception of those coming under subsections (b), (d), (e), and (f) of Section 4, Immigration Act of 1924 (43 Stat. 155; 44 Stat. 812; 45 Stat. 1009; 46 Stat. 854; 47 Stat. 656; 8 U.S.C. 204), all Chinese persons entering the United States annually as immigrants shall be allocated to the quota for the Chinese computed under the provisions of Section 11 of the said Act. A preference up to 75 per centum of the quota shall be given to Chinese born and resident in China.

SEC. 3. Section 303 of the Nationality Act of 1940, as amended (54 Stat. 1140; 8 U.S.C. 703), is hereby amended by striking out the word "and" before the word "descendants," changing the colon after the word "Hemisphere" to a comma, and adding the following: "and Chinese persons or persons of Chinese descent."

From Public Laws, Public Law 199, Chapter 345, 78th Congr., 1st sess., pp. 600–601

Orientals Find Bias Is Down Sharply in United States (1970)

When J. Chuan Chu came to the United States as a student at the end of World War II from his home in North China, he had trouble finding a place to live. Having an Oriental face, he discovered, was a liability.

But Mr. Chu, with an engineering degree from the University of Pennsylvania, has now risen to become a vice-president of Honeywell Information Systems. He lives today in the wealthy Boston suburb of Wellesley, near his concern's headquarters. "If you have ability and can adapt to the American way of speaking, dressing, and doing things," Mr. Chu said recently, "then it doesn't matter anymore if you are Chinese."

His story reflects a quiet, little-noted American success story—the almost total disappearance of discrimination against the 400,000 Chinese- and 500,000 Japanese-Americans since the end of World War II and their assimilation into the mainstream of American life.

Some Chinese have been left behind in the nation's depressed Chinatown ghettos, unable to speak English or too old, too poorly educated, or too fixed in their traditional ways to be assimilated.

And some younger Asian-Americans have become increasingly sensitive, like blacks and Indians, to what they consider white Americans' patronizing attitude toward them. They resent the tourists in Chinatown who politely ask if they can speak English. They indignantly reject the old Oriental stereotype of the slant-eyed, pig-tailed Chinaman, eating chop suey and mumbling "Ah-so." And they insist that many whites, behind a façade of believing in equality, are still prejudiced.

But the great majority of Chinese- and Japanese-Americans, whose humble parents had to iron the laundry and garden the lawns of white Americans, no longer find any artificial barriers to becoming doctors, lawyers, architects, and professors.

Some have achieved national reputations, a feat unimaginable twenty years ago: I. M. Pei and Minour Yamasaki as architects, Gerald Tsai as head of the Manhattan Fund; Tsung Dao Lee and Chen Ning Yang as Nobel Prize winners in physics; S. I. Hayakawa as president of San Francisco State College, and Daniel Inouye as Senator from Hawaii.

With one Senator and two Representatives, the Japanese may well be the nation's most overrepresented minority.

In interviews with dozens of Chinese and Japanese Americans, from executives like Mr. Chu to militant students in Chinatown, very few complaints of discrimination in jobs, housing, or education could be found.

Many people below thirty could not recall a single personal instance of discrimination. The Los Angeles Housing Opportunities Center, which helps people who feel discriminated against, reports that it has had only one complaint from an Oriental in the last three years.

Some prejudice still exists. Mr. Chu, for example, was told last year that he would not be allowed to join the Wellesley Country Club.

NO ORIENTAL MEMBERS

A spokesman for the club, in a telephone interview, denied that the club discriminates against people of any race. He said that he could not recall Mr. Chu's case. However, he also said that the club at present had no members of Oriental ancestry.

Most of the problems confronting Asian-Americans today are more subtle. Dr. Ai-li Chin, a Chinese sociologist at the Massachusetts Institute of Technology, who is doing a study of the Chinese experience in the United States, feels that "discrimination against Orientals has definitely diminished." "In any statement you make about prejudice you must be very careful," she feels. "But for most Chinese the problem is not so much physical barriers, as it is for blacks, as it is the question of identity. Who are you as a Chinese in the United States." This is particularly true, Dr. Chin believes, for the younger people who have grown up in the United States and have an Oriental face but do not speak their parents' language.

REJECT OLD STEREOTYPE

"Ironically, at the same time as prejudice has diminished, some of these younger people have now begun to become concerned about white Americans' attitudes toward them," Dr. Chin, a diminutive, soft-spoken woman points out. "They refuse to accept, as their parents did, the old humiliating Oriental stereotype."

Under the influence of the Black Panthers and Young Lords, some young Chinese have organized radical groups with names like the Boxers and the Red Guards to try to stop tourists from visiting New York's and San Francisco's Chinatowns. "This is our community, it is not a zoo" reads one sign in the Boxers' dingy store-front headquarters in New York.

Even the old stereotype, however, has undergone a metamorphosis. The pig-tailed coolie has been replaced in the imagination of many Americans by the earnest, bespectacled young scholar.

"My teachers have always helped me because they had such a good image of Chinese students," recalled Elaine Yuehy, a junior at Hunter College whose father used to run a laundry. " 'Good little Chinese kid,' they said, 'so bright and so well behaved and hard-working.'" Her comment was echoed by many of those interviewed.

For many years, from the time the first Chinese came to California in the 1850s, prejudice and discrimination against Orientals were very real indeed. Many were barred from obtaining citizenship. In California, where the great majority settled, none born outside the United States were allowed to own land.

1854 REPORT IS QUOTED

A report written by the San Francisco Board of Aldermen in 1854 typified the nineteenth-century American view. "The Chinese live in a manner similar to our savage Indians," the report said. "Their women are the most degraded prostitutes and the sole enjoyment of the male population is gambling." The aldermen recommended "the immediate expulsion of the whole Chinese race from the city."

The ultimate indignity came during World War II when thousands of Japanese on the West Coast were interned in concentration camps and their property sold for 10 cents on the dollar. Many Japanese-Americans feel that white Americans' guilt over the internment has helped lead to their increased acceptance since the end of the war.

Another factor, cited by Dr. Chin, "is the general growth in awareness of racial problems since the end of World War II." Dr. Chin points to the beneficial effect of the Negro civil rights movement, with its fair housing laws. The old California law barring foreign-born Orientals from owning land was ruled unconstitutional by the California State Supreme Court in 1952 after a test case brought by a Japanese lawyer. And the McCarran Act of 1952 made foreign-born Orientals eligible for citizenship.

RESPECT FOR ACHIEVEMENTS

Dr. Chin also feels that the respect Chinese and Japanese have gained by their recent achievements in the professions has helped ease discrimination. Where before the war San Francisco's Chinese were all crowded into Chinatown and

Los Angeles' Japanese were confined to a small area in west Los Angeles, today they have spread out over all parts of their cities.

According to Jeffrey Matsui of the Japanese American Citizens League, Los Angeles, 150,000 Japanese have been able to move into exclusive communities like Bel Air, Beverly Hills, and Pacific Palisades. Two judges and the county coroner are Japanese. Mr. Matsui reported that although Japanese on the West Coast still have some difficulty finding executive or sales jobs, which require large amounts of personal contact, they have no trouble getting jobs as secretaries, accountants, doctors, or engineers. Before the war they were largely restircted to working as gardeners or small farmers.

The situation is much the same across the country. Chicago's 14,000 Japanese live in every section of the city and its suburbs. "There used to be discrimination here," said the Rev. Shinei Shigefuji, minister of the Midwest Buddhist Church, "but I don't think there's much now."

LIKE WHITES IN SOUTH

In the South, Orientals are now considered whites rather than Negroes. Young Chinese and Japanese growing up in such widely scattered areas as Richmond, Durham, N.C., and Atlanta remember attending white schools and going in the white entrance to movie theaters.

In Augusta, Georgia, where a group of Chinese laborers was brought in 1910 to dig the Augusta Canal, their descendants have gone to college and become pharmacists, doctors, and insurance salesmen: in its small way, a typical American immigrant success story.

But for the minority of Chinese who have not been assimilated, Chinatown, behind the glitter of its red-tile store fronts and pagodalike roofs is a slum. In San Francisco's Chinatown, with 50,000 people the nation's largest, 45 percent of the families live below the federal poverty level of a $3,700 annual income; 15 percent are unemployed; 60 percent share a bathroom with another family or have none at all.

Half of the people cannot speak or read English in the heart of Chinatown, nearly half have never been to school. Employment for many means long hours sewing dresses in backroom sweatshops at wages below the legal minimum.

STILL CONTROLLED BY ELDERS

Control in Chinatown rests as it always has with the mysterious family and district associations, ruled by elders who see no need to change their old patterns. Some younger Chinese radicals, like those in the Boxers and Red Guards, blame white racism for the situation. But discrimination appears to be much less of a factor than old age, preference for Chinese tradition, and difficulty with English. Japanese-Americans, who have not clung so closely to their traditional ways, have not encountered the Chinatown problem.

"We resent ignorant Americans coming in here and staring at us as if we were animals," explained Richard Lee, a twenty-year-old resident of New York's Chinatown. "But we're not really discriminated against. If you can speak English you can get through school and get a job like any American."

"We still have problems," said Mr. Lee, who wears blue jeans and lets his straight black hair grow long over his ears, "but they are more internal problems, problems of what you are, than of discrimination."

Looking around his tiny, cramped room at a picture of Raquel Welch, he said: "Our parents suppressed this identity problem for themselves, but we think about it a lot. Chinese have always considered that they are Chinese no matter where they are. Now we have to figure out what this means for us."

"Orientals Find Bias Is Down Sharply in U.S.," the *New York Times*, December 13, 1970

The Subtlety of Prejudice (1971)

Prejudice against the Orientals in America is no longer gross or blatant as in the past. Nevertheless, it is still ubiquitous although now couched in very sophisticated, subtle forms. Unfortunately, to many observers not sensitive to the new nuances of prejudice, there is the frequent misinterpretation that there is no longer any discrimination against Orientals.

The *New York Times* article of December 13, 1970, by Fox Butterfield, is an example of such misinterpretation. There is no question that the racial milieu was more oppressive in the 1940s and 1950s, when many Chinese-Americans with bachelor's degrees and even advanced university degrees could not find work in white companies, and when they could not purchase homes in the "nicer" residential areas. But this improvement has not been achieved solely by "chance." Due to the civil rights legislation of 1964, reinforced by Executive Order 11246 of September 25, 1965, companies with government contracts (including Honeywell Information Systems and virtually all other major corporations) must now pursue an affirmative action program to hire, recruit, train, and promote minority group members.

Younger Asian-Americans—in contrast to their elders who were grateful just to be in America and who were also silent for fear of deportation—expect the full rights and privilege of citizenship, not second-class status. True, many Chinese, "whose humble parents had to iron the laundry and garden the lawns of white Americans," encounter fewer barriers to becoming doctors, lawyers, architects, and professors, but it is also true these same professionals have not been able to become members of the San Francisco Board of Supervisors, Board of Education, or any other key commissions. From private industry to government agencies, Orientals in San Francisco (despite their reputed superior educational qualifications and 14 percent population) still are underrepresented in executive, managerial, supervisory, sales, personnel, and highly paid craft positions such as ironworkers, operating engineers, plumbers, and electricians.

Like the Blacks and Chicanos, conditions have improved substantially within the last two decades and it is now easier to cite a few "success" stories. But a few cases, whether they be Willie Mays, Mayor Carl Stokes, Wilson Riles, S. I. Hayakawa, or Gerald Tsai, do not prove barriers are no longer in existence. More appropriately, the question should be posed, "Why is it that so few minorities have been able to 'make it' in the system?"

The *New York Times* article states, "It is interesting that in interviews with dozens of Chinese- and Japanese-Americans from executives . . . to militant students in Chinatown, very few complaints of discrimination in jobs, housing, or education could be found." Perhaps if the *New York Times* would have sent a representative to the FEPC hearing in San Francisco on December 10, when over twenty individuals testified for three hours on problems of discrimination faced by Chinese-Americans, the conclusion drawn would have been a different one.

It is indeed unfortunate that many Orientals, who have been the direct beneficiaries of state–federal programs for equal employment opportunities, are not aware of the forces which have opened up the doors to job opportunity. It is not simply a case of, "If you have ability and can adapt to the American way of speaking, dressing, and doing things, then it doesn't matter any more if you are Chinese." Quite the contrary. Equal Employment Opportunity programs have stressed to corporations the obligation to be more tolerant of the cultural diversity presented by the various ethnic groups and subcultures of the society whether it be a Black with an Afro (hairdo) or an Oriental with an accent. For example, corporations are required to eliminate culturally biased tests such as the Wonderlic unless the tests can be demonstrated to be directly related to actual performance required on the job. In addition, minority group members have frequently been added to recruitment and promotional panels to ensure greater objectivity and to reduce the chances of racial or cultural bias. Most importantly, corporations must now set goals and timetables to consciously and deliberately seek out minority group applicants in areas where there is a current underutilization.

The *New York Times* notes that many Chinese may unknowingly perceive a crisis of identity rather than prejudice. In reality, however, the issues of discrimination, identity, and alienation are closely interconnected and in many ways inseparable. Identity crises exist because Orientals are told that if they just act white, they will be treated accordingly, but subconsciously they know that being Chinese still means they will not be allowed to join the Elks Club, "Wellesley Country Club," etc. Even if they should live in a wealthy, exclusive suburb armed with a university degree, professional licence, and great hope, the question persists whether they will be treated and accepted as equals.

We all know of many Orientals who in their quest for acceptance have rejected their Oriental identity and heritage. It is indeed a heavy price to pay for admission to a group that one must reject one's own background since this is a form of self-hatred. Even more vital and critical, Orientals are distinguished by certain physical traits and characteristics unique to Orientals. Even if an Oriental should go to the extreme of changing his name from Wong to Wright, and have surgery performed to make his eyes more oval in conformity to Western ideals of beauty, there will always be some Caucasian who will remind him that "all Orientals look alike."

From East/West, The Chinese American Journal, January 6, 1971, "The Subtlety of Prejudice," by James W. Chin

The Myth of Assimilation (1970)

The civil rights movement in this country in the last decade has contributed to a renewed awareness of social and economic justice among the rising generations; recent immigration, too, has awakened new concepts of dignity and justice, quite opposite to the established and widely held "defeatist" attitude.

But a large portion of our community still suffers under the weight of poverty, overcrowding, high rates of unemployment and underemployment, and inadequate city services. It is time that a community-wide effort be launched to assure equal employment opportunities for the Chinese and for all races. Without proper employment no "human" standard of living will ever be available to those in our community who are forced to live "ten-in-a-room" and who are unable to properly feed their children.

Limited occupational choices and employment opportunities and unfair promotional practice, in both private and public sectors, have always been the way of life for the Chinese in the United States. Most Chinese have achieved limited economic success and a certain amount of immunity toward discrimination and therefore tend to become insensitive and indifferent to the problem of job discrimination and often highly hostile to the unsuccessful majority that seeks equality and justice.

Over the years, the Chinese community has shown a tendency to overlook the relation between poverty and job discrimination.

It is both timely and significant, therefore, that an organization such as Chinese for Affirmative Action (CAA) requests "representatives of the Chinese community to . . . form a viable group as our first attempt to eliminate injustices against the Chinese people."

No doubt, a few Chinese will continue to insist that there is *no* employment problem in our community. The myth of "assimilation" and "widespread success" continues to flourish, particularly among those insensitive to the suffering of others.

We, however, do not find equal employment opportunity for all Chinese in the areas singled out by the CAA: construction, hotel, mass media, finance, and civil service. These trades and occupations, by the way, comprise well over 65 percent of the job market in San Francisco.

Chinese should be allowed to freely enter these jobs, if

qualified, and major employers in these areas should do their share in rectifying the present unjust state of affairs by opening their doors. Language and cultural differences, without adding job discrimination, already limit job opportunity for thousands of Chinese in San Francisco.

Efforts to remove additional unfair barriers toward meaningful employment must be supported by the entire community. We commend the aims of the CAA and urge all concerned and responsible citizens to take part in and support the organization.

> An editorial from *East/West, The Chinese American Journal*, July 15, 1970

Job Discrimination in San Francisco (1970)

"I believe this hearing is the first ever held for one of the Asian communities in California. It is long overdue. I am sure the commission will agree with us at the end of this two-and-a-half hour hearing that our people and resources have been exploited, our social and economic problems deliberately ignored or suppressed, our rights denied, and our hopes and aspirations destroyed by continuing harassment and intimidation. We come to assert our rights and to find effective means of rectifying both past and current wrongs committed against our people."

With these statements L. Ling-chi Wang set the tone of subsequent testimonies for a December 10, 1970, State Fair Employment Practice Commission (FEPC) hearing in San Francisco. The hearing was organized by the Chinese for Affirmative Action (CAA) of which Wang is a co-chairman.

Harriet Haber, director of the Clay Street YWCA, pointed out that although there are about 100,000 Chinese or 14 percent of the entire San Francisco population, recent studies on the local civil service in San Francisco by the Human Rights Commission show that only about 4 percent of the city's employees are Chinese. Haber also stated that minorities are rarely found in appointed positions.

Several individuals demonstrated anti-Asian bias in many

local unions and the construction industry. Quailand Tom, president of the Greater Chinatown Community Services, pointed out that a local plumbing union in 1963 had no Chinese members. Today there are only two. Frank Quinn, regional director of the Federal Equal Employment Opportunity Commission, showed that Asians comprise about 1 percent of the work force in the local construction industry. Quinn cited a union official who stated that the Chinese were too small for construction work. Quinn refuted the individual by stating that the Chinese were big enough to build the Great Wall of China and the transcontinental railroad in America.

James Chinn, an advisor to the FEPC, showed that in a random election of three San Francisco companies, Orientals are completely absent from the officials, managers, professionals, technicians, and sales categories. "The highest positions occupied by an Asian are office and clerical. The employment profiles reflected in the cases cited are not typical. Despite the fact that Orientals are inordinately industrious, ambitious, reliable, and studious, they nevertheless have found it difficult, if not impossible, to achieve full participation or mobility in this society."

Numerous other discriminatory incidents were cited by individual complainants. Representatives from the offices of Congressman Philip Burton, State Senator George Moscone, and Assemblymen John Burton, Willie Brown, and March Fong, all indicated support for the Chinese.

Lamber Choy, a CAA co-chairman, ended the hearing with six recommendations:

1. FEPC should print publicly in Chinese and Spanish and hold hearings at ethnic communities in the evening, not during working hours.
2. FEPC should hire a bilingual staff.
3. FEPC should review the construction industry periodically.
4. FEPC should investigate Mayor Alioto's office (allegedly no Chinese on his staff).
5. FEPC should remunerate ethnic people who can little

afford to lose pay when testifying.
6. FEPC should include provisions for Asians and their community in FEPC staff and commission training.

Little response was elicited from the eight members (two absent) of the state FEPC. Pier Gherini, commission chairman, indicated that more community input was needed and that Congressmen must be made aware that processes take money before things can be done. Mark Guerra, commission member, stated that he was a better man for having heard the testimonies.

After the hearing, in response to a question about what specific action FEPC would take, Gherini replied that further meetings are in order and that the commission may have to be reinstituted on a full-time basis.

An audience member queried about her reaction to the hearing replied, "I don't feel the need to pay taxes for a commission whose only function seems to be to agree that we [Chinese] have problems. I can perform that function myself."

From *Third World News*, I, no. 12, January 11, 1971

The Fair Employment Practice Commission Asian Discrimination Hearing (1970)

"Orientals are inordinately 'industrious, reliable, and smart in school' but like Avis Rent-A-Car, 'being only number two,' Chinese must try harder to prove their middle class Americanism." Author of this quote, from "A Legacy of Prejudice," December 2 issue of *East/West* newspaper, James W. Chin, spoke last Thursday night to the Asian Studies 33 class [at San Francisco State College]. Mr. Chin, an advisor to the Fair Employment Practices Commission, spoke about the San Francisco Asian Community's presentation before the Fair Employment Practices Commission (FEPC). This hearing will be held Thursday, December 10 from 2:00 to 4:00 P.M. at 455 Golden Gate Avenue, Room 1194, San Francisco.

The presentation, coordinated by the Chinese Affirmative

Action group, came about when five Asians were denied promotions to the positions of senior health inspectors for the city and county of San Francisco. They were all qualified according to their examination scores. One of the five had scored the highest on the written examination, then was placed in the lowest level because he presumably lacked the ability to deal with the public. According to Mr. Chin's personal experience with this man, there was no lack of ability. Mr. Chin also indicated that all five had graduated from the University of California at Berkeley, School of Public Health, and that some of the Caucasians selected over them had not more than high school diplomas.

The main purpose of the hearing is to inform the commissioners and public of the fact that Asians do have problems; they have not "made it." It also provides an opportunity for Asians to come together and actively voice their opinions.

Specific problems this hearing would like to present include the need for Asian-American consultants for the FEPC staff. A second problem is the need for in-service training of FEPC staff in Asian-American problems.

Mr. Chin also spoke generally about discrimination in hiring. He feels there is a need for active displays of fair employment practices, such as actually hiring and promoting minorities, not just the passive "I'm not prejudiced," with poor minority hiring records. There should also be minority members on the selection panels. This way, when minorities are interviewed, there is someone on the panel who understands and relates to the applicants' responses. This minimizes the chances of discrimination through ignorance.

Mr. Chin welcomes attendance or participation in the hearing. If anyone has information, that is, if you know someone or have personally been involved in discriminatory hiring or promoting or would like to attend the hearing, contact George Kagiwada at the Asian American Studies Division Office in Building B, Aggie Villa, 752-3625.

From *Third World News*, December 7, 1970, by Thomas Yang Chinn and Shirley Takemori

Orientals Complain of Examination Bias (1970)

A "Chinaman's chance" is no chance—a dead horse at the gate, hopeless, scratched. You're not in the running. So when a Civil Service Commission examiner called you a Chinaman, what chance do you have?

For the first time in the city's history, five Oriental health inspectors from the San Francisco Department of Public Health dared protest against the Civil Service Commission, claiming they were victims of discrimination in promotional examinations.

The five complainants, Donald Chan, Chong D. Koo, George Kusaba, Wilbur Lee and William Wong filed charges with the State Fair Employment Practice Commission which were heard on September 3 and 4.

Last year thirty-two candidates for senior and/or principal food and environmental health inspectors took oral and written examinations. Fourteen passed the written exams to qualify for the oral tests leading to seven permanent openings.

HIDDEN BIAS

The five Orientals passed the written, but failed the oral exams. And this is, the five charged, because of a hidden bias and cultural differences of the examiners.

The oral tests were the same at those given in all Civil Service examinations for promotions to supervisory and administrative positions.

One thousand points are given in the examinations with 500 for the written portion, 400 for the oral interviews, and 100 points given by supervisors for meritorious services.

The basis for oral scoring is based on personal traits, education, experience, and overall evaluation.

All five of the complainants are graduates of the University of California and qualified by education, training, and experience in their speciality fields.

Chong D. Koo, one of the inspectors, complained that his examiner asked him if he did "what all Chinamen do, play the lottery," when Koo told him he went to Reno occasionally in his leisure time.

He identified the examiner as A. Henry Bliss, associate professor in public health at the University of California in Berkeley.

Koo objected to the use of the word "Chinamen."

TOUGH

Dr. Bliss was cited by other complainants as tough and formal, yet relaxed with those who scored high in the oral. This was indicated in the replays of the test tapes. Successful candidates were put at ease with innocuous exchanges of patter before questioning. Another point brought up was that one of the high scorers was a former student of Dr. Bliss.

The other two examiners, William H. Renner, a senior inspector from San Mateo, and Kenneth Pool, a shellfish specialist with the public health service, knew some of the successful candidates who are members of the National Association of Sanitarians. After a lunch break one of the examiners greeted a candidate by his first name as they entered the examination room.

Pool also came in for criticism at the hearing when George Kusaba, one of the complainants who is of Japanese descent, said he was "unnerved" by Pool's remark on his war record.

Kusaba, who was interned at the start of World War II, served in the U.S. Army in the last year of conflict. Pool commented, "I see you got in at the tail end of the war." Kusaba considered the comment a racial slur.

SUBTLE

Another of the complainants, Wilbur Lee, testified at the hearing, "Discrimination is not something you can wrap your fingers around and say, 'Here it is.' It's subtle, a singular experience."

According to Lee, there was a wide range of treatment extended the promotion candidates. For some, the length of interviews ran only eight minutes. Lee was questioned for half an hour.

FEPC attorney Charles E. Wilson charged that the oral examinations were manipulated to accommodate certain candidates. He also pointed out that the normal cut-off point for civil service examinations at 70 percent was dropped to 60 percent in this case.

Charts were exhibited at the hearing to substantiate the charge that grades were maneuvered in the oral test to upgrade and downgrade final scores.

In the case of John O'Rourke, who barely passed the written exam at 350.30, tying for the last position in the field of fourteen for senior inspector, was first in the orals at 367.47, for a total of 717.77 and a job.

On the other hand, Wilbur Lee, who ranged number one in the principal inspector written test, was last in the oral, to cut his gross points to 696.45 and out of contention.

PADDED

The graphs revealed a same pattern for the Orientals who scored high in written exams but ridiculously low in the orals, with the oral score padded for those candidates who won promotions.

It was pointed out that the uneven scoring extended to a white candidate also.

The civil service provides the oral appraisal board with a suggested scale to score candidates on pertinent experience and education. A breakdown of the oral tests showed that the scoring deviated from the suggested rate by as much as 5.5 points. And always in favor of candidates needing points to compensate for a low written exam grade.

The five Oriental complainants realized that they are sticking out their necks in challenging the Civil Service Commission in complaining to the FEPC. But they feel that the days of the stoic, passive Asian who suffers in silence is over. Uncle Tong is dead.

From *East/West, The Chinese American Journal,* September 16, 1970, "Orientals Complain of Job Bias," by Ken Wong

The Hearing of the "Orientals Five" (1970)

East/West:

It was never meant to hit the headlines like the trials of the "Chicago Seven" and the "Los Sietes." But the Orientals Five discrimination hearing will long reverberate throughout the Asian community for some time to come.

Of course, it was not a "trial" but an informal hearing before the California State Fair Employment Practice Commission at State Building on September 3 and 4. Its significance lies in the fact that this is the first open hearing on discrimination charges filed by persons of Oriental ancestry in the FEPC's eleven-year history. Within a week, Chairman P. Gherini will hand down a decision.

The gist of the case has been well publicized and need not to be repeated here. However, to avoid confusion the reader should be made aware that the oral examination where alleged discrimination was involved covered two different job classifications: principal health inspector and senior health inspector. And while the case is still pending, the San Francisco Civil Commission has already appointed the seven highest Caucasian candidates to respective positions. Should the FEPC decision favor the Orientals a new oral examination will be held and a new set of eligible lists will be established.

The feeling of loneliness and uncertainty was evident among the Five during the second day of the hearing. They shouldn't be. They received plenty of moral support not only from the Chinese fellow workers but also from the few Chinese professionals in civil rights. Among the twenty or so observers there were Attorney Gordon Lau, James Chin of Department of Defense Contract Compliance, Stanley Lim of San Francisco Human Rights Commission, and Leonard Kiang of Economic Development in Chinatown. James Chin, by the way, is on the FEPC's Technical Advisory Committee on Testing.

Before the tapes were played during the second day of the hearing an unusual move was made by Stanley Lim of Human Rights. Lim suggested to the hearing panel that expert witnesses knowledgeable of employment problems of Orientals should be called to testify. It was rejected by Chairman Gherini on grounds it was not connected to the case.

During the replay of the oral tapes, Dr. Harry Bliss' remark on Chong Koo "... I suppose you like to play the lotteries like all good Chinamen ..." was heard twice. This is one of the main contentions of the discrimination charges leveled by the Orientals. Koo emphasized that he took offense at the use of the word "Chinamen." Of course, another oral board member, Kenneth Pool, a U.S. public health official, commented on the Japanese-American George Kusaba's service record "you're caught at the tail end of the draft ..." got Kusaba all "shook up" as he testified. These two incidents seem to have casted some impact on the hearing panel.

FEPC attorney Charles Wilson's eloquent summation really tells it like it is. Wilson, a black, cited the case as a prime example of maneuvering and manipulation by the San Francisco Civil Service to get the people they want and to get rid of the person they don't want. The five Orientals are victims of this system, he said.

Wilson then gave two examples of how this is being done. According to testimonies submitted, J. O'Rourke, a Caucasian candidate, finished last in the field of fourteen in the Senior Health Inspector written exam, but the oral panel scored him so high he became the number three man on the final list. On the other hand, Wilbur K. Lee, top scorer in the Principal Health Inspector exam and number two man in the written Senior Inspector series, finished last and thirteenth, respectively, by virtue of the low oral scores.

Another example of inequity in scoring: a Caucasian who has eighteen years of appropriate experience received ninety-four points in experience rating while Japanese-American Kusaba, who has a total of nineteen years of qualified experience, got eighty-nine points. Need I say more?

It was reported that the CACA (Chinese American Citizens Alliance) sent a protest telegram to the Los Angeles Civil Service Commission to support the appointment of a

Chinese chief sanitarian in Los Angeles. I wonder did they do the same for the Chinese here? We do not have an organization like the NAACP or the Urban League; maybe a civil rights division ought to be incorporated into the CACA or the Chinese Six Companies?

Whatever the outcome of this hearing may be, one thing is certain: the so-called silent minority need not to be silent anymore. The Chinese has a beautiful phase about citizen's protest—*"fu p'ing tse ming."* That's exactly what Messrs. Lee, Koo, Kusaba, Chan and Wong did. They have every reason to be proud of the action they took. No doubt it has caused them much mental anguish and frustration. I say it's better to get it out of your chest.

Right on!

—Kai M. Lui

From *East/West, The Chinese American Journal*, September 16, 1970

Red Tape or Racism: The Strange Case of Mr. Ching (1971)

The appointment of Francis Ching, top-ranking candidate for the position of Director of Arboreta and Botanical Gardens for Los Angeles County, was delayed again as the County Board of Supervisors granted a request made by the twenty-five-man Board of Governors for the Arboreta and Botanical Gardens for additional time to assess the "public relations and social abilities" of candidates for the position.

It was the second time in less than three months that Ching, a Hawaiian of Chinese descent, topped the civil service list, only to have his appointment denied. The latest delay was granted on March 11, after Maurice Machris, president of the Board of Governors, claimed that he learned of the results of the latest civil service examination for the position only a few days earlier. The examination results had been public knowledge for more than a week.

Machris, when requesting the delay, stated, "It is an important job that involves the image of the people of Los Angeles

County. We just can't go by some pieces of paper concerning a man's qualifications."

A few days after the delay was granted, the Board of Governors scheduled a luncheon for March 26. Candidates for the directorship were invited to give fifteen-minute talks on any subject of their choice. The luncheon was to be followed by cocktails at the home of one of the Governors.

"It was all very social," Ching told *Gidra* reporters after the luncheon. He added that candidates were never questioned about their views concerning the position of director.

The job, which pays from $18,628 to $25,704 a year, became vacant on January 1, when Dr. William Stewart left to take a position with the Pacific Tropical Botanical Gardens of Hawaii.

CHING PLACES FIRST

The selection of a new director is in the hands of the twenty-five-man Board of Governors of the Arboreta and Botanical Gardens, which is composed of citizens appointed by members of the County Board of Supervisors. The Board of Supervisors acts on recommendations submitted to it by the Board of Governors. (Two Asian Americans, Kay Iizuka of Gardena and John Fukushima of Los Angeles, are members of the Board of Governors.)

The first civil service examination was given on September 19. Aside from Ching, the only other person to pass the exam was Dr. John Beard, director of Kings Botanic Gardens in Perth, Australia, who was highly regarded by several of the Governors. He was so highly regarded, in fact, that he was allowed to take the examination a week before the publicly announced date.

Ching placed first, followed by Beard. However, the Board of Governors passed over Ching and nominated Beard for the position. Beard was ultimately rejected by the Board of Supervisors because he did not possess U.S. citizenship.

In selecting Beard over Ching, the Board of Governors, in contrast with its latest stand, felt that personal interviews with the candidates were unnecessary. Ching wrote personal letters to all twenty-five governors expressing a desire to meet personally with them to discuss the job and his qualifications. He received no replies. Board president Machris denied ever receiving such a letter.

After Beard's rejection, the Board of Governors decided to scrap the results of the first examination, arguing that the examination failed to produce the three candidates customarily required.

A second examination was scheduled for February 13 with requirements on administrative experience that were eased somewhat to attract more candidates. Machris also requested that this examination include questions relating to "the public relations and social aspects of the candidates."

Ching again finished atop the list, only to have his appointment delayed to enable the Governors to evaluate his "public relations and social abilities" at the March 26 luncheon.

RACIAL PREJUDICE CHARGED

The situation is complicated by charges made by Dr. H. Hamilton Williams, a Negro biologist in turfgrass research and education, that Ching is racially prejudiced. Williams, himself a candidate for the directorship until he failed to make the civil service list after the first examination, also accused the Civil Service Commission of "ineptness in examination procedures which resulted in severe breaches of professionalism."

Ching responded to Williams' accusations of racial prejudice by stating that of the top six supervisory positions he has filled in the last year, two went to Negroes, two to Mexican-Americans, and two to whites. He also chided the Board of Governors for not granting him an opportunity to answer the charges brought by Williams.

"I am very disappointed," says Ching, "but I have been fighting for a year and I am not going to quit now. I think I am fully capable of doing the job. I am the only one who has gone through two examinations. I am not bitter to anyone. I intend to keep cool and do my job."

Things are rapidly coming to a head. Some members of the Board of Governors have said loudly and publicly that they won't appoint Ching "if he is the last candidate in the world." Many people in the Asian American community, including more than a dozen members of JUST (Japanese United in Search of Truth) Committee of Noguichi-case fame, are following the case closely. "We won't stand idly by . . . if the situation arises, we'll move," stated a member of the group.

And so the stage is set for the April 7 meeting of the Board of Governors, when the Board may decide its own fate, along with that of Francis Ching.

Late Bulletin: The County Board of Supervisors appointed Francis Ching after transferring the power of appointment from the Board of Governors to themselves. The Governors selected Henry Hellmers, who placed second to Ching in the latest examination, but were overruled by the Board of Supervisors. Maurice Machris, president of the Board of Governors, resigned in protest.

From *Gidra*, April 17, 1971

A Human Rights Commission Reports on Civil Service Job Bias (1969)

Job discrimination against minority groups in the form of underrepresentation at all levels, except at the low-paying, nontechnical and semiskilled levels, still exists in San Francisco civil service is the conclusion of a lengthy report, "Racial and Ethnic Employment Pattern Survey of City and County of San Francisco Employees," released on September 10 by the Human Rights Commission (HRC). The report, prepared by Francisco J. Aviles, State Department of Human Resources Development, shows that out of a total of 19,261 city employees, 13,525 or 70.3 percent are whites, 4,054 or 21 percent blacks, 549 or 2.9 percent Spanish-surnames and 834 or 4.3 percent Chinese and Japanese. (These figures do not include employees in the Unified School District, Housing

Authority and S.F. Redevelopment Agency.) This short article is *not* a report on the survey, but a study on the results of the survey with special emphasis on the Chinese.

PROCEDURES AND METHODOLOGY

The survey, conducted in December 1969, covered employees, both "permanent" and "temporary," in sixty-eight departments or subdivisions, and was based on master payroll tapes with data on ethnic origin and position level on each employee added to the final tabulation. Results of the survey are printed in three tables: Table I, "Summary of Occupational Categories by Racial/Ethnic Distribution—All City Employees," Table II, "Summary of Occupational Categories by Racial/Ethnic Distribution—By Departments," and Table III, "Summary by Monthly Salaries (Gross)." Occupational categories are patterned after those used by the U.S. Commission on Civil Rights. Each category is broken down by ethnic origins and position levels: entrance, promotive and appointive, indicating how employees gained their present civil service classifications. Racial/ethnic information includes White, Negro, Spanish-origin, Oriental (Japanese and Chinese), Filipino, American Indian and other nonwhite. This system of ethnic breakdown regrettingly renders any study on Chinese employees in civil service impossible, if not outright confusing. For example, the lone Oriental in managerial position in the Department of Park and Recreation (total employees: 1,227) is a Korean or the only Oriental in the same position in the Mayor's Office happens to be a Japanese. The monthly salaries table collaborates well with the table on occupational categories. Information on civil service salary range for each category, if given, could be very useful. The assumption that the city's population has 12 percent black, 10 percent Spanish-surname and 10 percent Oriental is false. Chinese population alone is at least 10 percent, not to mention the Japanese, Koreans, Filipinos and Indo-Chinese.

OCCUPATIONAL CATEGORIES

Here is the ethnic breakdown of all city employees, by percentages, in the ten occupational categories:

Managerial (397 employees): white: 90.4; black: 4.3; Spanish-surname: 1.7; Oriental: 8.1.

Technical (675): white: 49.3; black: 31.3; Spanish-surname: 4.3; Oriental: 8.7.

Clerical (2,682): white: 73.6; black: 11.9; Spanish-surname: 3.6; Oriental: 8.7.

Craftsmen (1,670): W: 91.1; B: 3.7; SS: 2.4: O: 2.2.

Operatives (1,958); W: 44; B: 51.4; SS: 1.6; O: 1.5.

Laborers (661): W: 51.7; B: 43.4; SS: 4.8; O: 0.2.

Uniformed Protective Services (3,596): W: 93.5; B: 3; SS: 2.9; O: 0.2.

Service Workers (2,758): W: 28.3; B: 61.9; SS: 4.3; O: 2.1.

Agricultural and Horticultural Workers (441): W: 86.1; B: 7.1; SS: 3.9; O: 1.7.

It is obvious that Chinese are underrepresented in every category and that most of the better paying jobs and positions of power are currently occupied by whites. The breakdown by position levels in each category further reveals that all minority employees score poorly in appointive positions. For example, in the managerial category, 80 are whites, 2 blacks, 3 Spanish-surnames and 2 Orientals. Appointive positions in the professional category similarly show that 534 are whites, 17 blacks, 6 Spanish-surnames and 21 Orientals. Only in three out of ten categories—professional, technical, and clerical— do the Chinese come close to semblance of fair representation. Finally, these figures support charges of discrimination leveled by Chinese for Affirmative Action (CAA) earlier this year.

DEPARTMENTAL PATTERNS

The following chart shows the number of Oriental (Chinese and Japanese) employees in all ten categories, in selected city departments:

Departments	Total	Oriental	% of Or.
Controller.............	362	68	18.8
Electricity.............	105	1	1.0
Fire	1,743	6	0.3
Juvenile Court..........	158	6	3.8
Library	442	87	19.7
Municipal Court	154	12	7.8
Muni Railway...........	2,646	57	2.2
Police.................	1,966	19	1.0
Port Commission........	377	8	2.1
Public Health—Central..	611	72	10.9
Emergency Hospital.....	95	0	0.0
Laguna Honda..........	1,070	29	2.7
General Hospital........	2,140	66	3.1
Building Inspection	134	18	13.4
Building Repair.........	384	7	1.8
Public Works—Engineer.	284	58	20.4
Street Cleaning.........	349	1	0.3
Street Repair	194	2	1.0
Recreation and Park	1,227	46	3.7
Sheriff	188	0	0.0
Social Services..........	1,305	100	7.7
Water..................	531	28	5.3
Youth Guidance	138	3	2.2

It could be seen from the chart that Chinese are found mostly in controller's offices, libraries, public health and public works, indicating traditional Chinese preference, not by choice, but by necessity, for accounting, engineering and architecture. Practically no Chinese are hired in essential protective services, such as police and fire departments and sheriffs' offices. No Chinese work in emergency hospitals. Youth guidance, juvenile courts, hospitals and social services could use more bilingual Chinese workers at all levels. Insufficient number of bilingual workers means Chinese-speaking taxpayers are getting shortchanged in services.

MONTHLY SALARIES

Uneven and, therefore, unjust distribution of taxpayers' money is inevitable in view of the employment patterns shown above. Table III shows that 8,657 white employees, compared with only 423 Orientals, have a monthly salary of over $800. Monthly salary, of course, depends on the type of job one gets. At this moment, the high-paying jobs seem to go almost exclusively to whites, as if no minority persons are qualified for those positions.

CONCLUSIONS

From this short study, the following conclusions emerge:

1. Survey method must be refined and ethnic origins sharply distinguished.
2. Discrimination against the Chinese still exists in city's civil service. Discrimination occurs in recruitment, hiring and promotion in every department.
3. Essential services for city's residents are unevenly distributed. Non-English speakers invariably are shortchanged.
4. Civil Service Commission must reexamine its recruitment, hiring, and promotion partices so that more minority workers could join civil service. At least 10 percent Chinese should be found in every major category, as CAA contends.

SAN FRANCISCO CIVIL SERVICE OCCUPATIONAL CATEGORIES

1. *Officials and Managers:* Administrative personnel who establish and/or administer broad policies and direct individual departments or special phases of an operation. Includes: officials, executives, middle management, department managers, executive secretaries, and kindred workers.

2. *Professional:* Specialized personnel with either college education or equivalent experience. Includes: accountants and auditors, social workers, editors, engineers, lawyers, li-

brarians and labor relations workers, investigators and inspectors, registered nurses, physicians, social scientists, computer programmers, and kindred workers.

3. *Technical:* Specialized personnel with a combination of basic scientific knowledge and manual skill usually obtained through two years of post high school education, or through equivalent on-the-job training. Includes: draftsmen, engineering aides, junior engineers, mathematical aides, licensed, practical, or vocational nurses, radio operators, photographers, scientific assistants, surveyors, technicians (medical, electronic, physical sciences), computer operators, barbers and beauticians, and kindred workers.

4. *Office and Clerical:* All clerical personnal, regardless of the level of difficulty, in which the activities are predominantly nonmanual. Includes: bookkeepers, cashiers, collectors (bills and accounts), messengers and office boys, office machine operators, shipping and receiving clerks, stenographers, typists, secretaries, key punch operators, telephone operators, and kindred workers.

5. *Craftsmen:* Manual workers of relatively high skill level having a thorough and comprehensive knowledge of the processes involved in their work. Exercise considerable independent judgment and usually receive an extesive period of training. Includes: foremen, the building trades, mechanics and repairmen, skilled machining occupations, electricians, engravers, heavy equipment operators, stationary engineers, tailors, and kindred workers.

6. *Operatives:* Workers who operate machine or processing equipment or perform other mechanical type duties of intermediate skill level which can be mastered in several weeks and requires limited training. Includes: apprentices (of all the skilled trades), operatives, delivery men, motormen, drivers, seamstresses, and kindred workers.

7. *Laborers:* Workers in manual occupations which generally require no special training. Includes: garage laborers, car washers and greasers, garbage and trash collectors, construction laborers, street and highway maintenance laborers, and kindred workers.

8. *Uniformed Protective Services:* Includes personnel of the police department, fire department, and the sheriff's office.

9. *Service Workers:* Workers in protective and nonprotective service occupations (excluding those employees listed under No. 8). Includes: attendants (hospital, other institutions, recreation, and personal service), hospital aides, orderlies, janitors, charwomen and cleaners, cooks, porters, elevator operators, guards, watchmen, and kindred workers.

10. *Agricultural and Horticultural Workers:* Includes: farmers, gardeners, tree toppers, landscaping and street planting supervisors, agricultural inspectors, groundkeepers, and kindred workers.

From *East/West, The Chinese American Journal,* September 23, 1970, by L. Ling-chi Wang

We Are All Americans (1971)

LAUNDRYMAN'S FAMILY

Mrs. Lee was born in Louisiana. She came from a New Orleans laundryman's family of seven sisters, one brother and two half-brothers.

The family record of accomplishment is one of which any father would be proud:

Four public school teachers, a registered nurse, a medical technician, an X-ray technician, a postal supervisor and two businessmen.

When Mrs. Lee came to California she found widespread discrimination against those of Chinese descent.

"There were many parallels between California Chinese and southern Negroes," she said. "On my public records, I saw racial designations changed from 'yellow' to 'white' while in Louisiana. But when I came to California, I once again had to write 'yellow.'

"From the original Constitution of California, education was said to be free for all persons. A little later, segregation of Mongolians crept in and continued throughout many districts of California."

SEGREGATED SCHOOL

Segregation was not limited to the distant past. Mrs. Lee pointed out that her husband attended a segregated school in Walnut Grove in southern Sacramento County, in the 1940s. This occurred even though he was a third-generation Californian.

The response to the discrimination came in unique form. The Chinese immigrant became determined to achieve in a scholarly way.

"Some suggest that the Chinese achieved because of discrimination more than in spite of it," Mrs. Lee said.

She does not totally accept this theory. But she believes the class divisions created did provide some motivation for one to excel academically in order to neutralize the effects of racial prejudice.

SEGREGATION EVEN TODAY

Segregation of Chinese students exists today in one school of the Sacramento City Unified School District, according to Mrs. Lee. The legally established limit which determines ethnic imbalance has been surpassed by Chinese in the Riverside School.

"There has been no attempt to balance Riverside ethnically," she explained, "probably because there is no problem in achievement. At Riverside School, achievement is among the highest of any school in the city.

"However, the problem, as I see it, is the language facility. If the children speak mostly Chinese at home and then their peers speak broken English at school, they have no model to emulate.

"Studies have shown that while Chinese are generally good achievers in most professions, they avoid those requiring proficiency in the English language."

From the *Sacramento Bee*, January 17, 1971

No Right to Bilingual Classes (1970)

Federal Judge Lloyd H. Burke has ruled that non-English-speaking Chinese schoolchildren in San Francisco have no legal right to special English language instruction in schools. A lawsuit was filed March 25 by thirteen Chinese-speaking parents on behalf of nearly 3,000 Chinese-speaking students who need special help in English in order to function adequately in regular classrooms.

According to Attorney Edward Steinmen of Neighborhood Legal Assistance, representing the parents and students, the case is on its way to the U.S. Court of Appeal. In view of the latest decision by Robert H. Finch, Secretary of HEW, . . . it now appears possible for the U.S. Office for Civil Rights to join the lawsuit or to ask Judge Burke to reopen the case. He made the ruling last Thursday.

The suit, filed in U.S. District Court, contends that to be denied special bilingual instruction in English is to be denied an education. According to a recent survey by the S.F. Unified School District, about 3,000 Chinese-speaking students, including nine of the plaintiffs, currently receive *no* special instruction at all. Of the remaining students, most—including four of the plaintiffs—receive such instruction from non-Chinese-speaking teachers, usually for less than one hour a day.

According to the complaint, the school system's failure to provide special bilingual instruction in English violates not only the plaintiff's constitutional and statutory rights to an education, but also their rights to learn English. The lawsuit seeks both injunctive and declaratory relief to require the school system and Board of Supervisors, named as defendants, to provide all Chinese-speaking students with a meaningful education.

A hearing was held May 12 before Judge Burke, former U.S. attorney in charge of, among other things, prosecuting thousands of immigration cases, many of them involving Chinese.

The defendants were represented by city attorney Ray Williamson, also well known to the Chinese community. However, the entire two-and-a-half hour proceeding was a seesawing exchange between Burke and Steinman, with Williamson listening on the sideline.

The judge said that "the defendants recognize the importance of an education and equal educational opportunities, and make education available to plaintiffs on the *same* terms and conditions as it is available to other groups within the school district." He added that the defendants "have made special efforts toward remedial education programs for Chinese-speaking students."

In handing down his decision, Judge Burke stated, "This Court fully recognizes that the Chinese-speaking students involved in this action have special needs, specifically the need to have special instruction in English. To provide such special instruction would be a desirable and commendable approach to take. Yet this Court cannot say that such an approach is legally required. On the contrary, plaintiffs herein seek relief for a special need—which they allege is necessary if their rights to an education and equal educational opportunities are to be received—that does not constitute a right which would create a duty on defendants' part to act. These Chinese-speaking students—by receiving the same education made available on the same terms and conditions to the other tens of thousands of students in the S.F. Unified School District—are legally receiving all their rights to an education and to equal educational opportunities. Their special needs, however acute, do not accord them special rights above those granted other students." On the request for bilingual teachers, the judge ruled, "Although this Court and both parties recognize that a bilingual approach to educating Chinese-speaking students is both a desirable and effective method, though not the only one, plaintiffs have no right to a bilingual education. Again, this Court is in no position to mandate that such instruction must be given by bilingual Chinese-speaking teachers; though desirable, there is no legal basis to require it."

No decision from the appellate court is expected for at least five months. The case could eventually reach the U.S. Supreme Court.

> From *East/West, The Chinese American Journal*, June 3, 1970, by L. Ling-chi Wang

Chinese and the Media *(1970)*

Media coverage of Chinese events has been neither accurate nor truly representative of the Chinese community in San Francisco. Those charges were made during a KNBR-NBC Radio panel discussion last Sunday evening between community and media spokesmen.

Dr. Dennis Wong, founding chairman of Project Concern, said, "Mass media is not really performing its duties . . . they have been neglecting the good things and efforts by fine people to improve the community." Dr. Wong noted that the media was instrumental in forming public opinion of communities.

Newspaper, television, and radio "continue to reinforce an image of the Chinese as foreigners; they are regarded as guests in a host country," said Loni Ding, of the Chinatown–North Beach Neighborhood Arts Program. "The Chinese are portrayed as peculiar, quaint, and mystifying," she said.

Moon Eng, new chairman of Asian Studies at San Francisco State College, said that media had failed to cover specific community movements; he cited the sparse coverage of the May 18 Asian Anti-War and Poverty demonstration in Chinatown as an example. "Media is forcing communities to turn to violence in an attempt to capture the kind of public attention necessary for the alleviation of social problems."

Eng also said that media did not focus on the issues that mattered to the Chinese community and that most events that were reported were from the "white perspective," or what would be important to the white community.

Ling-chi Wang, co-director, Ford Foundation Research

Grant on Chinatown Problems, said that the media coverage of Chinese had been influenced by the negative U.S. relationship with China. "We are not really dealing with a minority," he said, adding that there was a close relationship between the 800 million Chinese in China and the 10 percent Chinese population in San Francisco.

Wang spoke of the failure of radio and television stations to make broadcast time available to the Chinese community.

Scott Blakey, urban affairs editor of the *San Francisco Chronicle*, suggested that the community and the media work together to find constructive ways of changing the traditional news coverage of minorities. "The young people," said Blakey, "would have to go to all the media and 'squeak until they get their share of the oil.'"

Blakey noted that the men who run the newspapers are sensitive to change, although, he admitted, that change would be slow in coming.

Victor Wong, photographer for KQED Newsroom, said that the Chinese community needed to increase its own press efforts to tell the outside media what Chinatown events needed coverage.

KNBR-NBC newsman Robert Lazich moderated the program, third in the KNBR series "Rap Session: Minorities vs. the Media."

From East/West, The Chinese American Journal, June 24, 1970, by Gimmi Park Li

Heard, But Not Seen (1970)

East/West:

I feel that I must set the record straight in reference to an article which appeared in the *San Francisco Chronicle* July 11. The article, "Job Bias Charge Denied," reported that KRON and KCBS denied that they have in any way discriminated against hiring Chinese-Americans.

After I graduated from San Francisco State College in 1954 with a radio-television/broadcasting degree, I was inter-

Have They Made It?—A Conclusion 253

viewed by all the Bay Area radio and television stations (including KRON and KCBS). Although I did not have any commercial experience, my college experience on the campus radio station was comparable to any radio-television graduate. I did not land a job for a couple of months, and each time the "we'll call you, don't call us" routine really meant "we can't hire you unless you are an artist or engineer, but not for on-the-air work, because, you see, you're Chinese."

I have now been in braodcasting for over sixteen years and fortunately there have been broadcasters such as Mr. William C. Dempsey, Mr. Philip G. Lasky, Mr. John Thompson, and Mr. William D. Pabst who were "color-blind" and gave me a job based upon my qualifications and ability. I don't think that I have disappointed them, since I have directed everything from pro-basketball to Romper Room. But only when it became obvious to me that I would never land an on-the-air job, did I turn to directing and I was first successful at KPIX and now at KTVU.

In 1958 or 1959, after several years of directing at KPIX, I applied for a job at KRON and was introduced by Mr. Vern Louden (a director for KRON) to Mr. Douglas Elleson, the program manager, "as one of the best young directors in the area." But while we talked, Mr. Elleson, for some reason, kept emphasizing the Chinese-Americans on the art department staff and the Chinese-Americans on the engineering staff. Needless to say, I did not land the director's job open.

Mr. Jim Simon of KCBS was quoted in the *Chronicle* article as saying he "has actively tried to recruit a Chinese-American broadcaster" and he speaks of one in Phoenix. I know of whom he speaks, for this young Chinese, Mr. Sam Chu Lin, called upon me a few years ago, because I was and am among a handful of Chinese-American television directors in the United States.

The gist of what I told him was that even as cosmopolitan as the San Francisco Bay Area seems to be, no radio or television station is going to hire an Oriental for on-the-air work. I advised Sam to turn to "behind the scenes" work. And if he really wanted on-the-air work he should stick with it and someday he'd make it. Sam has now been quite successful on

CBS radio feeds and on KOOL-TV on-air work in Phoenix. For your information, Mr. Simon and Mr. See, only a couple of months ago I spoke to Sam Chu Lin in regard to the news personnel changes here at KTVU, and I know that a phone call from either of you would bring him running.

The phrase "Equal Opportunity Employer" used by Mr. See and Mr. Simon are nice words to hear, but for the Chinese-American, it still means behind the scenes in broadcasting. One picture would truly be worth a thousand of your words.

Sincerely yours,
George Lum
Director

From <i>East/West, The Chinese American Journal,</i> July 15, 1970

Discrimination Is a Subtle Thing (1971)

East/West:

Your recent editorials (December 2 and 16) in support of the position of Mr. Irvin Lai and the Chinese American Citizens Alliance, Los Angeles Lodge, to overcome bias against people of Chinese descent was most heartening. The Chinese American Citizens Alliance has a long history of crusading for the rights of the Chinese people in the United States and especially in seeking equitable immigration laws. Social problems are ever changing and we of the Alliance endeavor to meet the needs and problems facing all of us.

More specifically and recently Los Angeles Lodge has been more active on many fronts such as participation in the creation of the Oriental Study Center at UCLA, raising funds for one of the local community hospitals, providing facilities for job agents and social workers who assist new immigrants, and supporting the County Coroner Thomas Noguchi in his fight to hold office. Further, the Lodge played a major role in assisting one of our own brothers to attain a promotion which was being denied him for political reasons despite the fact that he was number one—eighteen points ahead of the next

Have They Made It?—A Conclusion

closest candidate—in a civil service examination in the County Health Department.

This brings us to the most recent incident involving Mr. Irvin Lai and the Bank of America. Presently, the Lodge is engaged in discussions with the bank in hopes that some program will be initiated in Los Angeles by the bank which will benefit the whole Chinese community. We have been informed by the Bank of America that they have awarded the construction contract and will not reopen bids. In any event, Mr. Lai would not be afforded the opportunity to bid even if new bids were permitted as he will not bid having brought attention to this situation, not so much for himself, but for the community at large.

We of the Lodge were most sorry to read a letter in your December 16, 1970, edition from a Los Angeles resident. His naïveté is most unfortunate and his inference on the character of Mr. Lai, shockingly irresponsible. Your reader is grossly ignorant of the facts, and ironically, guilty of the very charge he made against your newspaper.

As you most discerningly pointed out in your December 16 editorial, "... discrimination is a subtle thing...." Because it is not obvious is no reason for deluding ourselves into believing that it does not exist nor reason for fearing to fight it.

Your reader has suggested that shouting and belligerent methods were employed. Nothing can be further from the truth. Mr. Lai, like the gentleman he is, wrote letters to the Bank of America and had several discussions with the management. The CACA Los Angeles Lodge wrote a letter to the bank, after reviewing the facts and correspondence from both Mr. Lai and the bank representatives.

Subsequently, this writer, as president of the Lodge, had several discussions with personnel of the bank, which are continuing as indicated above. If these are belligerent methods, there is no civilized approach to disagreement.

What effect will all this have on other minority contractors, your reader asks. A most salutary one we believe. Before this situation arose, it was indicated by the bank that they knew of no Chinese contractors who could do work of this type required. They are now keenly aware of the many capable contractors of Chinese descent in this area. No one is asking for an advantage. Mr. Lai, as do all of us, only wishes to have the opportunity to compete.

If you have readers who are unaware of the many existing social problems but have an open mind and are willing to do something constructive, let this be an open invitation for them to join us. They may learn of the problems of recent immigrants, their children, the aged, the exploited, and the need for adult education. They undoubtedly will be inspired by the fine young people in the Oriental Study Center at UCLA, the numerous tutorial projects, and the Chinatown Youth Council, to mention a few.

Membership in the Alliance is open to all males of Chinese descent, who are United States citizens, twenty-one years of age, self-supporting and above all, of good moral character and intestinal fortitude. The purpose and object of our Alliance are, "To form a more perfect body; to inculcate the principles of Charity, Justice, Brotherly Love, and Fidelity among the members; to promote the general welfare and happiness of its members and the Chinese communities; to quicken the spirit of American patriotism; to ensure the legal rights of its members; and to secure equal economic and political opportunities for its members," and the cardinal principles upon which our Alliance is founded, are, "To fully enjoy and defend our American citizenship; to cultivate the mind through the exchange of knowledge; to effect a higher character among the members; and to fully observe and practice the principles of Brotherly Love and mutual help. It is imperative that no member shall have sectional, clannish, tong, or party prejudices against one another, or to use such influences to oppress fellow members."

Nowland C. Hong
President,
Los Angeles Lodge
Chinese American Citizens Alliance

From *East/West, The Chinese American Journal*, February 17, 1971

The Culture and Trade Center and Unfair Hiring (1970)

The following is extracted from a series of three editorials broadcast on San Francisco's KGO-TV last month. The series, delivered on the air by editorial director Herb Levy, not only details some of the problems of Chinese workers, but also offers suggestions which may help the construction trades avoid similar instances of discrimination in the future.

The Chinese community thanks KGO for its social awareness and for its efforts to bring problems such as this one before the public for general consideration and discussion.

This graceful twenty-seven-story building which towers above historic Portsmouth Square in the heart of Chinatown is a significant contribution to the economy of San Francisco. It is also a constant and galling reminder to the Chinese that they face job discrimination in every way possible.

In constructing this building, now 90 percent completed, no more than ten Chinese workers were employed at any one time. This constituted about 6 percent of the work force. Many reasons were given why they weren't employed. Such things as they are not adaptable to the building trades; they are too small in structure. But the fact remains that these are descendents of workers who were adaptable and large enough to build the great western railroads of one hundred years ago. And thousands of years ago, their ancestors conceived and built the Great Wall of China, one of seven wonders of the ancient world.

And yet, with this tremendous heritage of construction, Chinese simply were not employed on a building which, ironically, carries the title Chinese Culture and Trade Center.

This so-called Chinese Culture and Trade Center building, in effect, is a 572-room Holiday Inn hotel. The Culture and Trade Center is confined to one floor. It got its name principally to tie in the fact that the building is located in the heart of Chinatown.

The hotel is on the site of the old Hall of Justice on land owned by the city of San Francisco. In contracting to build the hotel, the city Human Rights Commission and the construction company agreed to do their best to hire Chinese and other minority workers for the job. But, as it turns out, very few Chinese or other minorities were hired. And the reason is simple. The building trade unions have historically shunned minorities for membership. In this case, it becomes particularly galling to the Chinese because this graceful structure carries the name of the Chinese Culture and Trade Center and yet it appears to exclude Chinese.

The Cahill Construction Company, which is building the structure, claims it is making a real effort to employ Chinese. The Chinese constitute 10 percent of San Francisco's population. Yet this project in the heart of Chinatown has never employed more than 6 percent Chinese workers.

San Francisco's Chinatown is a ghetto in every sense and, like any ghetto, the people who live there have a hard time finding a job. Job discrimination against Chinese is widespread despite the fact that the Chinese helped build San Francisco. The construction work on the so-called Chinese Culture and Trade Center is an example.

We have pointed out the problems concerning job discrimination, now we offer some soltuions. In the first place, we believe that any time anything is built on city-owned property, there must be no discrimination whatsoever in hiring. We believe there should be legally binding and court-enforceable agreements to cover this. Secondly, we believe that the "model cities" program, a federally funded rehabilitation project, should be instituted for Chinatown at the earliest possible moment. And thirdly, we believe both employers and unions should do their best to employ minority workers, not just on a tokenism basis but on a meaningful level.

From the Chinese community standpoint, the construction of the so-called Culture and Trade Center building is a good example of tokenism. And so long as job discrimination exists, the Chinatown ghetto will always remain a depressed and degraded area.

From *East/West, The Chinese American Journal,* August 19, 1970

A Chance for Chinese Laborers (1970)

A $13 million, twenty-seven-story structure in the heart of Chinatown is scheduled for completion in November this year. The 572-room Holiday Inn hotel—with a five-level, 460-car garage—is also called the Chinese Culture and Trade Center because the entire third floor—20,000 square feet—will be used "to provide the proper atmosphere and facilities for the development of cultural perspective, self-awareness, and community understanding and participation among Americans of Chinese ancestry."

However, a quick survey of the work force on the construction site reveals that only three Chinese apprentices out of a total of more than 220 journeymen and foremen—that is, 1.3 percent Chinese—are on the payroll even though the surrounding population is almost 100 percent Chinese and the building is labeled a Chinese Culture Center.

That there is incessant discrimination against the Chinese, exploitation of community resources, and deliberate disregard of the agreement set forth in the Affirmative Action Program (AAP) is beyond dispute. Cahill Construction Company, the general contractor, the unions with which Cahill has agreements in the construction project, and the San Francisco Redevelopment Agency, headed by Justin Herman, must be held responsible for failing to comply with the guidelines of the AAP—a program designed to recruit, hire, train, and retain minority workers in building trades, especially in projects involving public property and funds.

The Center stands at the site of the old Hall of Justice, across from the historic Portsmouth Square. Through an agreement between the city of San Francisco and Justice Enterprises, Inc., a group of some three hundred investors, the Center's space on the third floor is made available under a sixty-year, $1-a-year lease. Construction and mortgage financing is by, respectively, First Western Bank and Connecticut General Life Insurance Company. Since the property belongs to the city's Redevelopment Agency and public funds are involved, both Justice Enterprises and Cahill Construction and all their subcontractors on the site are required by federal law and city ordinance to carry out an Equal Employment Opportunity Policy and an Affirmative Action Program based on nine points:

1. Cooperate with the unions with which the general contractor and the developer have agreements in the development of programs to assure qualified members of minority groups equal opportunity in employment in the construction trades;

2. Actively participate individually or through an association in joint apprenticeship committees to achieve equality of opportunity for minority group applicants to participate in the apprenticeship programs;

3. Actively seek and sponsor members of minority groups for preapprenticeship training;

4. Assist youths with minority group identification to enter each apprenticeship program;

5. Improve opportunities for the upgrading of members of the construction force;

6. Seek minority group referrals or applicants for journeymen positions;

7. Make certain that all recruiting activities are carried out on a nondiscriminatory basis;

8. Make known to all contractors, subcontractors, employees, and all sources of referral the general contractor and developer's Equal Employment Opportunity Policy; and

9. Encourage minority group subcontractors and subcon-

Have They Made It?—A Conclusion

tractors with minority representation among their employees to bid for subcontracting work.

In his letter to Harold Moose, President of Justice Enterprises, on November 10, 1967, Justin Herman stated that the Redevelopment Agency "has the role of enforcement of these contract obligations and desires to provide appropriate assistance and support." In addition, both Cahill and Justice were to submit periodical reports on the implementation of the AAP to the Redevelopment Agency and the Human Rights Commission (HRC) for review and evaluation.

At a preaward Equal Employment Opportunity Conference November 28, Cahill and Justice agreed to the terms outlined above and subsequently detailed their plans in letters to the Redevelopment Agency on November 30 and December 26, 1967. It was on the basis of this agreement that Cahill and Justice were awarded the contracts. Cahill adopted the same AAP it was then using for the construction of the University of San Francisco's School of Nursing. Charles Kollerer was designated as Cahill's Equal Opportunity Officer.

Justice, in spelling out its AAP, stressed that "the greatest opportunity for employment for minority groups in connection with our project would be in the period after the prime contractor had completed construction of the building." Justice noted, "There will be a significant amount of construction performed by the various lessees of our building, and in addition, there will be a large number of permanent new jobs created by these lessees." Charles Slutzkin, project manager for Justice, was assigned to see that the AAP is carried out. Benson I. Hattem is a compliance officer for the Redevelopment Agency. William Becker and Stanley Lim represent the Human Rights Commission for the same purpose.

Representatives of the Chinese community met with representatives of Cahill and Justice January 10, 1969, and expressed the desire of the community to participate in the work force of the construction of the Culture Center. After eighteen months of continuous negotiations, there are only three Chinese apprentices and one laborer working on the construction site. In March 1970 Cahill employed at the Chinese Culture Center site 77 journeymen carpenters (69 white, 3 Spanish and 5 black), but maintained only 3 apprentices (2 Chinese and 1 Caucasian). It is instructive to note that the ratio between journeymen and apprentices in building trades is generally 5:1; state law requires a minimum of 8:1. Cahill furthermore fails to bring its subcontractors in compliance with the AAP as required by the contract. For example, Charles B. Farrow Company, one of about thirty subcontractors on the Culture Center site, had a total of 80 journeymen electricians citywide (4 Spanish, 2 black, and 74 white) against 8 apprentices (1 black and 7 white). Rafael Painting, another subcontractor, had 18 foreman and 60 journeymen painters citywide with neither Chinese nor apprentices in the second half of 1969.

In addition to the underutilization of apprentices and therefore, noncompliance with the AAP, the token Chinese apprentices have been reportedly subjected to continuous harassment, humiliation, and dismissal. Some have been fired allegedly for being "too lazy," "can't follow orders," or "don't have time to train apprentices." Others have been called "chinks" and "Chinamen" by co-workers. In short, Cahill and most of its subcontractors have made no attempt to hire minority workers and apprentices as required by the AAP and have failed to submit periodic work force survey forms to the Redevelopment Agency and the HRC. In fact, evidence shows that they have systematically excluded Chinese and deliberately ignored the AAP. The Redevelopment Agency to date has taken no action against Cahill and its delinquent subcontractors; efforts by the HRC have been largely ignored.

Systematic exclusion of Chinese workers and noncompliance with the AAP in Chinatown is not limited to the construction of the Chinese Culture Center. For example, Northwest Construction Company, the general contractor for the Northeast Health Center on top of the Broadway tunnel, has also been ignoring the AAP. Similarly, the construction of the Senior Citizens Housing (Mason and Pacific) and of the police station (Vallejo and Stockton) was completed with public funds without any efforts to hire and train Chinese workers.

Projects outside of Chinatown are being constructed without any Chinese participation, even though Chinese make up about 10 percent of the San Francisco population. With San Francisco actively undergoing renewal programs, systematic exclusion of the Chinese from building trades means reduction of employment opportunity for hundreds if not thousands of Chinese.

> From *East/West, The Chinese American Journal,* May 27, 1970, by L. Ling-chi Wang

Unreasonable: Meat and Poultry Inspection (1970)

NEW YORK—Chinatown's purveyors of cooked meats and poultry have termed as "unreasonable," the current on-the-spot inspection of their supplies by N.Y. State authorities.

Among other things, the inspectors object to the retailers' custom of unrefrigerated, exposed displaying of the cooked food for sale. Also, the heads and feet of the animals should be removed before preparation, the inspectors say.

Chinese merchants point out that this is a lack of sensitivity to Chinese religious practice. "Chickens, for instance, are always presented with head and feet intact at religious ceremonies," one spokesman said. "Sanitation is their concern," he continued. "Well, we clean our products very well."

The purveyors also take issue with the fact that they are charged for the time spent by the State inspectors on the premises.

"That's forcing me to put an extra man on my payroll," one merchant complained.

The N.Y. Chinese Chamber of Commerce has taken the lead in exploring the possibility of prevailing on the N.Y.

State authorities to take a more reasonable and realistic attitude in the enforcement of the regulations.

"First, let's research the regulations," a spokesman said. "Right now, we're yelling in the dark."

From the *Chinese-American Times*, October 1970

San Francisco Chinatown Is Blamed for Drugs (1970)

On December 1, 1970, the strike-torn *Independent Journal*, the major paper in the Marin County, reported in a headline article that the Chinese in San Francisco are "not just running chop suey parlors," but also are engaged in disseminating hard drugs, such as morphine and heroin, into Marin County through the Black and Mexican-American communities. The allegation was made by Peter Niblo of the Federal Bureau of Narcotics in San Francisco while addressing the San Rafael Rotary Club on the subject "Profit of Red China and Communist Countries on Opiates and Drugs Shipped to Our Country." He dismissed immediately that popular belief that drugs in this country originate in the People's Republic of China. He said, "There is no evidence of drugs coming out of Red China. I wish we were as little permissive as the Chinese are. I don't think they put up with it." Contrary to this popular myth, according to Niblo, most opium is grown in the mountains where Laos, Burma, and Thailand meet, refined in Bangkok, Thailand, or Singapore, and sold in Hong Kong. "Oddly enough, the countries which are making opium are countries with which we have good diplomatic relations and extensive aid programs," he said. In addition to the Indochinese nations, he mentioned Turkey as a major grower and France and Mexico as large-scale suppliers, both also allies of the United States.

The purpose of this short article is not to give a report of drug traffic, but to demonstrate, through the report of one person, how deeply embedded the prejudice is against the Chinese in the United States, how this prejudice manifests itself publicly, and how the Chinese are adversely affected daily by such prejudicial allegations.

TRADITIONAL HOSTILITY AND DISTRUST

Historically, Chinese have always been blamed for just about every evil that existed in this country. It is, therefore, not surprising to read reports and hear popular beliefs that the current drug problem in the United States is caused by drugs shipped deliberately from Red China in view of the hostile relation between the United States and the People's Republic of China. This hostile relation has led to general hostility toward and distrust of Chinese-Americans in the United States as witnessed in J. Edgar Hoover's statement before the U.S. Congress last year about the Chinese-American being susceptible to recruitment by Red China. Within the Chinese community, many are forced to become super-patriots, like some of the Nisei during the World War II, in order to prove their unquestionable loyalty and anti-Communist stand and to avoid any suspicion by the U.S. government and hostility from the American public. (The community, to this date, has not forgotten the incarceration of the Japanese-Americans in 1943.) Combine this intimidating political climate with historical discrimination against the Chinese; the Chinese have been cut off from social, political, and economic activities in the United States, and have been left with neither civil rights nor self-respect. This phenomenon, in part, explains why the Chinese remains mysterious to, if not ignored by, the American public, and the Chinese community as a whole has been largely an apolitical community in the United States.

CHINESE AS SMUGGLER AND SUPPLIER

It is, therefore, not surprising that the American public attributed generally all drugs to be from its enemy, China. It is equally unsurprising that once the myth was exploded, the Chinese community in the United States becomes the new scapegoat. According to Niblo, the drugs grown in Asia are smuggled off ships by Chinese sailors who carry off a small amount each time they go ashore. "They are hard to catch," he said. It is difficult, according to Niblo, to get informers in the tightly knit Chinese community and Chinese are schooled in the science of smuggling. It is in this connection that Niblo alleged that hard drugs that enter America seem to emanate from Chinatown in San Francisco where the Chinese are "not just running chop suey parlors."

The deep prejudice against the Chinese is implicit in Niblo's allegation. The negative effect of this statement on the general public and on suburban, white, middle-class parents with teen-age children having drug problems cannot be exaggerated. Many of these parents can now blame all the drug problems on the Chinese in Chinatown, especially on those Chinese who run restaurants: Chinese in Chinatown are guilty of smuggling drugs into Marin County and poisoning its youth. To make this allegation convincing and simple to understand, Niblo exploited a popular stereotype of the Chinese—Chinese are inscrutable. All Chinese, according to him, are "schooled in the science of smuggling." This explanation, reinforced by stereotype image, satisfies any uncritical mind and reduces a complicated drug traffic problem instantly into a simple answer.

Peter Niblo, a federal official, has made an irresponsible statement and unfounded allegation. He owes the Chinese community a public apology. He must publicly retract or correct his statement and present the public with facts rather than unfounded generalizations and fancies. In my opinion, he must be publicly reprimanded and dismissed from his post.

From East/West, The Chinese American Journal, December 23, 1970, by L. Ling-chi Wang

Are Asian GIs Gooks? (1970)

(The following is a first-person story of one Asian's experiences in the army, told through an interview with the former

Have They Made It?—A Conclusion

GI, a twenty-year-old New York City youth named Sam Choy. The interview appeared in *Getting Together*, the New York Chinatown-based youth publication, and was conducted by representatives of the youth group, I Wor Kuen.)

How old were you when you enlisted in the army?
About 17, I was a junior in high school.

How come you enlisted?
Well, y'know, I didn't like school, and they said the army would make a man out of you and give you a skill . . .

How long was it before you were sent to Vietnam?
I didn't even know I was going to fight. I just wanted to leave and learn to be a man. They said they would teach me a skill.

What happened?
First I went to boot camp for six months. I was the only Asian in camp. It wasn't too bad. When we got the call to Vietnam, half the company didn't show up.

A half? What happened to them?
I don't know. I never found out.

Where were you stationed?
Duk Foi, a small supply post. I don't even know where it was; they never told us. I was with a combat unit, up next to the front lines. I was heavy equipment operator. They didn't want me to be on the front lines; they didn't trust me.

Were you the only Asian in the unit?
Yes.

What kind of treatment did you receive?
Well, a couple of days after, the Viet Cong started shelling us. Then the other GIs started making comments about me looking like the Viet Cong.

How did you react?
I didn't do nothing. I was just doing a job. This went on and got worse. They asked me what I was doing on their side; I told them I was just doing a job. I didn't have any political awareness.

When was this harassment the worst?
Right after the GIs got back from patrol. They really gave it to me. They started asking me where I was born, where my

parents were born, if I was a Communist. They even asked me what I thought about China. They thought I could turn traitor any time.

What kind of job did you have at the base?

They made me the cook. The mess sergeant was mean. He made me do all these things and kept bossing me around. I couldn't take it any more. One day I go so mad I threw a knife on the floor after he called me a Chink. He ordered me to pick it up. I refused. He started yelling at me. He kept yelling all kinds of remarks, like "slant-eyed Chinaman," "gook," "Chink," and he went on and on. I just got madder. So he went to get the staff sergeant. I went to get my rifle. I waited for them to come back and when they did they started to sweet talk me to give my rifle up. I said, "If you come any closer, I'll shoot." I fired a warning shot and they froze. Then I left the tent and the corporal came after me. He tried to grab my rifle. I fired once and he froze; he was scared as hell. Then the MPs came and I shot at them, too. I had bad eyes so I missed. By this time I was near the perimeter of the base and was thinking of joining the Viet Cong; at least they would trust me. But the MPs sent for tanks and armored carriers to come after me, and I got caught.

They beat me up and sent me to the hospital for observation. They knew they were wrong but they put me up for court-martial.

Did you have any friends to help you out?

No, the only friends I had were the blacks. They couldn't do anything, though, they were just regular GIs and even if they did, they'd get in trouble. They used to protect me from the white GIs when they picked on me. Like, I took showers only with the blacks for protection and because they were my friends.

How long was it before the court-martial?

They sent me to Long Binh stockade first. That's where all the GI dissenters were.

How was it?

The place was bad. The conditions were unfit for animals. Everybody was in a cage. Most of the dissenters were black;

they were there because they refused to fight any more. The place was so bad they had a riot. It lasted all night and into the morning. The black GIs were beating up the guards and smashing everything. They were getting back for all the treatment they had been given. The army had to surround the camp before it stopped.
How long were you in Long Binh?
Four months. They were preparing my case.
Where did your court-martial take place?
Pleiku, Vietnam.
Who were the judges?
They had a board of majors and colonels.
Hos long was the court-martial?
Three hours.
What was the charge?
Aggravated assault and culpable negligence.
Did anybody know what was happening to you?
No, they censored all my mail. I couldn't even tell my parents.
What happened next?
The Army sentenced me to eighteen months of hard labor at Fort Leavenworth. There was a maximum sentence of seven years but they made a deal with me. If I pleaded guilty then I would only get eighteen months.
How was Leavenworth?
Fort Leavenworth is the worst place in the world. They beat me up every day, like a time clock. It makes me mad and sick to think about it. Right now, I don't want to think about it any more.
When did you get out?
I only served nine months. I kept quiet, so they discharged me.
Is there anything else?
One thing: I want to tell all the Chinese kids that the army made me sick. They made me so sick that I can't stand it.

From *Third World News*, April 26, 1971

Notes to Introduction

1. H. R. Isaacs, *Scratches on Our Minds* (New York, 1958), p. 111.
2. B. Schrieke, *Alien Americans* (New York, 1936), p. 10.
3. Samuel E. W. Becker, *Humors of a Congressional Investigation Committee (1877)*, p. 11.
4. Shrieke, *Alien Americans*, p. 11.
5. Gary B. Nash and Richard Weiss, *The Great Fear* (New York, 1970), p. 110.
6. Mary Robert Coolidge, *Chinese Immigration* (New York, 1909), p. 96.

7. Becker, *Humors*, p. 15.
8. Mark Twain, *Roughing It*, II (New York, 1870), pp. 128–129.
9. Carey McWilliams, *Brothers Under the Skin* (Boston, 1951), p. 96.
10. Shien-Woo Kung, *Chinese in American Life* (Seattle, 1962), p. 69.
11. *United States v. Ju Toy* (1905).
12. Bret Harte, "John Chinaman," quoted in Isaacs, *Scratches*, p. 114.
13. Bruno Lasker, *Race Attitudes in Children* (New York, 1929), p. 140.
14. Isaacs, *Scratches*, p. 123.
15. *New York Times*, December 13, 1970.
16. *East/West, The Chinese American Journal*, December 2, 1970, p. 6.
17. *Sacramento Bee*, January 17, 1971, p. 23.
18. *East/West*, January 6, 1971, p. 6.
19. C. Marden, *Minorities in American Society* (New York, 1952), p. 194.
20. Isaacs, *Scratches*, p. 71.
21. Quoted in Marden, p. 194, from an editorial in *The Chinese Journal* (New York), December 1, 1950.
22. Quoted in *East/West*, December 16, 1970, p. 1.
23. U.S., Congress, *Senate Miscellaneous*, 45th Congr. 2d sess.

Notes to Chapter 12

1. Elmer C. Sandmeyer, *The Anti-Chinese Movement in California*, Illinois Studies in the Social Sciences, XXIV, no. 3 (1939), p. 45.
2. See Part 2, "Overt Agitation," p. 104.
3. Mary R. Coolidge, *Chinese Immigration* (New York, 1909), p. 83.
4. Carey McWilliams, *Brothers Under the Skin* (Boston, 1951), p. 97.
5. U.S., Congress, Senate, *Exclusive of Chinese Laborers*, 57th Congr., 1st sess., Sen. Doc. 162, a note sent by Wu Ting Fang to John Hay, to be transmitted to Congress October 10, 1901.
6. J. W. Foster, "The Chinese Boycott," *Atlantic Monthly*, 97 (January 1906), p. 122.

Notes to Chapter 2

1. Bruno Lasker, *Race Attitudes in Children* (New York, 1929), p. 140.
2. Richard T. La Piere, "Attitudes vs. Actions," *Social Forces,* XIII, no. 2 (December 1934), pp. 230–237.
3. *New York Times,* February 17 and 19, 1952.
4. Mary R. Coolidge, *Chinese Immigration* (New York, 1909), p. 95.
5. Dorothy Jones, *The Portrayal of China and India on the American Screen, 1896–1955,* Center for International Studies (M.I.T., 1955), p. 24.

Notes to Chapter 3

INTRODUCTION

1. Sidney L. Gulick, *American Democracy and Asiatic Citizenship* (New York, 1918), p. 32.
2. Alexander McLeod, *Pigtail and Gold Dust* (Idaho, 1871), p. 198.
3. Elmer C. Sandmeyer, *The Anti-Chinese Movement in California,* Illinois Studies in the Social Sciences, XXIV, no. 3, 1939, p. 97.
4. U.S., Congress, House Rep. 255, 52nd Congr., 1st sess.
5. *School and Society,* Vol. 28 (1928), p. 389.
6. *Treaty of Trade Consuls, and Emigration,* concluded July 4, 1868, and *Convention Between the United States of America and the Empire of China,* signed at Washington, D.C., March 17, 1894.

THE ANTI-CHINESE OUTBREAKS IN SEATTLE (1885–1886)

1. George Kinnear, *Anti-Chinese Riots at Seattle, Wn., February 8th, 1886* (Seattle, 1911), p. 3. Also see Foster Rhea Dulles, *China and America* (Princeton, 1946), pp. 78 ff.
2. Seattle *Post-Intelligencer,* September 17, 1885.
3. *Ibid.,* September 11, 1885.
4. *Ibid.,* September 11–20, 1885, *passim;* Seattle *Call,* October 5, 24, 26, 1885.
5. Letter, *Post-Intelligencer,* September 19, 1885.

6. Kinnear, *Anti-Chinese Riots,* p. 3.
7. *Post-Intelligencer,* October 6, 1885.
8. *Call,* September 21, 1885.
9. Seattle *Star,* September 28, 1885.
10. *Call,* September 21, 1885.
11. September 11, 1885.
12. October 3, 1885. Also see Orange Jacobs, *Memoirs* (Seattle, 1908), p. 138.
13. J. C. Haines, quoted in *Post-Intelligencer,* September 24, 1885; *Call,* September 25, November 19, 1885; R. Jacob Weisbach, quoted in *Star,* September 28, 1885; W. H. White, U.S. Attorney, to A. H. Garland, Attorney-General, September 8, December 5, 1885; T. J. Hamilton, U.S. Marshal, W.T., to Garland, March 6, 1886; Department of Justice File No. 980–8218, 10017, 2024 (microfilm, University of Washington library). Hereafter all references to this file will read DJ 980.
14. *Call,* September 17, 1885; T. H. Cann, quoted in *ibid.,* September 21, 1885.
15. Roger S. Greene, quoted in *Post-Intelligencer,* October 6, 1885.
16. *Ibid.,* September 16, 1885.
17. *Call,* October 14, 27, 28, 1885; *Post-Intelligencer,* November 24, 1885.
18. September 17, 1885.
19. September 21, 1885.
20. For examples, see September 25, 26, 1885.
21. September 17, 1885.
22. October 24, 1885.
23. October 2, 3, 1885.
24. See *Post-Intelligencer* and *Call,* September 1885, *passim.*
25. *Call,* September 21, 1885.
26. *Post-Intelligencer,* September 23, 1885.
27. *Idem.*
28. *Ibid.,* September 24, 1885.
29. *Star,* September 29, 1885. For a defense of this Congress, see *Call,* October 5, 1885.
30. *Post-Intelligencer,* October 2, 1885.
31. *Star,* October 2, 1885.
32. October 2, 1885.
33. *Call,* October 5, 1885.
34. *Post-Intelligencer,* October 7, 1885.

Notes 275

35. *Call*, October 5, 1885.
36. *Idem*.
37. *Ibid*., October 9, 1885; *Star*, October 9, 1885.
38. *Post-Intelligencer*, October 6, 9, 1885.
39. For details, see *Call*, October 6, 8, 1885; *Post-Intelligencer*, October 8, 1885.
40. *Post-Intelligencer*, October 6, 1885.
41. *Call*, October 5, 1885.
42. *Ibid*., October 10, 1885.
43. *Ibid*., October 12, 1885.
44. *Ibid*., October 16, 1885.
45. C. B. Bagley Collection (University of Washington library).
46. *Post-Intelligencer*, October 16, 18, 1885.
47. *Call*, October 19, 1885.
48. *Star*, October 23, 1885.
49. *Post-Intelligencer*, October 25, 1885.
50. *Call*, November 2, 1885.
51. *Ibid*., November 3, 1885.
52. *Ibid*., November 4, 1885.
53. Department of State: Miscellaneous Letters, November 1885, Part I (National Archives). The *Star* vigorously denounced it; November 5, 1885.
54. Telegram, November 5, 1885; Bagley Collection.
55. *Call*, November 5, 1885.
56. *Post-Intelligencer*, November 6, 1885.
57. *Call*, November 5, 1885.
58. *Post-Intelligencer*, November 6, 1885.
59. *Call*, November 6, 1885.
60. *Post-Intelligencer*, November 6, 1885.
61. *Call*, November 6, 1885; *Post-Intelligencer*, November 6, 7, 1885.
62. For details, see *Call*, November 9, 1885.
63. *Call*, November 7, 1885.
64. *Post-Intelligencer*, November 8, 1885.
65. *Call*, November 10, 1885.
66. See certified Gordon Hardward Co. bill, November 1885, for $1,162.24; Bagley Collection.
67. *Call*, November 7, 1885.
68. *Post-Intelligencer*, November 8, 15, 1885.
69. Telegram, William C. Endicott to General John Gibbon, November 7, 1885, File No. 5820–1885, The Adjutant Gen-

eral's Office, Principal Records Division, War Department Archives (National Archives). Hereafter cited as AGO 5820–1885.
70. November 7, 1885; AGO 5820–1885.
71. Telegram, H. C. Wood, Asst. Adj. Gen., to General R. G. Drum, Adj. Gen., U.S. Army, November 7, 1885; AGO 5820–1885.
72. Telegram, De Russy to Wood, November 8, 1885; AGO 5820–1885.
73. *Call*, November 9, 1885.
74. Telegrams, De Russy to Wood, Wood to Drum, November 8, 1885; AGO 5820–1885.
75. Telegram, Wood to Drum, November 8, 1885; AGO 5820–1885.
76. Telegram, Gibbon to Endicott, November 9, 1885; AGO 5820–1885.
77. *Post-Intelligencer*, November 10, 1885.
78. *Call*, November 10, 1885.
79. November 9, 1885.
80. Telegram, Gibbon to Drum, November 12, 1885; AGO 5820–1885; *Post-Intelligencer*, November 10, 1885.
81. *Call*, November 17, 1885.
82. *Ibid.*, November 10, 1885.
83. November 9, 16, 1885.
84. November 27, 1885.
85. November 8, 15, 1885.
86. Telegram, General John Pope to Philip H. Sheridan, November 13, 1885; AGO 5820–1885.
87. November 8, 1885.
88. November 8, 1885, *passim*.
89. Telegram, Gibbon to Endicott, November 9, 1885; AGO 5820–1885.
90. *Call*, November 16, 1885. For a severe criticism of the ministers, see *Star*, November 16, 1885.
91. *Call*, November 11, 14, 1885.
92. November 11, 1885; DJ 980–9497.
93. November 23, 1885; DJ 980–9733.
94. *Call*, November 18, December 5, 1885.
95. *Ibid.*, December 7, 1885.
96. *Ibid.*, November 14, 1885.
97. November 12, 1885.
98. November 19, 1885.

99. *Post-Intelligencer*, November 21, 1885.
100. For examples, see *Call*, December 1, 3, 5, 1885.
101. November 9, 1885.
102. November 11, 1885.
103. November 22, 1885.
104. November 29, 1885.
105. For details, see *Call*, December 7, 1885; and *Post-Intelligencer*, December 20, 1885.
106. *Call*, December 3, 1885.
107. *Ibid.*, December 5, 1885.
108. *Ibid.*, February 6, 1886.
109. Journal of the House of Representatives of Washington Territory, 1885-1886, p. 53 (typescript, University of Washington library). Hereafter cited as House Journal.
110. *Ibid.*, January 13, 1886, p. 194.
111. *Idem.*
112. *Ibid.*, January 20, 1886, pp. 236-239.
113. *Ibid.*, p. 235.
114. *Star*, January 25, 1886.
115. *Post-Intelligencer*, January 23, 1886.
116. *Star*, January 25, 1886.
117. *Post-Intelligencer*, January 26, 1886.
118. Journal of the Council of Washington Territory, 1885-1886, January 22, 1886, pp. 185-186, 189, January 27, 1886, p. 232 (typescript, University of Washington library).
119. House Journal, January 25, 1886, p. 282.
120. January 23, 1886.
121. January 25, February 2, 1886.
122. *Post-Intelligencer*, January 27, 1886.
123. *Idem.*
124. *Call*, January 4-16, 1886.
125. He later denied having spoken in the vein attributed to him in the newspapers. Cann to G. M. Haller and "other friends," February 9, 1886; G. O. Haller Collection (University of Washington library).
126. *Call*, February 8, 1886.
127. *Post-Intelligencer*, February 7, 1886.
128. *Call*, February 8, 1886.
129. This narrative of the February days is based primarily on the news columns of the *Post-Intelligencer* and the *Call* except when otherwise designated. Both newspapers blended full coverage and a reasonable regard for fact, unlike most avail-

Notes 278

130. able secondary accounts. When the two dailies differed, it will be noted.
130. *Post-Intelligencer*, February 9, 1886. The *Call* boasted, however, that there was not a "single case of disorder or violence," and that "every care and comfort" was bestowed upon the Chinese; February 8, 1886.
131. *Post-Intelligencer*, November 8, 1885.
132. Kinnear, *Anti-Chinese Riots*, p. 14.
133. Formal printed copy; Bagley Collection. Interestingly enough, Judge Roger S. Greene wrote in pencil on the bottom of this copy the following: "I had nothing to do with the foregoing. It was issued by the Governor without consulting me."
134. February 7, 1886; AGO 5820–1885.
135. Text, Thomas A. Mercer Collection (University of Washington library).
136. *Call*, February 8, 1886; *Post-Intelligencer*, February 9, 1886.
137. The wounded included James Murphy, a special police officer, Bernard Mulrane, a member of Engine Company No. 2, George Smith, an unemployed coppersmith, C. Schreiber, an unemployed laborer, and Charles G. Stewart, an unemployed woodsman; *Post-Intelligencer*, February 9, 1886. Stewart died the next day; *ibid.*, February 10, 1886.
138. Text, Mercer Collection. This prevented the serving of warrants on Thomas Burke and other deputies, charging them with murder; *Post-Intelligencer*, February 9, 1886.
139. Granville O. Haller, Military Documents 1840–1889 (University of Washington library).
140. *Post-Intelligencer*, February 9, 1886; *Call*, February 8, 1886.
141. *Call*, February 9, 1886; *Post-Intelligencer*, February 10, 1886.
142. Telegram, February 7, 1886; AGO 5820–1885.
143. Endicott had refused on the ground that troops could not be sent "except upon last emergency. It would seem that with the force you have, order can and should be maintained." Telegram, Endicott to Squire, February 8, 1886; AGO 5820–1885.Squire did not receive this message. Telegram, Squire to Endicott, February 13, 1886; AGO 5820-1885. Yet Endicott had telegraphed Gibbon on February 8 to hold himself in readiness to go to Seattle, "if necessary"; AGO 5820–1885. Apparently Gibbon was to survey the situation.

144. February 8, 1886; AGO 5820–1885.
145. For examples, see Mercer Collection.
146. Copy; AGO 5820–1885.
147. Telegram, Drum to Gibbon, February 9, 1886; AGO 5820–1885.
148. Telegram, Gibbon to Drum, February 16, 1886; AGO 5820–1885; *Post-Intelligencer*, February 11, 1886.
149. Kinnear, *Anti-Chinese Riots*, p. 10.
150. *Post-Intelligencer*, February 11, 1886.
151. Telegram, Gibbon to Drum, February 16, 1886; AGO 5820–1885. Also see Gibbon to Drum, February 11, 1886; AGO 5820–1885; *Post-Intelligencer*, February 11, 1886; *Call*, February 13, 15, 1886.
152. This group comprised fugitives from the Puyallup coal mines; Diary of James G. Swan, Vol. 39, February 12, 14, 1886 (University of Washington library).
153. *Call*, February 15, 1886.
154. February 11, 1886; Mercer Collection.
155. February 12, 1886; Mercer Collection.
156. Telegram, February 12, 1886; Mercer Collection.
157. Squire to Cleveland, February 22, 1886; AGO 5280–1885; *Call*, February 23, 1886.
158. Telegram, February 23, 1886; AGO 5820–1885.
159. Telegram, Greene to A. H. Garland, Attorney-General; DJ 980–1318.
160. Telegram, Gibbon to Drum, February 24, 1886; AGO 5820–1885.
161. Telegram, Gibbon to Drum, March 11, 1886; AGO 5820–1885. According to a March 25, 1886, notation, the February 16 telegram was missing from the files.
162. Telegram, Gibbon to Drum, March 31, 1886; AGO 5820–1885.
163. Telegram, Drum to Gibbon, April 2, 1886; AGO 5820–1885.
164. Telegram, Drum to Gibbon, April 20, 1886; AGO 5820–1885.
165. Telegram, Gibbon to Drum, April 22, 1886; AGO 5820–1885.
166. Telegram, Drum to Gibbon, April 23, 1886; AGO 5820–1885.
167. Gibbon to H. Clay Wood, April 23, 1886; AGO 5820–1885.
168. AGO 5820–1885.
169. May 4, 1886; China: Notes to Department of State, II, 6 (National Archives).
170. May 4, 1886; AGO 5820–1885; Endicott to Bayard, May 5,

1886; Department of State, Miscellaneous Letters, May 1886, Part I (National Archives).
171. Bayard to Chang Yen Hoon, May 5, 1886; China: Notes from Department of State, I (National Archives).
172. Telegram, J. C. Kelton, Asst. Adj. Gen., to Gibbon, May 5, 1886; AGO 5820–1885.
173. Gibbon to Kelton, May 5, 1886: AGO 5820–1885.
174. Telegram, Gibbon to Kelton, May 8, 1886; AGO 5820–1885. But also see Major General O. O. Howard to Drum, May 17, 1886; AGO 5820–1885.
175. Quoted in *Post-Intelligencer,* July 9, 1886.
176. For accounts of election meetings, see *Post-Intelligencer,* July 9, 11, 1886.
177. *Ibid.,* July 11, 1886.
178. *Ibid.,* July 10, 1886.
179. *Call,* February 8, 1886.
180. *Post-Intelligencer,* July 13, 1886.
181. *Ibid.,* July 11, 1886.
182. Telegram, Gibbon to Drum, July 20, 1886; AGO 5820–1885.
183. Telegram, Drum to Gibbon, August 13, 1886; AGO 5820–1885.
184. Telegram, Gibbon to Drum, August 18, 1886; AGO 5820–1885.
185. Telegram, Drum to Gibbon, August 19, 1886; AGO 5820–1885.
186. Special Order No. 142, August 19, 1886; AGO 5820–1885.
187. *Post-Intelligencer,* June 6, 1886.
188. *Ibid.,* September 28, 1886.
189. *Ibid.,* June 6, 1886. Also see W. H. White to A. H. Garland, March 10, 1886; DJ 980–2017.
190. White to Garland, August 9, 1886; DJ 980–5662.
191. *Post-Intelligencer,* September 3, 1896.
192. *Ibid.,* September 28, 1886.

ANTI-CHINESE RIOTS IN WASHINGTON (1885–1886)

1. Hunt, *History of Tacoma,* I, p. 356.
2. *Ibid.*
3. Snowden, *History of Washington,* IV, p. 319.
4. Hunt, *History of Tacoma,* I, p. 357.
5. Bagley, *History of Seattle,* II, p. 457.
6. Kinnear, *Anti-Chinese Riots in Seattle,* p. 3.

7. Snowden, *History of Washington*, IV, pp. 520–521.
8. Hunt, *History of Tacoma*, I, p. 365. Bagley, *History of Seattle*, II, p. 459.
9. Snowden, *History of Washington*, IV, pp. 326–327. Kinnear, *Anti-Chinese Riots in Seattle*, p. 5.
10. Snowden, *History of Washington*, IV, p. 328.
11. Hunt, *History of Tacoma*, I, pp. 372–374.
12. Snowden, *History of Washington*, IV, p. 329.
13. Bagley, *History of Seattle*, II, p. 466.
14. Kinnear, *Anti-Chinese Riots*, pp. 4–6.
15. *Ibid.*
16. *Ibid.*
17. Bagley, *History of Seattle*, II, p. 467. Kinnear, *Anti-Chinese Riots*, p. 7.
18. Kinnear, *Anti-Chinese Riots*, p. 8.
19. Snowden, *History of Washington*, IV, p. 343.
20. Kinnear, *Anti-Chinese Riots*, pp. 9–10.
21. *Ibid.*, p. 12.
22. Bagley, *History of Seattle*, II, p. 476.

Notes to Chapter 4

1. Quoted in J. W. Foster, "The Chinese Boycott," *Atlantic Monthly*, 97 (January 1906), p. 126.

BIBLIOGRAPHIES

Cowan, Robert Ernest, and Boutwell Dunlop. *Bibliography of the Chinese Question in the United States.* San Francisco: 1909.

Griffin, Appleton P. Clark. *Select List of References on Chinese Immigration.* Washington: 1904.

Lum, William Wong. *Asians in America: A Bibliography.* Davis: University of California, 1969.

———. *Asians in America: A Bibliography—Supplement I.* Davis: University of California, 1970.

———. *Asians in America: A Bibliography of Master's Theses and Doctoral Dissertations.* Davis: University of California, 1970.

———, and Mari Imamura, *Asians in America: A Bibliography—Supplement II.* Davis: University of California, 1970.

CURRENT PERIODICALS

Amerasia Journal (quarterly), Yale Asian American Students Association, Box 3374, Yale Station, New Haven, Conn. 06520.

Bridge Magazine (bimonthly), The Basement Workshop, Inc., New York, N.Y.

Chinese-American Times (monthly), 215 Park Row, New York, N.Y. 10038.

Chinese Awareness (monthly), published in association with the Chinatown Youth Council, 971 Chungking Road, Los Angeles, Calif. 90012.

East/West, The Chinese-American Journal (weekly), San Francisco, Calif.

Gidra (monthly), published by Gidra, Inc., a registered nonprofit organization, P.O. Box 18046, Los Angeles, Calif., 90018.

New Bridge (bilingual monthly), P.O. Box 5743, Station F., Vancouver 12, B.C., Canada.

Rodan (monthly), Asian American Publications, Inc., 1808A Sutter Street, San Francisco, Calif.

Yellow Journalism, The News Monthly of the Asian American Student Alliance, Asian American Student Center, FO 4–181, 6101 East 7th Street, Long Beach, Calif., 90810.

BOOKS

Allport, Gordon. *The Nature of Prejudice.* Reading, Mass.: Addison-Wesley Publication Co., 1958.

Barth, Gunther. *Bitter Strength: A History of the Chinese in the United States 1850–1870.* Cambridge, Mass.: Harvard University Press, 1964.

Becker, Samuel E. W. *Humors of a Congressional Investigation Committee 1877.* Washington, D.C.

Bromley, Isaac Hill. *The Chinese Massacre at Rock Springs, Wyoming Territory, September 2, 1885.* Boston, Mass.: Franklin Press; Rand, Avery & Co., 1886.

Brown, F. J., and J. S. Roucek (eds.). *One America: The History, Contributions, and Present Problems of our Racial and National Minorities,* third edition. Englewood Cliffs, N. J.: Prentice-Hall, Inc., 1952.

Cattell, Stuart H. *Health, Welfare, and Social Organizations in Chinatown, New York City.* New York: Community Service Society, 1962.

Cayton, H. R., and A. O. Lively. *The Chinese in the United States and the Chinese Christian Church.* New York: National Council of Churches of Christ, 1955.

Chinn, Thomas W. (ed.). *A History of the Chinese in California: A Syllabus.* San Francisco: Chinese Historical Society of America, 1969.

Coleman, Elizabeth. *Chinatown, USA.* New York: John Day, 1946.

Condit, Ira M. *The Chinaman as We See Him.* Chicago: F. H. Revell Co., 1900.

Coolidge, Mary R. *Chinese Immigration.* New York: Henry Holt & Co., 1909.

Daniels, Roger, and Harry H. L. Kitano. *American Racism: Exploration of the Nature of Prejudice.* Englewood Cliffs, N. J.: Prentice-Hall, Inc., 1970.

Dickson, M. S. *American History for Grammar Schools.* New York: Macmillan, 1926.

Gibson, Otis. *The Chinese in America.* Cincinnati: Hitchcock and Walden, 1877.

Gulick, Sidney L. *American Democracy and Asiatic Citizenship*. New York: Charles Scribner's Sons, 1918.

Hoy, William. *The Chinese Six Companies*. The Chinese Consolidated Benevolent Association, 1942.

Hsu, Francis L. K. *American and Chinese: Two Ways of Life*. New York: Henry Schuman, 1953.

Isaacs, H. R. *Scratches on Our Minds: American Images of China and India*. New York: John Day, 1958.

Jones, Dorothy. *The Portrayal of China and India on the American Screen, 1896–1955*. Center for International Studies, Cambridge, Mass.: M.I.T., 1955.

Kinnear, George. *Anti-Chinese Riots in Seattle, 1885–1886*. Seattle: G. Kinnear, 1911.

Kung, Shien-Woo. *Chinese in American Life: Some Aspects of Their History, Status, Problems, and Contributions*. Seattle: University of Washington Press, 1962.

Lasker, Bruno. *Race Attitudes in Children*. New York: Henry Holt & Co., 1929.

Lee, Calvin. *Chinatown U.S.A.: A History and Guide*. New York: Doubleday, 1965.

Lee, Rose Hum. *The Chinese in the United States of America*. Hong Kong: Hong Kong University Press, 1960.

Li, Tien-Lu. *The Congressional Policy of Chinese Immigration*. Nashville, 1916.

Liu, Kwang-Ching. *Americans and Chinese*. Cambridge: Harvard University Press, 1963.

Lyman, Stanford M. *The Asians in the West*. Reno, Nevada: Desert Research Institute, 1970.

McKenzie, R. D. *Oriental Exclusion*. Chicago: University of Chicago Press, 1928.

McLeod, Alexander. *Pigtail and Gold Dust*. Idaho: Caxton Printers, Ltd., 1871.

McWilliams, Carey. *Brothers Under the Skin*. Boston: Little, Brown & Co., 1951.

Mar, Dave. *I Am Yellow (Curious)*. Davis: University of California Asian American Research Project, 1969.

Mar, David, and Joyce Sakai (eds.). *Asians in America*, Selected Student Papers. Davis: University of California, 1970.

Marden, C. *Minorities in American Society*. New York: American Book Co., 1952.

Memmi, Albert. *The Colonizer and the Colonized*. New York: Orion Press, 1965.

Miller, Stuart C. *The Unwelcome Immigrant; the American Image of the Chinese, 1785–1882*. Berkeley: University of California Press, 1969.

Myers, A. J. *Literature for Children and Its Influence in Religious Education*. 1926.

Nash, Gary B., and Richard Weiss. *The Great Fear: Race in the Mind of America*. New York: Holt, Rinehart, & Winston, 1970.

Palmer, A. W. *Chinatown: Orientals in American Life*. New York: Friendship Press, 1934.

Remer, C. F. *A Study of Chinese Boycotts with Special Reference to their Economic Effectiveness*. Baltimore: Johns Hopkins Press, 1933.

Rohmer, Sax. *The Insidious Dr. Fu-Manchu*. New York: McKinlay, Stone, & Mackenzie, 1913.

———. *The Return of Dr. Fu-Manchu*. New York: McKinlay, Stone, & Mackenzie, 1916.

———. *Tales of Chinatown*. New York: Doubleday, Page, & Co., 1922.

Sandmeyer, Elmer Clarence. *The Anti-Chinese Movement in California*, Illinois Studies in the Social Sciences, XXIV, no. 3, Urbana: University of Illinois Press, 1939.

Schrieke, B. *Alien Americans: A Study of Race Relations*. New York: Viking Press, 1936.

Selvin, David F. *The Other San Francisco*. New York: The Seabury Press, 1969.

Seward, George F. *Chinese Immigration in Its Social and Economic Aspects*. New York: Charles Scribner's Sons, 1881.

Simpson, George E., and J. Milton Yinger. *Racial and Cultural Minorities*, revised edition. New York: Harper & Row, 1958.

Stonequist, E. V. *The Marginal Man, a Study in Personality and Cultural Conflict*. New York: Charles Scribner's Sons, 1937.

Sung, Betty Lee. *Mountain of Gold: The Story of Chinese in America*. New York: Macmillan, 1967.

Williams, S. Wells. *Chinese Immigration*. New York: Charles Scribner's Sons, 1879.

Whitney, James A. *The Chinese and the Chinese Question*. New York: Tibbals Book Co., 1888.

Wollenberg, Charles. *Ethnic Conflict in California History:* Los Angeles: Tinn-Brown, 1970.

ARTICLES

Chang, Francis. "An Accommodation Program for Second Generation Chinese," *Sociology and Social Research*, XVIV (July–August 1934), pp. 541–583.

Chen, K. F. "Overseas Chinese in the United States," *Far Eastern Economic Review*, 25 (July 1958), pp. 142–144.

Chong, Janet. "Sorry, But You're Chinese," *Asia* (February 1944), p. 61.

Corbally, John. "Orientals in Seattle Schools," *Sociology and Social Research*, XVI (September–October 1931), pp. 61–67.

Culin, Stewart. "Customs of the Chinese in America," *Journal of American Folklore*, III, no. 10 (1890), pp. 347–352.

Foster, J. W. "The Chinese Boycott," *Atlantic Monthly*, 97 (January 1906), pp. 118–127.

Graham, Virginia Taylor. "The Intelligence of Chinese Children in San Francisco," *Journal of Comparative Psychology*, I, no. 1 (February 1926), pp. 43–71.

Hayner, Norma S., and Charles M. Reynolds. "Chinese Family Life in America," *America Sociological Review* (October 1937), pp. 630–637.

Iyenaga, Toyokichi. "Discrimination with Reference to Citizenship and Land Ownership," *Proceedings of the Academy of Political Science* (July 1917), Vol. 7, pp. 565–569.

Johnson, Emory R. "Chinese and Japanese in America," *Annals of the American Academy of Political and Social Science*, XXXIV, no. 2 (September 1909), pp. 1–203.

Karlin, Jules Alexander. "The Anti-Chinese Outbreaks in Seattle, 1885–1886," *Pacific Northwest Quarterly*, XXXIX, no. 2 (April 1948), pp. 103–129.

Kwoh, Beulah Ong. "The Occupational Status of American-Born Chinese Male College Graduates," *American Journal of Sociology*, 53 (November 1947), pp. 192–200.

La Piere, Richard T. "Attitudes vs. Actions," *Social Forces*, XIII, no. 2 (December 1934), pp. 230–237.

Lew, T. T. "China in American School Textbooks," *Chinese Social and Political Science Review*, VII, no. 3, 1923.

Ling, Pyau. "Causes of Chinese Emigration," *Annals of the American Academy of Political and Social Science*, 39 (January 1912), pp. 74–82.

Louis, K. K. "Problems of the Second Generation Chinese," *Sociology and Social Research* (January–February 1932).

Lush, H. H. "Real Yellow Peril," *North American Review*, 186 (November 1907), pp. 375–383.

Lyman, Stanford. "Marriage and the Family Among Chinese Immigrants to America, 1850–1960," *Phylon*, 29, p. 4.

McWilliams, C. "Racism on the West Coast," *New Republic*, 110 (May 29, 1944), pp. 732–733.

Nutting, H. C. "Immigration from the Orient," *Nation*, 98 (June 18, 1914), pp. 724–725.

Saniford, P., and R. Kerr. "Intelligence of Chinese and Japanese Children." *Journal of Educational Psychology*, 17, 1926, pp. 361–367.

Saturday Evening Post. "People Nobody Wants" (May 9, 1942). "Why No Chinese American Delinquents" (April 30, 1955), p. 12.

Von Kaltenborn, Hans. "Land Ownership by Aliens," *Proceedings of the Academy of Political Science*, 7 (July 1917), pp. 570–575.

Whiteside, T. "Wet Wash Chinatown," *New Republic* (December 23, 1946), pp. 872–874.

Wilcox, W. P. "Anti-Chinese Riots in Washington," *Washington Historical Quarterly*, XX, no. 3 (July 1929), pp. 204–211.

Young, P. V. "Support of the Anti-Oriental Movement," *Annals of the American Academy of Political and Social Science*, 34 (September 1909), pp. 231–238.

ACKNOWLEDGMENTS

The editor and publisher gratefully acknowledge permission to quote the following articles:

"Anti-Chinese Riots in Washington," from *The Washington Historical Quarterly*, 20, no. 3 (July 1929), pp. 204–12. Reprinted by permission.
"Orientals Find Bias Is Down Sharply in U.S.," from *The New York Times*, December 13, 1970. Copyright © 1970 by The New York Times Company. Reprinted by permission.
"Red Tape or Racism: The Strange Case of Mr. Ching," from *Gidra*. Reprinted by permission.

Photos on pages 2–3 (of insert): from *Judge*, June 17, 1882; pages 1 (top), 4–5, 6, 7, 8: courtesy New York Public Library.